Excel 2007 PivotTables Recipes

A Problem-Solution Approach

Debra Dalgleish

Apress®

Excel 2007 PivotTables Recipes: A Problem-Solution Approach

Copyright © 2007 by Debra Dalgleish

ISBN-13 (pbk): 978-1-59059-920-4

ISBN-10 (pbk): 1-59059-920-9

Printed and bound in the United States of America 9 8 7 6 5 4 3 2 1

Lead Editor: Tom Welsh
Technical Reviewer: Roger Govier
Editorial Board: Steve Anglin, Ewan Buckingham, Tony Campbell, Gary Cornell, Jonathan Gennick,
    Jason Gilmore, Kevin Goff, Jonathan Hassell, Matthew Moodie, Joseph Ottinger, Jeffrey Pepper,
    Ben Renow-Clarke, Dominic Shakeshaft, Matt Wade, Tom Welsh
Project Manager: Beth Christmas
Copy Editor: Marcia Baker
Associate Production Director: Kari Brooks-Copony
Production Editor: Katie Stence
Compositor: Linda Weidemann, Wolf Creek Press
Proofreader: Liz Welch
Indexer: Brenda Miller
Artist: April Milne
Cover Designer: Kurt Krames
Manufacturing Director: Tom Debolski

Distributed to the book trade worldwide by Springer-Verlag New York, Inc., 233 Spring Street, 6th Floor, New York, NY 10013. Phone 1-800-SPRINGER, fax 201-348-4505, e-mail orders-ny@springer-sbm.com, or visit http://www.springeronline.com.

For information on translations, please contact Apress directly at 2855 Telegraph Avenue, Suite 600, Berkeley, CA 94705. Phone 510-549-5930, fax 510-549-5939, e-mail info@apress.com, or visit http://www.apress.com.

The source code for this book is available to readers at http://www.apress.com.

Contents at a Glance

Contents

■CHAPTER 5   Grouping and Totaling Pivot Table Data 101

About the Author

DEBRA DALGLEISH is a computer consultant in Mississauga, Ontario, Canada, serving local and international clients. Self-employed since 1985, she has extensive experience in designing complex Microsoft Excel and Microsoft Access applications, as well as sophisticated Microsoft Word forms and documents. Debra has led hundreds of Microsoft Office corporate training sessions, from beginner to advanced level.

In recognition of her contributions to the Excel newsgroups, Debra has been awarded a Microsoft Office Excel MVP each year since 2001. You can find a wide variety of Excel tips and tutorials, and sample files, on her Contextures web site at www.contextures.com/tiptech.html.

About the Technical Reviewer

 **ROGER GOVIER** is an independent IT consultant based in the UK, where he specializes in developing solutions for clients utilizing Excel worksheet functions and VBA programming.

Following an Honours B.Sc. in Agricultural Economics and Business Management, Roger gained considerable hands-on management experience by running companies both for himself, and for other private and public companies. During this time Roger developed many accounting skills and focused on control through the better utilization of company data.

Roger has been involved with computing from 1980 and, since 1997, most of his work has centered on Excel. Microsoft recently awarded Roger the prestigious Most Valuable Professional (MVP) status as recognition of his Excel skills and help to the community through newsgroups.

Acknowledgments

Many people helped me as I worked on this book. Above all, love and thanks to Keith, who convinced me I could do it again, and to Jason, Sarah, Neven, and Dylan for providing a few hours of diversion from the task at hand.

Thanks to the wonderful people at Apress: Dominic Shakeshaft, who helped develop the original book's concept and who edited a few chapters; my editor, Tom Welsh, whose input and support was much appreciated; and project manager Beth Christmas, who kept us all on track. Special thanks to Roger Govier, for his insightful comments and excellent suggestions during the technical review, and to Mandy and Jack for their generosity in sharing such a valuable resource (again). Thanks to my copy editor, Marcia Baker, who polished the text, and to production editor, Katie Stence, who made sure everything looked just right on the printed page.

Many thanks to Dave Peterson, from whom I've learned much about Excel programming, and who graciously commented on some of the code for this book. Thanks to Jon Peltier, who convinced me to start writing about pivot tables, and who is always willing to exchange ideas and humor. Thanks also to Ron Coderre and Tom Ogilvy, who generously shared their creative code. Thanks to all those who ask questions and provide answers in the Microsoft Excel newsgroups, and who were the inspiration for many of the recipes in this book.

Thanks to my clients, who remained patient as I juggled projects and writing, and who continue to challenge me with interesting assignments, especially when pivot tables are part of the solution.

Finally, thanks to my parents, Doug and Shirley McConnell, and my sister, Nancy Nelson, for their continued love and support. And thanks also to Brad, Robert, and Jeffrey Nelson for checking all those bookstores.

Introduction

Excel's pivot tables are a powerful tool for analyzing data. With only a few minutes of work, a new user can create an attractively formatted table that summarizes thousands of rows of data. This book assumes you know the basics of Excel 2007 and pivot tables, and it provides troubleshooting tips and techniques, as well as programming examples.

Who This Book Is For

This book is for anyone who uses pivot tables, and who only reads the manual when all else fails. It's designed to help you understand the advanced features and options that are available, as you need them. If you're familiar with pivot tables in previous versions of Excel, this book may help you apply the new features introduced in Excel 2007.

Experiment with pivot tables, and if you get stuck, search for the problem in this book. With luck, you'll find a solution, a workaround, or, occasionally, confirmation that pivot tables can't do what you want them to do.

How This Book Is Structured

Chapters 1 to 10 contain manual solutions to common pivot table problems, and they alert you to the situations where no known solution exists. Chapter 11 has sample code, for those who prefer a programming solution to their pivot table problems, and for the settings that can only be adjusted programmatically. The following is a brief summary of the material contained in each chapter.

- Chapter 1, Creating a Pivot Table:

  Issues you should consider when planning a pivot table and preparing the source data. Using data from multiple worksheets. Creating an Excel Table from the source data and understanding the new PivotTable Field List.

- Chapter 2, Sorting and Filtering Pivot Table Data:

  Understanding how data sorts in a pivot table, creating custom sort orders, and ensuring new items sort correctly. Filtering labels for text, dates, and values; applying multiple filters to a field; filtering for top items; and applying dynamic filters.

- Chapter 3, Calculations in a Pivot Table:

  Using the summary functions and custom calculations, creating calculated items and calculated fields to expand the built-in capabilities, modifying formulas, listing all formulas, and adjusting the solve order.

- Chapter 4, Formatting a Pivot Table:

  Applying and customizing PivotTable Styles, retaining formatting, applying Report Layouts, and formatting numbers. Applying conditional formatting, such as data bars, icon sets, and color scales.

- Chapter 5, Grouping and Totaling Pivot Table Data:

  Grouping dates, to compare results by year, quarter, month, or week. Grouping numbers or text labels, to summarize data. Preventing errors when grouping dates or numbers, creating multiple subtotals, and displaying multiple values for a field.

- Chapter 6, Modifying a Pivot Table:

  Changing the pivot table layout, showing all items for a field, clearing old items from the field drop-downs, hiding items with no data, and allowing drag-and-drop in the worksheet layout.

- Chapter 7, Updating a Pivot Table:

  Refreshing the pivot table, refreshing automatically, reconnecting to the source data, locating and changing the source data, and deferring a layout update.

- Chapter 8, Pivot Table Security, Limits, and Performance:

  Preventing users from changing the pivot table layout, connecting to a password-protected data source, using security features, addressing privacy issues, and understanding pivot table limits.

- Chapter 9, Printing and Extracting Pivot Table Data:

  Printing headings on every page, adjusting the print area, and starting each item on a new page. Using the Show Details feature to extract underlying records, using the GetPivotData worksheet function to extract pivot table data, turning off the GetPivotData feature, and using cell references in GetPivotData formulas.

- Chapter 10, Pivot Charts:

  Planning and creating a pivot chart, creating normal charts from pivot table data, creating multiple series for years, creating a combination chart, and locating the source pivot table.

- Chapter 11, Programming a Pivot Table:

  Recording and using macros, modifying recorded code. Sample code for automatically deleting created sheets, changing report filters in related pivot tables, preventing layout changes, refreshing automatically when source data changes, and identifying and changing the pivot cache.

Prerequisites

The solutions in this book are written for Microsoft Excel 2007. A working knowledge of Excel 2007 is assumed, as is familiarity with pivot table basics. Sample code is provided in Chapter 11, and some programming experience may be required to adjust the code to conform to your workbook setup.

For an introduction to pivot tables in Excel 2007, see *Beginning Pivot Tables in Excel 2007,* by Debra Dalgleish; Apress, 2007.

Downloading the Code

Sample workbooks and code are available for download from the Apress web site at www.apress.com.

Contacting the Author

You can send comments to the author at ddalgleish@contextures.com and visit her Contextures web site at www.contextures.com.

CHAPTER 1

■■■

Creating a Pivot Table

Even though you've likely created many pivot tables in Microsoft Excel, you sometimes encounter problems while setting them up. You may be familiar with creating pivot tables in Excel 2003, but you have upgraded to Excel 2007, and you can't find all the familiar commands and option settings. After you create a pivot table, perhaps its layout isn't as flexible as you'd like, or perhaps you have trouble connecting to the data source you want to use. This chapter discusses the issues you can consider as you plan the pivot table, set up the source data, and connect to the source. Other topics include working with data on separate worksheets, and using the PivotTable Field List.

1.1. Planning a Pivot Table: Getting Started

Problem

You've been asked to create a pivot table to summarize your company's sales data, and you aren't sure what issues to consider before you create it. You've created pivot tables before, but this one will be used in an executive presentation, and you want to ensure that the pivot table is going to work smoothly and be problem-free.

Solution

If you spend some time planning, you can create a pivot table that is easier to maintain and that clearly delivers the information your customers need. When planning a pivot table, you should consider several things, as the following outlines.

Where Is the Source Data Stored?

Many pivot tables are created from a single Excel Table, usually in the same workbook as the pivot table. Others are created from an external source, such as a database query, or online analytical processing (OLAP) cube.

To create a meaningful pivot table, you need current, accurate data. Is the source data in your workbook updated by you on a regular basis? Or is the source data stored elsewhere?

If others are using the pivot table, and the data is not stored in the workbook, will they have access to the source data when they want to refresh the pivot table? If the source data is password protected, will all users know the password?

How Frequently Will the Source Data Be Updated?

If the source data will be updated frequently, you may want a routine that automatically refreshes the pivot table when the workbook is opened. If the data is stored outside the workbook, and updated occasionally, will you be notified that the data has changed and that you need to refresh the pivot table?

Does the Source Data Include All the Information You Need?

The source data may contain all the information that you want in the pivot table. However, you may need to report on other fields. For example, if variance from actual to budget is required in the pivot table, is variance a field in the source data? If not, you'll need to calculate that in the pivot table, or add variance to the fields in the source data.

If fields are missing from the source data, can they be calculated at the source, or will they be calculated in the pivot table? Adding calculations to a large pivot table may cause any updates to be very slow, and they may have different results than doing line calculations in the source data.

1.2. Planning a Shared Pivot Table

Problem

As part of the annual budget process, you've been asked to create a pivot table that summarizes the previous year's sales data and make the results available to other employees. Although you've made several pivot tables for your own use, you aren't sure what to consider when making a pivot table for wider distribution.

Solution

If a pivot table is to be shared with others, here are some things to consider.

Will All Users Need the Same Level of Detail?

Some users may require a top-level summary of the data. For example, the senior executives may want to see a total per region for annual sales. Other users may require greater detail. The regional directors may want to see the data totaled by district, or by sales representative. Sales representatives may need the data totaled by customer, or by product number.

If the requirements are varied, you may want to create multiple pivot tables, each one focused on the needs of a particular user group. If that's not possible, you'll want to create a pivot table that's easy to navigate, and adaptable for each user group's needs.

Is the Information Sensitive?

Often, a pivot table is based on sensitive data. For example, the source data may contain sales results and commission figures for all the sales representatives. If you create a pivot table from the data, assume that anyone who can open the workbook will be able to view all the data. Even if you protect the worksheet and the workbook, the data won't be secure. Some passwords can be easily cracked, allowing the protection to be bypassed. This weakness is described in Excel's Help files, under the heading, "Protect worksheet or workbook elements."

It includes the warning, "Element protection cannot protect a workbook from users who have malicious intent."

When requiring a password to open the workbook, use a strong password, as described in the Microsoft article "Strong Passwords: How to Create and Use Them," at `www.microsoft.com/protect/yourself/password/create.mspx`.

▪**Note** A strong password contains a mixture of upper- and lowercase letters, numbers, and special characters (such as $ and %), and is at least six characters long.

For sensitive and confidential data, the pivot table should only be based on the data that each user is entitled to view. You can create multiple Excel Tables, in separate workbooks, and create individual pivot tables from those. It requires more time to set these up, but it is worthwhile to ensure that privacy concerns are addressed. You can use macros and naming conventions to standardize the source data and the pivot tables, and to minimize the work required to create the individual copies.

Another option is to use secured network folders to store the workbook, where only authorized users can access the data. Also available in Excel 2007 is *Information Rights Management,* a file-protection technology that enables you to assign permissions to users or groups. For example, some users can have Read permission only and won't be able to edit, copy, or print the file contents. Other users, with Change permission, can edit and save changes. You can also set expiry dates for the permissions to limit access to a specific time period. To learn more about Information Rights Management, see Excel's Help files, and check out "Information Rights Management in the 2007 Microsoft Office system" at `www.microsoft.com/office/editions/prodinfo/technologies/irm.mspx`. The Security for the 2007 Office System article discusses the security technologies available in Excel, as well as other Office programs, in the downloadable Word file available at `http://go.microsoft.com/fwlink/?LinkID=85671`.

Will the Information Be Shared in Printed or Electronic Format?

If the information will be shared in printed format only, the security issues are minimized. You can control what's printed and issued to each recipient. If the information is to be shared electronically, it's crucial that confidential data not be included in any pivot table that's being distributed to multiple users.

Will the Pivot Table Be in a Shared Workbook?

Many features are unavailable in a shared workbook, including creating or changing a pivot table or pivot chart. Users will be able to view your pivot table, but they won't be able to rearrange the fields or select different items from the drop-down lists.

If the workbook contains a formatted Excel Table, it cannot be shared, so you wouldn't be able to use this feature as a source for your pivot table. As described in Section 1.4, a formatted Excel Table offers many benefits, such as automatically expanding to include new rows. In a shared workbook, you would need another method of ensuring that all new data is included in the pivot table's source data.

Also, protection can't be changed in a shared workbook, so you can't run macros that unprotect the worksheet, make changes, and then reprotect the worksheet.

Will Users Enable Macros in Your Workbook?

If your pivot table requires macros for some functionality, will users have the ability to enable macros? In some environments, they may not be able to use macros. Will that have a serious impact on the value of your pivot table?

1.3. Preparing the Source Data: Using Excel Data

Problem

The sales manager sent you an Excel workbook that contains last year's sales orders, and wants you to create a pivot table to summarize the data. You had problems with the last pivot table you created and couldn't get the totals you wanted. To avoid similar problems this time, before creating the pivot table, you want to ensure the data is set up correctly. This problem is based on the sample file named ProductSales.xlsx.

Solution

Probably the most common data source for a pivot table is Excel data, in the same workbook as the pivot table. The data may be contained in only a few rows of records or there may be thousands of rows. No matter how much data there is, some common requirements exist when preparing to create a pivot table from the Excel data.

Organizing the Data in Rows and Columns

The Excel data should be organized in a table of rows and columns, as shown in Figure 1-1. This shows the first few rows of data from the sample file named ProductSales.xlsx.

	A	B	C	D	E	F	G	H
1	Date	SalesRep	Region	Product	Cost	Units	Dollars	
2	6–Jan–07	Jones	East	Pencil	2.99	95	284.05	
3	23–Jan–07	Kivell	West	Binder	4.99	50	249.5	
4	9–Feb–07	Jardine	West	Pencil	2.99	36	107.64	
5	26–Feb–07	Kivell	West	Binder	4.99	27	134.73	
6	15–Mar–07	Sorvino	West	Pencil	2.99	56	167.44	
7	1–Apr–07	Jones	East	Binder	4.99	60	299.4	
8	18–Apr–07	Andrews	West	Pencil	2.99	75	224.25	
9	5–May–07	Jardine	Central	Pencil	2.99	90	269.1	
10	22–May–07	Thompson	West	Pencil	2.99	32	95.68	

Figure 1-1. *Data organized in a table of rows and columns*

- Each column in the source data must have a heading. You will be unable to create a pivot table if any of the heading cells are blank.

- No completely blank rows should be within the source data.

- No completely blank columns can be within the source data. Each column must contain at least an entry in the heading cell. If you need the column to appear blank, you can type a heading, such as **Blank1**, and format the font with a color that matches the cell fill color.

Tip Select a cell in the source data, and then while holding down the Ctrl key, press the A key to select the current region. If all the source data isn't selected, blank rows or columns are probably within the data. Locate and delete them, or enter data in them.

- Each column should contain the same type of data. In Figure 1-1, Column G contains sales amounts in currency. Column C contains region names in text. Column A contains order dates.

- Create a separate column for each type of data that you want to analyze in the pivot table. For example, put City and State in separate columns, instead of storing City and State together, in one column. This lets you view totals by either city or state in the pivot table.

- The source data should be separated from any other data on the worksheet, with at least one blank row, and one blank column between it and the other data. Ideally, have only the source data on the worksheet, and move other data to a separate worksheet.

- If rows or columns within the source data are manually hidden, you can leave them hidden. The pivot table will be based on all rows and columns, whether they're hidden or visible.

Tip If columns are hidden, check that they contain data in the heading cells, or you won't be able to create a pivot table from the source data.

Removing Totals and Subtotals

- Remove any total calculations at the top or bottom of the source data, or separate the calculations from the data by inserting one or more blank rows.

- If the Subtotal feature is turned on in the source data, remove the subtotals. If your source data has automatic subtotals, you'll get an error message when you try to create the pivot table. The Subtotal command is on the Ribbon's Data tab.

- Remove any manually entered subtotals within the source data, to prevent inaccurate totals in the pivot table.

- If the source data has a filter applied, you can leave it on. The pivot table will be based on all data, whether it's hidden or visible.

Creating an Excel Table from the Worksheet Data

- As a final step in preparing the Excel source data, you should format the worksheet data as an Excel Table, to activate special features in the source data, such as the capability to automatically extend formulas as new rows are added to the end of the existing data. Instructions for creating an Excel Table are in Section 1.4.

1.4. Preparing the Source Data: Creating an Excel Table

Problem

You've just upgraded from Excel 2003, where you used the Excel List feature to prepare your data for use as pivot table source data. You've discovered that the List feature is no longer available, and you want to find an equivalent feature in Excel 2007. This problem is based on the sample file named ProductSales.xlsx.

Solution

In Excel 2007, you can create a formatted Excel Table from the data. This replaces the Excel List feature found in Excel 2003, and it includes many new features that will make pivot table creation and updating easier.

To create the Excel Table, organize your data in rows and columns, as described in Section 1.3. Then follow these steps to create the Excel Table.

1. Select a cell in the source data, and on the Ribbon, click the Insert tab.

2. In the Tables group, click the Table command (see Figure 1-2).

Figure 1-2. *The Table command on the Insert tab of the Ribbon*

3. In the Create Table dialog box, confirm that the correct range is shown for the table, and then select a different range if necessary.

4. Leave the check mark in the box for My Table Has Headers, and then click OK.

When it's created, the Excel Table is given a default name, such as Table1. You can rename the formatted Excel Table, so it will be easy to identify each table if multiple Excel Tables are in the workbook. This helps to ensure that you select the correct source data when you're creating pivot tables. To name the Excel Table, follow these instructions.

1. Select a cell in the formatted Excel Table, and on the Ribbon, click the Design tab.

2. At the left end of the Ribbon, in the Properties group, type a one-word name, such as **SalesData**, in the Table Name box (see Figure 1-3).

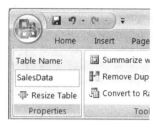

Figure 1-3. *Table Name in the Properties group*

How It Works

Using the Excel Table feature makes it easier to maintain the source data for a pivot table. In an Excel Table, if you add rows or columns, the new data is automatically included when you update the pivot table. If you base a pivot table on unformatted source data, new rows or columns may not be detected, and you would have to manually adjust the source data range each time new data is added, or create a dynamic range in the Name Manager. Or, you might forget to adjust the source data range to include the new data, and the pivot table could then show inaccurate results.

If you add columns to an Excel Table, column headings, such as Column1, are automatically added for you. This feature ensures you won't see errors caused by blank heading cells if you try to create or update a pivot table based on the Excel Table. You can change the default column headings to something more descriptive, if you prefer.

Another advantage of using a formatted Excel Table is this: the column headings remain visible when you scroll down the worksheet. This makes identifying the columns easier as you work in a large Excel Table. When the heading row is no longer visible on the worksheet, the column headings are displayed in the column buttons at the top of the worksheet.

An Excel Table's heading cells contain drop-down lists that let you quickly and easily sort and filter the data in the table. This feature can help you review the data before creating a pivot table or when troubleshooting a pivot table. For example, you can sort the values, to quickly spot the highest and lowest amounts in the table, or you can filter the data to view one region's sales records.

■**Note** The drop-down filter lists are only available when the heading row of the Excel Table is visible. Press Ctrl+Home to return to the top-left cell.

1.5. Preparing the Source Data: Excel Field Names Not Valid

Problem

You entered your company's sales order data on an Excel worksheet, and you want to create a pivot table from that data. On the Ribbon's Insert tab, you clicked the PivotTable command, and selected a source range in the Create PivotTable dialog box. When you clicked the OK button, a confusing error message appeared: "The PivotTable field name is not valid. To create a PivotTable report, you must use data that is organized as a list with labeled columns. If you are changing the name of a PivotTable field, you must type a new name for the field." You haven't named any fields, and you aren't sure what the message means. This problem is based on the sample file named `FieldNames.xlsx`.

Solution

One or more of the heading cells in the source data may be blank and, to create a pivot table, you need a heading for each column. To locate the problem, try the following:

- In the Create PivotTable dialog box, check the Table/Range selection carefully to ensure you haven't selected extra columns that are blank.

- Check for hidden columns within the source data range, as they may have blank heading cells.

- Select each heading cell and view its contents in the formula bar; text from one heading may overlap a blank cell beside it.

- Unmerge any merged cells in the heading row.

Tip If you create a formatted Excel Table from your Excel data, as described in Section 1.4, column headings are automatically entered for columns where there are blank heading cells.

1.6. Preparing the Source Data: Using Filtered Excel Data

Problem

The district manager for the Central district asked you to create a pivot table with the data for that district only. You filtered the sales order data, so only the records for the Central region are visible on the worksheet. When you created the pivot table, using the filtered range as the source, all the regions' records were included, instead of just the visible records for the Central region. This problem is based on the sample file named `Filter.xlsx`.

Solution

A pivot table includes all the items from the source data, even if the data has an AutoFilter or Advanced Filter applied, or if rows or columns have been manually hidden. Instead of filtering the list in place, you could use an Advanced Filter to extract specific records to another workbook, and then base the pivot table on the extracted data.

1.7. Preparing the Source Data: Using an Excel Table with Monthly Columns

Problem

The district managers sent you their year-end sales data, and you copied it from the separate workbooks into one sheet in a new workbook, so you can create a pivot table to summarize all the data. The worksheet has a column for each month (see Figure 1-4), and you're having trouble creating a flexible pivot table from this source data. Each month becomes a separate field in the PivotTable Field List, and getting the layout you want in the pivot table and creating annual totals is difficult. Figure 1-4 shows the data from the sample file named MonthlyData.xlsx.

	A	B	C	D	E	F	G	H	I	J	K	L	M
1	Product	Jan	Feb	Mar	Apr	May	Jun	Jul	Aug	Sep	Oct	Nov	Dec
2	Lamps	35	786	911	459	480	595	923	310	470	928	118	953
3	Fans	144	688	63	710	129	147	158	294	833	898	371	146
4	Heaters	209	5	754	793	351	457	701	612	939	680	471	400
5	Vacuums	39	144	642	919	555	446	917	98	382	993	495	279
6	Toasters	94	324	115	501	47	770	817	282	272	780	394	26
7	Blenders	668	455	819	96	986	185	966	165	107	59	760	101

Figure 1-4. *Data organized in monthly columns*

Solution

When organizing your source data, decide how you want to summarize the data in the pivot table. What headings would you like to show at the left, as Row Labels? What headings should appear across the top of the pivot table, as Column Labels? What numbers do you want to sum?

Using the data shown in Figure 1-4, you might want to summarize the data for each product, for each month, and create an annual total. The products' names are listed in Column A, with the column heading Product. Product will become a field name when you create a pivot table, and the product names will be items in the Product field. In the pivot table, you could add the Product field to the Row Labels area, and the product names would be listed there.

However, the columns with month names as headings, such as Jan and Feb, will cause problems when you create the pivot table. Each month will be a separate field, and the values in its column will be the items in that field. If each month is a separate field, the pivot table will not automatically create a total for the year; you would have to create a calculation for the annual total.

You should rearrange the data, using actual dates (if available) or month names, in a single column, with the sales amounts all in one column (see Figure 1-5). Instead of 13 columns (Product and one for each of the 12 months), the revised list will have three columns: Product, Month, and Quantity. This will *normalize* the data and allow you to create a more flexible pivot table.

	A	B	C
1	Product	Month	Quantity
2	Lamps	Jan	35
3	Lamps	Feb	786
4	Lamps	Mar	911
5	Lamps	Apr	459
6	Lamps	May	480

Figure 1-5. *Normalized data with month names in one column*

Normalization is a process of organizing data to remove redundant elements, such as multiple columns for similar data. For information on normalization, you can read the Microsoft Knowledge Base article "Description of the Database Normalization Basics" at http://support.microsoft.com/kb/283878. Although the article refers to Microsoft Access, it is relevant when organizing your data for use in a pivot table. The same principles apply, because you want the ability to summarize your data by specific fields, or to sort and filter the items in a pivot table, just as you would in an Access database.

The following technique automates the normalization process for you. It creates a pivot table from the existing list, and combines all the Month columns into one field. Then, the Show Details feature is used to extract the source data in its one-column format. The original data is not affected.

Adding the PivotTable and PivotChart Wizard

To use this technique, you need the PivotTable and PivotChart Wizard, which was used to create pivot tables in Excel 2003 and earlier versions. This is not on the Ribbon, but you can add it to the Quick Access Toolbar (QAT).

■**Tip** You can also open the PivotTable and PivotChart Wizard by using the keyboard shortcut Alt+D, P.

---

1. Right-click the QAT, and click Customize Quick Access Toolbar.

2. In the Choose Commands From drop-down list, choose Commands Not in the Ribbon.

3. Scroll down the alphabetical list of commands, and then click PivotTable and PivotChart Wizard.

4. Click the Add button to add the command to the QAT.

5. Click OK to close the Excel Options dialog box.

Normalizing the Data for a Single Text Column

Assuming you have a simple list, as in the sample file MonthlyData.xlsx, with one column of text (product names) and twelve columns of monthly sales figures, follow these steps:

1. Select a cell in the list, and then click the PivotTable and PivotChart Wizard command on the QAT (or press Alt+D, P).

2. In Step 1, select Multiple Consolidation Ranges, select PivotTable as the kind of report, and then click Next.

3. In Step 2a, select the I Will Create The Page Fields option, and then click Next.

4. In Step 2b, click in the Range box, and then select your worksheet list, including the headings, and then click the Add button.

5. Leave the other settings at their defaults, and then click the Finish button.

6. A pivot table appears on a new worksheet in the workbook, with a PivotTable Field List that contains only three fields: Row, Column, and Value.

7. In the PivotTable Field List, remove the check marks from the Row and Column fields, to remove them from the pivot table layout.

8. In the pivot table that was created, double-click the cell below the Count of Value heading. Double-clicking is the shortcut for the Show Details feature and it creates a list of underlying data on a new worksheet.

▆Tip You can filter the Value column in the table that was created, to remove any rows with blank Value cells. From the drop-down list in the Value column, choose (Blanks). Delete the filtered rows, and then from the drop-down list in the Value column, choose Clear Filter from Value.

---

9. In the resulting table of data, rename the heading cells as Product, Month, and Amount.

▆Tip This normalized list will be used as the source for your new pivot table. Make a backup copy of the file, and then you can delete the original list and its pivot table. You can also delete the sheet that contains the pivot table used in Step 9.

---

10. Create a pivot table from the normalized list, with Product in the Row Labels area, Month in the Column Labels area, and Amount in the Values area. Because there's only one value field, the Row Grand Total will automatically sum the Months. In the old version of the pivot table, with 12-month fields, you had to create a calculated field to sum the months.

Normalizing the Data For Multiple Text Columns

If you have two or more text columns, you should concatenate them before using the normalization technique. For example, if you have columns for Name and Region, as in the sample file MonthlyDataReg.xlsx, follow these steps:

1. Insert a blank column after Region, with the heading **NameRegion**.

2. In cell C2, enter the following formula, which combines the Name and the Region, with a dollar sign between them. Later, the dollar sign is used to separate the Name and Region into two columns.

        =A2 & "$" & B2

3. Copy the formula down to the last row of data.

4. Follow Steps 1 to 9 in the previous "Normalizing the Data instructions," using columns C:O as the source range for the pivot table.

5. In the resulting list of data, rename the heading cells as NameRegion, Month, and Amount.

6. Select Column A (NameRegion), and move it to the right of the other columns. This prevents it from overwriting the other columns when you separate Name and Region in the next step.

7. With the NameRegion column selected, click the Data tab on the Ribbon.

8. In the Data Tools group, click Text to Columns (see Figure 1-6).

Figure 1-6. *Text to Columns command on the Ribbon*

9. Under Original Data Type, select Delimited, and then click Next.

10. Under Delimiters, check the Other option and, in the text box, type a $ sign. This splits the text at the $ sign in each cell. In the Data Preview window, you can see how the data will look after it's split.

11. Click Finish to split the text into two columns.

12. Add headings to the name and region columns, and then move them to the left, if desired.

13. Create a pivot table from the normalized list, with Name and Region in the Row Labels area, Month in the Column Labels area, and Amount in the data area.

1.8. Preparing the Source Data: Using an Access Query

Problem

The sales manager has asked you to create a pivot table from sales orders stored in a Microsoft Access database. You will create reports that summarize the sales orders by product and color, or by customer location, and show the total quantities and total dollars. The person who manages the database will create a query in the database for you to use as the data source. This person has asked what fields you want to include in the query.

Solution

In the Access query, include all the fields you want in the pivot table, and create calculated fields if required, as the following describes.

- Include any lookup tables in the query, and add the descriptive field names to the query output, instead of using ID numbers or codes. For example, suppose an OrderDetail table includes a product number. Another table (Products) in the database contains the information about each product number, such as the product name and color. In the query, add both tables, and then join the Product number field in the two tables. In the query grid, include fields from the OrderDetail table, such as Quantity; and from the Products table, include descriptive fields, such as Product Name and Color.

- In the Access query, create calculated fields for any line calculations you want summarized in the pivot table, such as `LineTotal:UnitsSold*UnitPrice`. Unless all products have the same unit price, this type of calculation cannot be done in the pivot table; it must be done in the source data.

- Do not include user-defined functions or functions specific to Microsoft Access. Although they're permissible within Microsoft Access, user-defined functions and some built-in Access functions, such as NZ, create an error (for example, "Undefined function 'NZ' in expression") when used outside Access. For more information on the Jet SQL expressions used to return the data to Excel, see "Microsoft Jet SQL Reference" at `http://office.microsoft.com/en-ca/assistance/CH062526881033.aspx`.

- Do not include parameters in the Microsoft Access query. In Access, you can use parameters instead of specific criteria in a query, and you are then prompted to enter the criteria when the query runs. However, you can't create a pivot table that's directly based on a parameter query or, in the pivot table, you will get the error message "[Microsoft][ODBC Microsoft Access Driver] Too few parameters. Expected 1." Instead, create a query without parameters and, in the pivot table, you can use filters to limit the data that's summarized.

For more information on Access queries, see "Queries" at `http://office.microsoft.com/en-us/access/CH100645771033.aspx`.

1.9. Preparing the Source Data: Using a Text File

Problem

The accounting department can provide you with a text file of the year-to-date transactions, which you can use as a data source for your pivot table. They've asked how you want the file set up, and you aren't sure what to tell them.

Solution

You can use a delimited or fixed-width text file as the data source for a pivot table, but it's usually easier to work with a delimited file because it requires only one setting to separate the fields. If using a fixed-width file, you have to specify the start position and length of each field.

   If possible, include field headings in the first row (see Figure 1-7), or you will have to add the headings before using the file as the source for your pivot table. Also, ensure a line-break character is at the end of each record. Figure 1-7 shows the first few rows of comma-delimited data in the sample file ProductSales.txt.

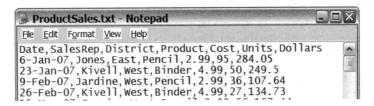

Figure 1-7. *Comma-delimited text file with headings*

1.10. Preparing the Source Data: Using an OLAP Cube

Problem

You want to base your pivot table on an OLAP cube that contains your company's sales data, but you aren't sure what to consider when creating the cube. You want to ensure the cube is designed to make the most of Excel's pivot table features.

Solution

A whitepaper is available for download on the Microsoft web site that can guide you or the person who is creating your OLAP cube: Excel 2007 Document: Designing SQL Server 2005 Analysis Services Cubes for Excel 2007 PivotTables www.microsoft.com/downloads/details.aspx?Familyid=2D779CD5-EEB2-43E9-BDFA-641ED89EDB6C.

   Although the whitepaper refers to SQL Server 2005 Analysis Services, the information will be useful to anyone creating an OLAP cube, from any source.

1.11. Creating the Pivot Table: Using Excel Data as the Source

Problem

You're familiar with creating pivot tables in Excel 2003, but you can't find the PivotTable Wizard on the Ribbon in Excel 2007. You want to create a pivot table from Excel data.

Solution

Before you create the pivot table, you should create an Excel Table from the data. This is a replacement for Excel Lists in Excel 2003, and it has many features that can make pivot table creation and updating easier. You can find instructions for doing this in Section 1.4. Then, follow these steps to create the pivot table.

1. Select a cell in the Excel Table and, on the Ribbon, under the Table Tools tab, click the Design tab.

2. In the Tools group, click Summarize with PivotTable, to open the Create PivotTable dialog box.

3. Under Choose the Data That You Want to Analyze, the option Select a Table or Range is selected, and the name of the Excel Table should appear in the Table/Range box.

4. Select the location for your PivotTable report—either a New Worksheet, or an Existing Worksheet—and then click OK.

5. An empty pivot table appears on the worksheet, at the location you selected. Add fields to the pivot table layout by checking the fields in the PivotTable Field List. The checked fields appear in the pivot table layout on the worksheet, and in the Areas section of the PivotTable Field List.

1.12. Creating the Pivot Table: Using Excel Data on Separate Sheets

Problem

You have an Excel Table with each region's sales on separate sheets in your workbook, and you want to combine all the data into one pivot table. All the sheets are set up identically, but each contains data for just one region. In the Create PivotTable dialog box, you can only select the data on one worksheet, so you can't create the pivot table from all the data.

Solution

Although you can create a pivot table from data on separate worksheets, the pivot table will have limited functionality, as described in the following "Notes" section. If possible, combine all the data on one worksheet, and then create the pivot table from that source data. To create a pivot table from data on separate worksheets, you must use the PivotTable and PivotChart

Wizard, which was used to create pivot tables in Excel 2003 and earlier versions. This is not on the Ribbon, but you can open it with a keyboard shortcut, or add it to the QAT, as described in Section 1.7.

Follow these steps to create the pivot table from data on separate worksheets, as in the sample file named MultiConsolSales.xlsx.

1. On the keyboard, press Alt+D, P, or, on the QAT, click the PivotTable and PivotChart Wizard.

2. In Step 1 of the PivotTable and PivotChart Wizard, select Multiple Consolidation Ranges, and then click Next.

3. In Step 2a, select one of the page options, and then click Next. For more information on the page options, see the following "Notes" section.

4. In Step 2b, click the Range box, select the first range, and then click Add, to add it to the All Ranges list.

5. Repeat Step 4 for each of the remaining ranges, to add it to the list.

6. If you chose "I Will Create The Page Fields," you can select each range, and assign field names, as described in the following "Notes" section.

7. Click Next and, in Step 3, select a location for the pivot table, and then click Finish.

8. If you created page fields, you can rename them on the worksheet, where they appear in the Report Filter area. For example, select the cell that contains the label Page1, and type **Salesperson**.

9. In the Column Labels drop-down list, hide any columns that contain meaningless data, such as Customer, which is a text field.

Notes

Creating a pivot table from multiple consolidation ranges enables you to create a pivot table from data in two or more separate Excel Tables. However, the result is not the same as a pivot table created from a single Excel Table. The first field is placed in the Row Labels area, the remaining field names are placed in the Column Labels area, and the values in those columns appear in the Values area. All the Values use the same summary function, such as Sum or Count.

You can hide or show the column items, and you can use the Report Filters to filter the data. However, there's no setting you can change that will make a pivot table created from multiple consolidation ranges look like a regular pivot table.

To get the best results when creating a pivot table from multiple consolidation ranges, ensure that all the ranges being used are identical in setup. Each Excel Table should have the same column headings, in the same order, and contain the same type of data. The ranges can contain different numbers of rows.

The first column will be used as Row Labels in the pivot table, so move the most important field to that position. In the `MultiConsolSales.xlsx` sample file, the Product field is in the first position, so the data is summarized by product.

In the PivotTable and PivotChart Wizard, after you select Multiple Consolidation Ranges as the data source, Step 2a asks, "How many page fields do you want?" You can let Excel create one page field, or you can create the page fields yourself. These appear as Report Filters in the pivot table.

Choosing Create a Single Page Field for Me

If you select this option, one page field is created automatically. In Step 2b of the PivotTable and PivotChart Wizard, you aren't presented with any options for creating the page fields. In the completed pivot table, there's one page field, and each range in the multiple consolidation ranges is represented as a numbered item—for example, Item1, Item2, and Item3.

This makes it difficult to determine which data you're viewing when you select one of the items from the drop-down list. However, if you're more interested in the total amounts than in the individual ranges, this is a quick way to create the page field.

Choosing I Will Create the Page Fields

If you select this option, you can create the page fields in Step 2b of the PivotTable and PivotChart Wizard. To create the page fields, follow these steps:

1. In Step 2b, select each range, and add it to the All Ranges list.

2. Select the number of page fields you want to create (zero to four). In this example, there will be two page fields.

3. In the All Ranges list, select the first range.

4. You'll use the first page field to show the salesperson names. In the drop-down list for Field One, type the name of the person whose range you have highlighted in the list.

5. Each salesperson works in one of your sales regions, and you'll use the second page field to show the region names. In the drop-down list for Field Two, type the region name for the person whose range you have highlighted in the list, as shown in Figure 1-8.

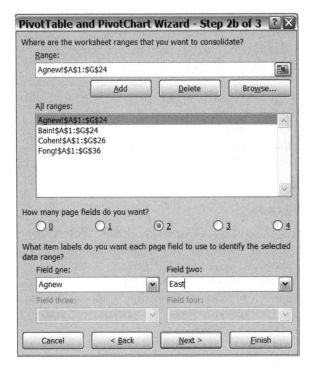

Figure 1-8. *Page fields for multiple consolidation ranges*

6. Select the next range in the All Ranges list, and then repeat Steps 4 and 5. Continue until all the ranges have page labels.

■**Tip** After you create a label, you can select that label from the drop-down list for subsequent entries.

---

7. Click Next, and then click Finish to close the PivotTable and PivotChart Wizard.

8. In the pivot table, the page fields you created are shown as Report Filters, with the labels, Page1 and Page2. You can change the labels by typing over them. Select the cell that has the Page1 label, and type **Salesperson**, and then select the cell that has the Page2 label, and type **Region**.

1.13. Creating the Pivot Table: Using the PivotTable Field List

Problem

You created a pivot table, but it's empty, and you can't drag the fields from the PivotTable Field List onto the worksheet layout, as you did in Excel 2003. When you add a check mark beside a field name in the PivotTable Field List, the field is automatically added to the pivot table layout, but you want to control where the fields are placed.

Solution

The PivotTable Field List lists all the fields available for the pivot table, and enables you to place the fields in specific areas of the pivot table. At the top of the PivotTable Field List is a list of the fields in your source data, in the same order they appear in the source data. At the bottom of the PivotTable Field List is the Areas section, with a box for each area of the pivot table layout; the Row Labels, the Column Labels, the Values, and the Report Filters.

When you add a check mark beside a field name in the PivotTable Field List, the field is automatically added to a default area of the pivot table layout, but you can move the fields to a different area if you choose. For example, to move a field from the Row Labels area to the Column Labels area, follow these steps.

1. In the PivotTable Field List, point to a field in Row Labels area.

2. When the pointer changes to a four-headed arrow, drag the field to the Column Labels area.

■Tip If you prefer to drag the fields onto the worksheet layout, as you did in earlier versions of Excel, you can change a pivot table option. Right-click a cell in the pivot table, and in the context menu, click PivotTable Options. In the PivotTable Options dialog box, click the Display tab, and add a check mark to Classic Pivot-Table Layout.

Another way to place a field in a specific area is to right-click the field name in the Pivot-Table Field List, and then select an area from the context menu (see Figure 1-9).

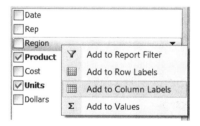

Figure 1-9. *PivotTable Field List context menu*

■Tip To remove a field from the pivot table layout, you can remove the check mark from its name in the Field List section, or drag it out of the Areas section in the PivotTable Field List.

How It Works

If you add a check mark to a numeric field in the PivotTable Field List, it is added to the Values area. If you add a check mark to a nonnumeric field, it is added to the Row Labels area. When checked, OLAP date and time hierarchies are automatically added to the Column Labels area.

You can add multiple copies of a field to the pivot table layout. One copy can be in the Row Labels, Column Labels, or Report Filters area, and one or more copies can be placed in the Values area. For example, you can add the Region field to the Row Labels area, and another copy of the Region field to the Values area, where it would become Count of Region.

If a field is already in a Row Labels, Column Labels, or Report Filters area, and you add that field to the area it's currently in, it will change to the new location. If you add that field to a different one of those areas, it moves to the different area. For example, if the Region field is the first of three fields in the Row Labels area, and you add it to the Row Labels area again, it will move to the third position in the Row Labels area. If you add the Region field to the Column Labels area, it will move from the Row Labels area to the Column Labels area.

For OLAP fields, you can only move hierarchies, attributes, and named sets to the Row Labels, Column Labels, and Report Filters areas. Measures, calculated measures, and Key Performance Indicators (KPIs) can only be moved to the Values area.

1.14. Creating the Pivot Table: Changing the Field List Order

Problem

Many fields are in the source data for your pivot table, and the PivotTable Field List shows the fields in the same order they appear in the source data. To make it easier to locate the fields in the long list, you would like the field list in alphabetical order.

Solution

You can change a pivot table option, to make the PivotTable Field List show the fields in alphabetical order.

1. Right-click a cell in the pivot table, and in the context menu, click PivotTable Options.

2. In the PivotTable Options dialog box, click the Display tab.

3. In the Field List section, select Sort A to Z, and then click OK (see Figure 1-10).

Figure 1-10. *Field List sort order*

■Tip To return the field list to its original order, select Sort in Data Source Order in the PivotTable Options Display tab.

CHAPTER 2

■■■

Sorting and Filtering Pivot Table Data

As you analyze data in a pivot table, you may want to rearrange the items in the Row Labels and Column Labels areas, or sort the summarized values, to focus on products that are selling the best, or districts that are doing poorly. Sorting the labels or the values lets you move the most important information to the top. You can also filter the labels or the values to limit the data summarized in the pivot table.

Unless otherwise noted, the problems in this chapter are based on data in the sample file named FoodSales.xlsx.

2.1. Sorting a Pivot Field: Sorting Row Labels

Problem

Three fields are in the Row Labels area of your pivot table: District, City, and Category, as shown in Figure 2-1. District, the first row field, is sorted alphabetically, and you want to sort the districts in ascending order by their total sales. The TotalSale field is in the Values area.

Sorting the row labels alphabetically or by values is simple when only one field is in the Row Labels area, but you sometimes have problems when multiple fields exist. This problem is based on the sample file FoodSales.xlsx.

Note If a pivot table has more than one field in the Row Labels area, the field that's last in the list is the *inner* field. All the remaining row fields are *outer* fields. In Figure 2-1, District and City are the outer row fields, and Category is the inner row field.

	Row Labels	Sum of TotalSale
2		
3	Row Labels ▼	Sum of TotalSale
4	⊟Central	33,847.08
5	⊟Chicago	33,847.08
6	Bars	7,745.03
7	Cookies	11,117.03
8	Crackers	7,812.14
9	Snacks	7,172.88
10	⊟East	131,482.83
11	⊟Boston	31,571.23
12	Bars	9,235.25
13	Cookies	6,691.61

Figure 2-1. *District and City are the outer row fields and Category is the inner row field.*

Solution

When a single field is in the Row Labels area, you can select any row label or value cell, and click the A-Z button on the Ribbon's Data tab to sort the labels. With multiple fields, the key to success lies in selecting an appropriate cell before sorting.

Sorting by Labels

To sort a field alphabetically, follow these steps:

1. Right-click a row label for the field you want to sort. For example, to sort the District field's labels, right-click the East label.

2. Click Sort, and then click Sort A to Z.

Sorting by Values

If the values or subtotals are visible, follow these steps to sort a field's row labels by their values:

1. Right-click a value cell or subtotal for the field you want to sort. For example, to sort the District field's values, right-click the subtotal for the Central district.

2. Click Sort, and then click Sort Largest to Smallest.

Only the row labels for the selected field will be sorted. For example, if you sort the district labels by their values, the city and category labels are unaffected. Also, the values are sorted within their group. For example, if you sort the categories by value, the categories listed under each city are sorted by value. As a result, the categories may appear in a different order under each city.

Sorting by Values with Hidden Subtotals

For an outer field in the Row Labels area, subtotals may be hidden. If the subtotals are not visible, additional steps are required to sort the row labels by their values. Follow these steps to sort a field's row labels by their values, in ascending order:

1. Right-click a row label for the field you want to sort. For example, to sort the City field's labels, right-click Boston.

2. Click Sort, and then click More Sort Options.

3. Under Sort Options, select Ascending (A to Z) by.

4. From the drop-down list, select the value field by which you want to sort. In this example, Sum of TotalSale would be the value field selected.

5. Click OK to close the Sort dialog box.

How It Works

In a pivot table, when you do an ascending sort, values are sorted in the following order:

1. Numbers (including dates, which Excel stores as numbers).

2. Text, in the following order: 0 1 2 3 4 5 6 7 8 9 (space) ! " # $ % & ( ) * , . / : ; ? @ [\ ] ^ _ ` { | } ~ + < = > A B C D E F G H I J K L M N O P Q R S T U V W X Y Z.

   Hyphens and apostrophes are ignored, except where two items are the same except for a hyphen. In that case, in an ascending sort, the item with the hyphen is sorted after the similar items without the hyphen. For example, Arrowroot would be listed before -Arrowroot.

3. Logical values (FALSE comes before TRUE).

4. Error values, such as #N/A and #NAME?. Unlike a worksheet sort, where error values are treated equally, error values in a pivot table are sorted alphabetically.

5. Blank cells.

2.2. Sorting a Pivot Field: New Items Out of Order

Problem

Your company has just started to sell binders, in addition to its existing products, and this morning you entered the first order for binders in your pivot table source data. The Product field is in the Row Labels area of the pivot table, and Quantity is in the Values area.

When you refreshed the pivot table, Binders appeared at the bottom of the Product list, instead of the top. It's also at the bottom of the drop-down filter list for the row labels. This makes finding the new product in the list difficult, and you'd like it sorted alphabetically with the other products. This problem is based on the sample file NewProduct.xlsx.

Solution

If a field's sort setting is set for Manual sort, new items will appear at the end of the drop-down list. This sort setting can occur if you manually rearrange the items in the Row Labels area. Follow these steps to sort the field in ascending order:

1. Right-click a cell in the Product field. For example, right-click the Envelopes cell.

2. Click Sort, and then click Sort A to Z.

When you sort the field, its sort setting changes from Manual to Sort Ascending or Sort Descending. This also sorts the drop-down list, and makes it easier for users to find the items they need.

2.3. Sorting a Pivot Field: Sorting Items Left to Right

Problem

In your pivot table, the City field is in the Column Labels area, the Product field is in the Row Labels area, and TotalSale is in the Values area. The city names in the column headings are sorted alphabetically.

You're planning a new marketing campaign for bran bars, and you want to focus on the cities with the highest sales for this product. You'd like to sort the values in the Bran row from left to right, so the city with the highest sales for bran bars is at the left. This problem is based on the sample file FoodSales.xlsx.

Solution

You can sort a row label by its values, left to right. In this example, the Bran product will be sorted by its TotalSale amounts. The column heading for the city with largest amount sold will be at the left.

1. In the pivot table, right-click a value cell in the Bran row.

2. Click Sort, and then click More Sort Options, to open the Sort By Value dialog box.

3. Under Sort Options, select Largest to Smallest.

4. Under Sort direction, select Left to Right. In the Summary section, you can see a description of the sort settings (see Figure 2-2).

5. Click OK to close the dialog box.

The TotalSale values for the Bran product are sorted largest to smallest, from left to right. The City column order has changed, and New York, which has the highest Bran sales, is at the left. Rows for other products may not be in descending order, because the column order has been set by the Bran product.

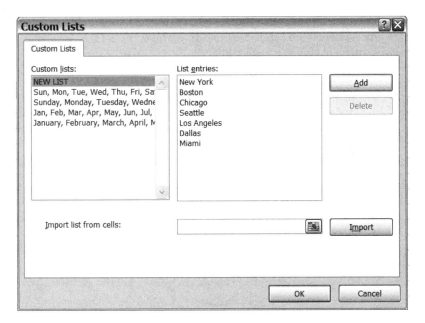

Figure 2-2. *Sort By Value dialog box*

2.4. Sorting a Pivot Field: Sorting Items in a Custom Order

Problem

In your pivot table, the City field is in the Row Labels area, and you would like the cities listed geographically instead of alphabetically. You can manually rearrange the city labels, but you would prefer to have them sorted automatically. This problem is based on the sample file FoodSales.xlsx.

Solution

In Excel, you can create custom lists, like the built-in lists of weekdays and months. For example, you could create a custom list of districts, department names, or reporting categories, and then use the custom lists to sort the items in your pivot table. This enables you to create reports that are tailored to your needs, quickly and easily.

Creating a Custom List

The entries for the custom list can be imported from a worksheet list, or typed in the Custom Lists dialog box. In this example, the list of cities is typed.

1. Click the Microsoft Office button, and at the bottom right, click Excel Options.

2. In the list of categories, click Popular, and in the Top Options for Working with Excel section, click Edit Custom Lists.

3. In the Custom Lists dialog box, under Custom Lists, select NEW LIST.

4. Click in the List Entries section, and type your list, pressing the Enter key after each item, to separate the list items (see Figure 2-3). In this example, the list is New York, Boston, Chicago, Seattle, Los Angeles, Dallas, Miami.

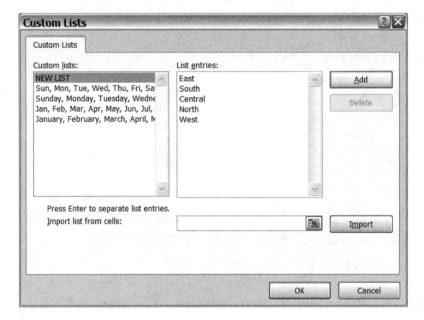

Figure 2-3. *Create a custom list by typing the entries.*

___

■Tip Instead of typing a list in the List Entries box, you can import the list from the worksheet by selecting the list and clicking the Import button.

___

5. Click OK twice, to close the dialog boxes.

Applying the Custom Sort Order

Follow these steps to apply the custom sort order to the City field:

1. Refresh the pivot table. If the City field is set for Automatic sort, it should change to the custom list's sort order.

2. If the City field is currently set for manual sorting, it won't sort according to the custom list order. To change it to automatic sorting, right-click a city label, click Sort, and then click Sort A to Z.

2.5. Sorting a Pivot Field: Items Won't Sort Correctly

Problem

One of your salespeople is named Jan, and her name always appears at the top of the SalesRep items, ahead of the names that precede it alphabetically. You can manually drag her name to the correct position in the row labels, but you'd like to know why her name is out of order, and how you can fix the problem. This problem is based on the sample file SalesNames.xlsx.

Solution

Jan goes to the top of the list because Excel assumes Jan means January, and is an item in one of Excel's built-in custom lists. Other names, such as May or June, would also go to the top of the list, because they're also in the custom list for months. Other words may not sort as expected if you have created other custom lists on your computer, as described in Section 2.4. For example, you may have created custom lists of districts or departments, and those lists take precedence when sorting labels in a pivot table.

   If you don't want to use custom lists when sorting in a pivot table, you can change a pivot table setting, to block their use.

■**Note**   Changing the Use Custom Lists When Sorting setting affects all fields in the active pivot table, not just a specific field.

---

   1. Right-click a cell in the pivot table, and click PivotTable Options.

   2. In the PivotTable Options dialog box, click the Totals & Filters tab.

   3. In the Sorting section, remove the check mark from Use Custom Lists When Sorting (see Figure 2-4), and then click OK.

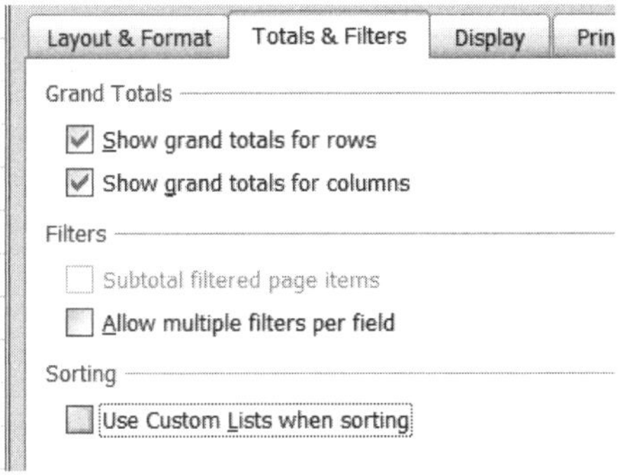

Figure 2-4. *Use Custom Lists When Sorting.*

Any custom sort orders in the pivot table are removed, and for fields that are set to automatic sorting, the labels are sorted in alphabetical or numerical order. To change a field to automatic sorting, right-click a label for the field, click Sort, and then click Sort A to Z.

2.6. Filtering a Pivot Field: Filtering Row Label Text

Problem

You're reviewing the sales of your company's mid-priced products and, in your pivot table, UnitCost and Product are in the Row Labels area, District is in the Column Labels area and TotalSale is in the Values area. You'd like to view only the data for the products with a unit cost between $0.40 and $0.70, but you don't want to uncheck all the other items in the UnitCost field's filter list. This problem is based on the sample file FoodSales.xlsx.

Solution

To limit what's displayed in the pivot table, you can filter the row labels. In this example, you filter to show only the unit costs within a specific range. To apply the filter, follow these steps:

1. Click the drop-down arrow in the Row Labels heading, and in the Select Field dropdown list, select UnitCost.

■**Tip** If you select a UnitCost row label before clicking the arrow, that field name will be the default selection in the drop-down list.

---

2. Click Label Filters, and then click Between.

3. In the Label Filter dialog box, leave the drop-down box with the selection Is Between. In the text box where the cursor is flashing, type **.4**, which is the minimum unit cost you want included.

4. In the second text box, type **.7**, which is the maximum unit cost you want included, and then click OK.

The filter is applied to the labels, and UnitCost labels between $0.40 and $0.70 are visible. A filter icon appears in the Row Labels drop-down arrow. Another filter icon appears to the right of the UnitCost field in the PivotTable Field List.

■**Note** The minimum and maximum values are included when the Between filter is used, so values of $0.40 and $0.70 are shown in the filtered results for this example.

How It Works

In addition to the Between filter, many other options exist for filtering the Label text, such as *Contains*, *Less Than Or Equal To*, and *Does Not End With*. Click any of these filters to open the Label Filter dialog box (see Figure 2-5).

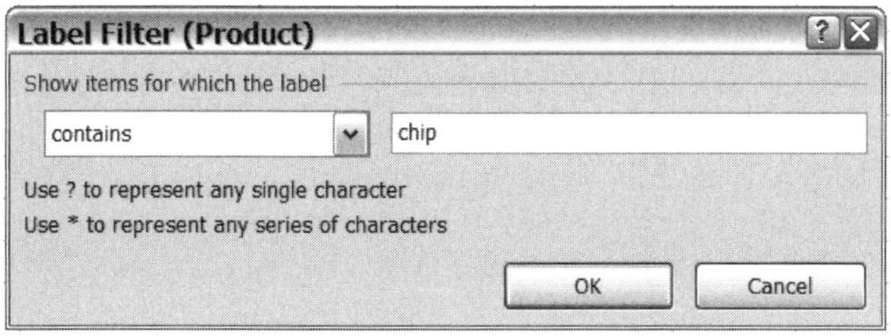

Figure 2-5. *Label Filter dialog box*

The drop-down list in the Label Filter dialog box shows the filter you selected. Depending on the filter you selected, there will be one or two text boxes in which you can enter your criteria. For example, if you filter the Product field, select the *Contains* filter, and type **chip** in the filter's text box, the Potato Chips and Chocolate Chip products would be visible in the product labels.

As indicated on the Label Filter dialog box, you can include an asterisk or a question mark in the criteria. These are *wildcard* characters that can make the criteria more flexible.

- The *`*`* *wildcard* represents any number of characters, including no characters. If you filter for Contains, and enter the criterion o*at, the products Chocolate Chip, Oatmeal Raisin, Potato Chips, and Whole Wheat would appear in the filtered labels, because each has the letters o and at, in that order.

- The *`?`* *wildcard* represents one character only. If you filter for Contains, and enter the criterion o?at, only the Chocolate Chip and Potato Chips would appear in the filtered labels, because they have the letters o and at, with exactly one character between those letters.

2.7. Filtering a Pivot Field: Applying Multiple Filters to a Field

Problem

As described in Section 2.6, you applied a filter to the UnitCost labels in the pivot table's row labels, so only the unit costs between $0.40 and $0.70 are shown. The unit cost for Chocolate Chip is in that range, but it's a special product, and you want to exclude its unit cost, 0.66, from the filtered results. When you open the filter list for UnitCost and remove the check mark for 0.66, the first filter is removed, and only Chocolate Chip is hidden by the filter. You want to keep the UnitCost label filter and add a manual filter for the special item. This problem is based on the sample file FoodSales.xlsx.

Solution

When a pivot table is created, its default setting is to allow only one filter at a time on each field. You applied a label filter to the UnitCost field, and it was automatically removed when you applied a manual filter on the same field. To allow more than one filter, you can change a setting in the pivot table options:

1. Right-click a cell in the pivot table, and then click PivotTable Options.

2. On the Totals & Filters tab, add a check mark to Allow Multiple Filters Per Field (see Figure 2-6), and then click OK.

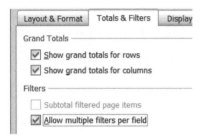

Figure 2-6. *Allow multiple filters per field.*

You can now click the drop-down arrow on the Row Labels heading and remove the check mark from the special product's unit cost. The label filter will be retained, and the manual filter will be added.

How It Works

Three types of filters can be applied to the row labels and column labels: label (or date) filters, value filters, and manual filters. If the Allow Multiple Filters Per Field setting is turned off, only one type of filter can be applied to a field. As soon as you apply a different type of filter, the first filter is automatically removed, without warning.

■**Note** Only one of each type of filter can be applied to a field. For example, even if the Allow Multiple Filters Per Field setting is turned on, you can only apply one label filter to the Product field.

If the Allow Multiple Filters Per Field setting is turned on, one of each type of filter can be applied to a field. You can filter the labels for a date range, or for specific text. Then, you can apply a manual filter, to exclude other items from the filtered results. Finally, you can filter the field based on its values, to show only the items with a row or column total over a specific amount, or in a set range.

To see the filters and sort options that were applied in the pivot table, you can point to the drop-down button on the Row Labels or Column Labels heading cell. In the pivot table shown in Figure 2-7, the UnitCost field has three filters applied, the City field has two filters applied, and the District field is sorted in ascending order.

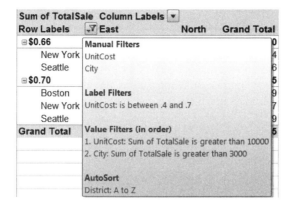

Figure 2-7. *Viewing the filter and sort details*

2.8. Filtering a Pivot Field: Filtering Row Label Dates

Problem

In your pivot table, you have sales results for all your sales districts, with District and Sales-Week fields in the Row Labels area and TotalSale in the Values area. At the beginning of each month, you have to prepare a report to summarize the data from the previous month. You'd like to find a quick way to select the SalesWeek items you need, so it's easier to create the report. This problem is based on the sample file FoodSales.xlsx.

Solution

When a date field is in the Row Labels or Column Labels area, you can filter the labels to show only the dates in a specific range, such as next week, or last month. To apply the filter, follow these steps:

1. Click the drop-down arrow in the Row Labels heading.

2. In the Select Field drop-down list, select the SalesWeek field.

3. Click Date Filters, and then click Last Month.

The filter is applied to the labels, and the pivot table now shows a summary of sales in the previous month. A filter icon appears in the Row Labels drop-down arrow, and another filter icon appears to the right of the SalesWeek field in the PivotTable Field List.

Tip In the PivotTable Options dialog box, on the Data tab, add a check mark to Refresh Data When Opening the File, to ensure the dynamic date range is up-to-date.

How It Works

There are two types of date filters—specific date range, and dynamic date range. When the filter criteria can change automatically, such as Last Week, or Next Month, it is called a *dynamic filter*. For other date filters, you use a comparison operator, such as Equals, or Between, and refer to a specific date or dates in the criteria (see Figure 2-8). When a comparison operator (Equals, Greater Than, Less Than, or Between) is used in a filter, it is called a *common filter*.

Figure 2-8. *Filter for a specific date range*

2.9. Filtering a Pivot Field: Filtering Values for Row Fields

Problem

In your pivot table, you have sales results for all your districts, with District in the Column Labels area, SalesWeek in the Row Labels area, and TotalSale in the Values area. You have removed all the filters from the pivot table, and now you'd like to view all the weeks in which the total sales are between $2000 and $5000. This problem is based on the sample file Food-Sales.xlsx.

Solution

You can filter the row grand total values, to show only the rows that meet the criteria.

■**Note** The Grand Total for rows does not have to be visible to use the Row Labels Value filters.

---

1. In the pivot table, click the arrow on the Row Labels heading.

2. Click Value Filters, and then click Between.

3. In the third box, enter 2000 as the minimum dollar amount and, in the fourth box, enter 5000 as the maximum dollar amount. The values entered in the minimum and maximum boxes will be included in the filter results. In this example, any weeks with total sales from 2000, up to and including 5000, will be shown.

■**Note** The values must be typed into the Value Filter dialog box. You can't use a cell reference to provide the criteria for a value filter.

---

4. Click OK, to apply the filter.

Only the weeks with total sales between the minimum value and maximum value (inclusive) remain visible.

Notes

The Row Labels Value filters can only be applied on the grand total for the row. Other values in the row cannot be filtered. For example, in the pivot table shown in Figure 2-9, you can't filter for SalesWeeks with a value greater than $1000 in the South District. You can only filter for SalesWeeks where the grand total value meets your criteria.

Sum of TotalSale	Colum ▾					
Row Labels ▾	Central	East	North	South	West	Grand Total
01-Feb-07	754	2,382	475	2,437	617	6,664
08-Feb-07	711	3,225	525	3,417	306	8,185
15-Feb-07	222	2,058	971	2,031	107	5,388
22-Feb-07	669	1,075	659	1,339	555	4,297
01-Mar-07	735	1,800	300	1,958	441	5,233
08-Mar-07	503	2,252	280	2,051	447	5,532

Figure 2-9. *Filter for grand total values only*

If you want to filter for values in a specific district, you can hide all the other districts, so the grand total reflects only the values for the visible district. Then, apply a filter, and it will show the results for the visible district.

2.10. Filtering a Pivot Field: Filtering for Nonconsecutive Dates

Problem

In your pivot table, the WorkDate field is in the Row Labels area and LbrHrs is in the Values area. You want to see the data from three nonconsecutive dates, when the service department was short-staffed. When you use the row label date filters, you can only select a consecutive date range, or one specific date. You can't select the three dates you need. This problem is based on the sample file Service.xlsx.

Solution

Instead of using the date filter options, you can manually select or deselect the items in the Row Labels drop-down list. You can use this manual filter option if you want to select specific items that can't be filtered by using a common or dynamic filter. To manually filter dates in the Row Labels filter list, follow these steps:

1. In the pivot table, click the arrow on the Row Labels heading.

2. In the list of dates, remove the check mark from Select All, to remove all the check marks from the list.

3. Add check marks to the dates you want to see, and then click OK.

The pivot table now shows results for work done on the selected dates, and you can focus on that data.

■**Note** A manual filter is retained if a filtered field is moved to the Report Filter area, but a label or value filter is removed.

2.11. Filtering a Pivot Field: Including New Items in a Manual Filter

Problem

In your pivot table, WorkDate is in the Row Labels area and LbrHrs is in the Values area. You manually applied a filter to the WorkDate field in the Row Labels area of your pivot table. When you updated the pivot table, some new dates appeared in the pivot table, even though they were not the dates selected in the manual filter. This problem is based on the sample file `Service.xlsx`.

Solution

You can change a setting in the WorkDate field, to specify if new items are included or not, when the field is manually filtered. To change the setting, and prevent new items from being included, follow these steps:

1. In the pivot table, right-click a cell in the WorkDate Row Labels, and click Field Settings.

2. On the Subtotals & Filters tab, in the Filter section, remove the check mark from Include New Items in Manual Filter, and then click OK (see Figure 2-10).

Figure 2-10. *Clear the Include New Items in Manual Filter check box.*

■**Tip** You can turn this setting on if you want to ensure that you notice new records when they're added, and you can manually deselect them after they appear.

2.12. Filtering a Pivot Field: Filtering by Selection

Problem

In your pivot table, the Product field is in the Row Labels area and UnitsSold is in the Values area. Frequently, you want to view a summary for two or three of the products, and you'd like a quick way to hide the other products. This problem is based on the sample file FoodSales.xlsx.

Solution

To quickly filter the labels in a pivot table, you can select one or more labels, and then use the selection to filter the pivot table. To filter for three of the Product labels, follow these steps:

1. Click a cell that contains one of the Product row labels you want to filter, to select that label.

2. Hold the Ctrl key on the keyboard, and click two other Product row labels, to select them.

3. Right-click one of the selected labels.

4. In the context menu, click Filter, and then click Keep Only Selected Items.

■**Note** At least one row label must remain visible.

Only the three selected products are visible, and all the other data is hidden. This is like manual filtering; if you look at the list of dates in the Row Labels drop-down, the three selected dates have check marks, and all the other dates have their check marks cleared.

Sometimes, you may want to hide a few selected items, and leave all the other items visible. Follow these steps to hide some items:

1. Select one label cell, or select a single block of label cells.

2. Right-click one of the selected cells.

3. In the context menu, click Filter, and then click Hide Selected Items.

This leaves all the labels visible, except the selected items.

2.13. Filtering a Pivot Field: Filtering for Top Items

Problem

In your pivot table, the Product field is in the Row Labels area, the District field is in the Column Labels area, and the UnitsSold field is in the Values area. The sales manager is preparing a forecast for next year, and he has asked you for a report that shows only the three products with the highest number of units sold. This problem is based on the sample file FoodSales.xlsx.

Solution

You can use the Top 10 Filter for the Product row labels, to filter the values. Follow these steps to apply the filter.

1. Right-click a cell that contains a Product row label, and in the context menu, click Filter, and then click Top 10.

2. In the Top 10 Filter dialog box, select Top from the first drop-down list, and in the second box, enter a **3**.

3. From the third box, select Items, and in the last box, select Sum of UnitsSold, and then click OK.

The pivot table shows only the three products with the highest number of units sold, based on the grand total for each row.

■**Note** If a tie occurs in the number of units sold, more than three products may be shown.

How It Works

Although the filter feature is called Top 10, you can use it to filter for the highest or lowest values, and you can choose a number other than 10. In the first drop-down list in the Top 10 Filter dialog box, you can choose Top or Bottom, to see either the highest or lowest values. In the second box, you can type any number, to limit the records that will be visible in the filtered pivot table. In the third drop-down list, you can select Items, Percent, or Sum. In the fourth drop-down list, you can choose one of the Value fields in the pivot table.

Filtering for Items

If you select Items in the third drop-down list, a specific number of items, with the highest or lowest grand total amounts, is displayed when you apply the filter. This number may be exceeded if ties are in the grand totals. For example, if you filter for the Top 2 Items, and three grand totals are tied for second highest, all three, plus the highest value, would be filtered.

Filtering for Percent

If you select Percent in the third drop-down list, items with the highest or lowest grand total amounts, that comprise the specified percent of the overall grand total, will be displayed when you apply the filter.

In the FoodSales.xlsx example, the pivot table has a grand total of 256,941 units sold. If you select to show the Bottom 20 Percent, you can see the products with the lowest grand totals for units sold, that combine to total at least 20 percent of that overall grand total, or approximately 51,000 units sold. The bottom six products have a total of only 42,517 units, which is less than 20 percent, so the bottom seven products are returned in the filter.

You could use this feature to determine where to focus your improvement efforts. Only a few clients or products may contribute to the top 10 or 20 percent of your sales, and several hundred comprise the remaining percent of sales. Using a top or bottom filter can help you identify those clients or products.

Filtering for Sum

If you select Sum in the third drop-down list, items with the highest or lowest grand total amounts, that total at least the specified sum, are displayed when you apply the filter.

In the FoodSales.xlsx example, if you selected to show the Top 100,000 Sum, when you apply the filter, you can see the products with the highest grand totals for units sold, that combine to total at least 100,000 units sold. Only two products, Potato Chips and Saltines, are returned in the filter, because these two have combined sales of 123,458.

2.14. Using Report Filters: Hiding Report Filter Items

Problem

The Product field is in the Report Filter area of your pivot table, and (All) has been selected from its drop-down list. The sales manager would like you to exclude the Cheese and Bran products from the report, and summarize all the other products. You don't see any way to hide some of the products in the Report Filter. Unlike the row and column labels, the Report Filter's drop-down list doesn't have check boxes to indicate which items to show and which to hide. This problem is based on the sample file FoodSales.xlsx.

Solution

You can change a setting in the Report Filter so it enables you to select items to show or hide. Follow these steps to change the setting:

1. Click the drop-down arrow for the Product Report Filter, and at the bottom of the item list, add a check mark to Select Multiple Items.

2. Remove check marks for the items you want to hide, and then click the OK button to close the list. At least one item must be selected, or the OK button won't be enabled.

The Report Filter will show (Multiple Items) instead of (All), if the Select Multiple Items option is turned on, and not all items are selected.

2.15. Using Report Filters: Filtering for a Date Range

Problem

The sales manager has asked for a report on the total sales for October. The SalesWeek field is in the Report Filter area of your pivot table, but you don't want to manually hide all the dates that aren't in October. The Filter Date feature isn't available when the SalesWeek field is in the Report Filter area. This problem is based on the sample file FoodSales.xlsx.

Workaround

If this is a one-time requirement, it might be quickest to remove the check mark from the (All) item in the Report Filter, and then check the October dates.

If you'll need frequent reports for a month's data, you could group the SalesWeek field, and then filter for a specific month, instead of individual dates. Follow these steps to group the dates:

1. Temporarily move the SalesWeek field to the Row Labels area. You can't group the dates while the field is in the Report Filter area.

2. Right-click one of the cells that contains a SalesWeek label, and then click Group.

3. In the Grouping dialog box, the earliest and latest dates in the SalesWeek field should automatically appear in the Starting at and Ending at date boxes.

4. In the By list, click Months, to select it. If other options are highlighted, click them, to deselect them. This groups all the data for each month, across multiple years. If you need to report on the years separately, also select Years in the By list.

5. Click OK to close the Grouping dialog box.

6. Move the SalesWeek field back to the Report Filter area, and then filter for October.

2.16. Using Report Filters: Filtering for Future Dates

Problem

The warehouse manager has asked you for a report that shows the product quantities for orders with future ship dates. In your pivot table, ShipDate is in the Report Filter area, Product is in the Row Labels area, and Units is in the Values area.

The date filters aren't available in the Report Filter, and you don't want to manually hide all the past dates in the ShipDate Report Filter. This problem is based on the sample file `Shipped.xlsx`.

Workaround

For some filtering problems, the best solution is to add a column to the source data. In the new column, you can enter a formula or a value, and use that data in the pivot table. In this case, a column can be added, with a formula to test if the ship date is later than the current date.

1. In the source data table, add a column with the heading ShipLater.

2. In the first data row of the new column, enter a formula that refers to the ShipDate in that row—for example, **=A2 > TODAY()**.

3. Copy the formula down to the last row of data. If the source data has been formatted as an Excel Table, the formula should automatically copy down to the last row in the table.

4. Refresh the pivot table, and add the ShipLater field to the Report Filter area.

5. From the ShipLater Report Filter drop-down list, select TRUE.

■**Note** Refresh the pivot table each day to see the current calculations for the ShipLater field. In the PivotTable Options dialog box, on the Data tab, you can add a check mark to Refresh Data When Opening the File.

■■■

CHAPTER 3

Calculations in a Pivot Table

In a pivot table, you can use functions like Sum, Count, or Average to summarize the fields you place in the Values area. You can also use custom calculations, such as Difference From, and Running Total, to show a different perspective on the data. For even greater flexibility, you can write your own formulas to create calculated fields and calculated items in the pivot table.

3.1. Using Summary Functions: Defaulting to Sum or Count

Problem

The sales manager sent you a workbook with sales data, and she asked you to create a pivot table from the data. You added the Product field to the Row Labels area, the District field to the Report Filter area, and Units and TotalSales to the Values area.

When you added the Units field to the Values area, it automatically used the Sum function, but when you added the TotalSales field to the Values area, it used the Count function. You're not sure why different functions were used for two fields that both contain numbers. This problem is based on the `OfficeSales.xlsx` sample file.

Solution

Perhaps blank cells were in the source data for the TotalSales field. If you add a number field to the Values area, the default summary function is Sum. However, if blank cells, or nonnumeric data, such as text or errors, are in the field, the Count function is used as a default.

■**Note** You cannot change the default summary function in a pivot table. Either Sum or Count will be used, depending on the field's contents.

After a field has been added to the Values area, you can change its summary function, unless the field is a calculated field, or the pivot table is based on an OLAP data source:

1. Right-click a cell in the field you want to change, and click Summarize Data By.

2. Click one of the functions in the menu (see Figure 3-1).

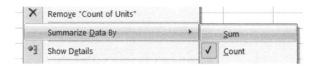

Figure 3-1. *Select a summary function.*

3. If the function you want is not visible, click More Options. Click a function in the Summarize Value Field By list, and then click OK (see Figure 3-2).

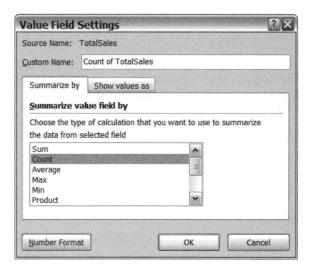

Figure 3-2. *The Value Field Settings dialog box with a list of summary functions*

■**Tip** You can add two copies of a field to the pivot table's Values area, and use a different summary function for each copy. For example, show the Sum of Units and the Average of Units.

How It Works

When you add a field to the pivot table's Values area, a list of 11 functions (listed as follows) is available to summarize the data. Only these functions are available when summarizing the pivot table data; other functions, such as Median, Mode, and Percentile, can be calculated from the source data, outside the pivot table.

The summary functions in a pivot table are similar to the worksheet functions with the same names, with a few differences as noted in the descriptions that follow.

Sum

Sum is the default summary function for numerical fields added to the pivot table's Values area, and it totals all the underlying values in the Values area. The result is the same as using the SUM function on the worksheet to total the values.

Count

Count is the default summary function when fields with nonnumeric or blank cells are added to the Values area. Like the COUNTA worksheet function, the pivot table Count function counts text, numbers, and errors. Blank cells are not counted.

Average

The *Average* function totals all the underlying values in the Values area, and it divides by the number of values. The result is the same as using the AVERAGE function on the worksheet to calculate the average (mean) of the values.

Max

The *Max* summary function shows the maximum value from the underlying values in the Values area. The result is the same as using the MAX function on the worksheet to calculate the maximum of the values.

Min

The *Min* summary function shows the minimum value from the underlying values in the Values area. The result is the same as using the MIN function on the worksheet to calculate the minimum of the values.

Product

The *Product* summary function shows the result of multiplying all the underlying values in the Values area. The result is the same as using the PRODUCT function on the worksheet to calculate the product of the values. The results of this function may be very large numbers and default to a Scientific number format. Excel only stores and calculates with 15 significant digits of precision, so after the 15th character you'll only see zeros.

Count Numbers

The *Count Numbers* summary function counts all the underlying numbers in the Values area. The result is the same as using the COUNT function on the worksheet. Blank cells, errors, and text are not counted.

StDev

Like the STDEV worksheet function, the *StDev* summary function calculates the standard deviation for the underlying data in the Values area.

If the count of items is one, a #DIV/0! error is displayed, because one is subtracted from the count when calculating the standard deviation.

There may be differences between the worksheet results and the pivot table results, because the worksheet function was improved in Excel 2003, but the pivot table function was not changed. For more information, see the Microsoft Knowledge Base article "Description of Improvements in the Statistical Functions in Excel 2003 and in Excel 2004 for Mac," at http://support.microsoft.com/default.aspx?kbid=828888.

StDevp

Like the STDEVP worksheet function, the *StDevp* summary function calculates the standard deviation for the entire population for the underlying data in the Values area. In Excel 2003, improvements were made to several statistical functions, including STDEV and STDEVP. See the previous "StDev" section for more information.

Var

Like the VAR worksheet function, the *Var* summary function calculates the variance for the underlying data in the Values area, and is the square of the standard deviation.

If the count of items is one, a #DIV/0! error is displayed, because one is subtracted from the count when calculating the standard deviation.

In Excel 2003, improvements were made to several statistical functions, including VAR and VARP. The Var and Varp summary functions have been improved when used in the interior of the PivotTable report, but not for grand totals for rows or columns. For more information, see the Microsoft Knowledge Base article "Excel Statistical Functions: VAR and VARP Improvements and Pivot Tables," at http://support.microsoft.com/default.aspx?kbid=829250.

Varp

The *Varp* summary function calculates the variance for the entire population for the underlying data in the Values area. In Excel 2003, improvements were made to several statistical functions, including VAR and VARP. See the previous "Var" section for more information.

Errors in the Source Data

The Count and Count Numbers functions handle errors as outlined earlier. For other summary functions, if errors are in the source data field, the first error encountered is displayed in the pivot table, and the total is not calculated. If subtotals, or row and column totals, are displayed, affected totals and subtotals display the error.

For example, the source data shown in Figure 3-3, from the sample file OfficeSalesError.xlsx, has two errors for West Binder data—a #REF! error and an #N/A error.

C	D	E	F	G
Region ▾	Item ▾	Cost ▾	Units ▾	TotalSales ▾
East	Pencil	2.99	95	284.05
West	Binder	#REF!	50	#REF!
West	Pencil	2.99	36	107.64
West	Binder	#N/A	27	#N/A
West	Pencil	2.99	56	167.44

Figure 3-3. *Errors in the sample source data*

The first error, #REF!, appears in the pivot table, when West Binder TotalSales are summed (see Figure 3-4). If the dates in the source Excel table were sorted in descending order, the #N/A error would be listed first, and would appear in the pivot table.

Sum of TotalSales	Colum ▾			
Row Labels ▾	Central	East	West	Grand Total
Binder	1,203	1,831	#REF!	#REF!
Desk	1,925		825	2,750
Pen		348	151	499
Pen Set	729	1,243		1,971
Pencil	1,094	451	595	2,141
Grand Total	4,950	3,874	#REF!	#REF!

Figure 3-4. *The first error in the source Excel table appears in the pivot table.*

3.2. Using Summary Functions: Counting Blank Cells

Problem

The sales manager sent you a workbook with sales data, and blank cells are in the District column for some records. You want to show a count of the blank District cells in the pivot table, so you can let the sales manager know how many records are incomplete.

You added the District field to the pivot table's Row Labels area, and another copy of the District field in the Values area, as Count of District. However, no count is showing for the blank districts (see Figure 3-5). This problem is based on the OfficeSales.xlsx sample file.

Row Labels ▾	Count of District
Central	12
East	18
West	9
(blank)	
Grand Total	39

Figure 3-5. *Blank cells are not counted in the Values area.*

Solution

The Count function doesn't count blank cells, so when you add the District field to the Values area, it has nothing to count for those blank records. Add a different field to the Values area, and use it for the count. For example, if the Units column in the source data has a value in every row, add Count of Units to the Values area (see Figure 3-6). With District in the Row Labels area, the count of blank Districts is calculated.

Row Labels ▾	Count of Units
Central	12
East	18
West	9
(blank)	4
Grand Total	43

Figure 3-6. *Use a different field to count blank cells.*

3.3. Using Custom Calculations: Difference From

Problem

Every morning, you download the regional sales data from your sales system. You'd like to use the pivot table to calculate each day's change from the previous day, to obtain the daily sales figures for each region.

In your pivot table, Date is in the Row Labels area, Region is in the Column Labels area, and Sum of Units is in the Values area, as shown in Figure 3-7. The example shown is from the RegionCalcs.xlsx workbook.

3	Sum of Units	Colum ▾			
4	Row Labels ▾	Central	East	West	Grand Total
5	09/01/2008	1,349	1,666	2,043	5,058
6	09/02/2008	1,563	1,899	2,562	6,024
7	09/03/2008	1,957	2,697	2,967	7,621
8	Grand Total	4,869	6,262	7,572	18,703

Figure 3-7. *The pivot table shows units sold to date for each region.*

Solution

To supplement the summary functions, custom calculations are available when summarizing data in a pivot table. In addition to the default normal calculation, custom calculations provide eight different ways of viewing the summary results. For this problem, use the Difference From custom calculation to compare each day's total to the previous day's total.

■**Tip** Custom calculations are only available for pivot tables based on non-OLAP sources.

---

1. Right-click a cell in the Values area, and then click Value Field Settings.

2. On the Show Values As tab, from the drop-down list for Show Values As, select Difference From.

3. You want to compare the results from one date to another, so for the base field, select Date.

■**Caution** If you select a base field that isn't in the Row or Column Labels area, all the results show an #N/A error.

---

4. You want to compare each date's results to the previous date's results, so for the Base item, select (previous) (see Figure 3-8), and then click OK.

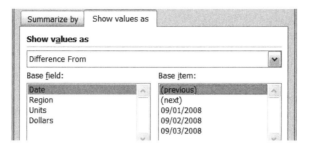

Figure 3-8. *Difference From settings*

The values in the pivot table change, to show the difference in values, from each date to the previous date. The row for the first date is empty, because there's no previous date with which to compare it. The remaining rows show the change from the previous day in units sold for each region (see Figure 3-9).

	Sum of Units	Column ▾			
	Row Labels ▾	Central	East	West	Grand Total
5	09/01/2008				
6	09/02/2008	214	233	519	966
7	09/03/2008	394	798	405	1,597
8	Grand Total				

Figure 3-9. *The custom calculation Difference From compares daily sales totals.*

How It Works

The Difference From custom calculation compares each item in the field to another item in the same field. In this example, (previous) was selected, so each day's total is compared to the previous day's total. If days are missing or hidden, the comparison is made to the previous visible day.

Instead of (previous), you could select (next) to compare each day to the next visible day's totals, or select a specific date to compare all days to the sales for the selected date.

Using the same sample data, you could select Region as the Base Field, and Central as the Base Item, to compare each region's sales to sales in the Central Region (see Figure 3-10).

	Sum of Units	Column ▾			
	Row Labels ▾	Central	East	West	Grand Total
5	09/01/2008		317	694	
6	09/02/2008		336	999	
7	09/03/2008		740	1,010	
8	Grand Total		1,393	2,703	

Figure 3-10. *The custom calculation Difference From, with Region as a base field*

3.4. Using Custom Calculations: % Of

Problem

You have monthly sales figures for each region, and would like to compare average sales for each region to the average sales in your strongest region.

In your pivot table, Date is in the Row Labels area, grouped by Month; Region is in the Column Labels area; and Sum of Units is in the Values area (see Figure 3-11). The example shown is from the RegionWeeks.xlsx workbook.

3	Sum of Units	Colum ▾			
4	Row Labels ▾	Central	East	West	Grand Total
5	Jan	3634	1757	3030	8421
6	Feb	1364	3728	1755	6847
7	Mar	2167	3257	1508	6932
8	Apr	2146	1757	1417	5320
9	Grand Total	9311	10499	7710	27520

Figure 3-11. *Sum of Units per Month per Region*

Solution

While using the custom calculations, you can use different summary functions for the data. For this problem, instead of Sum, you can use Average and the % Of custom calculation.

1. Right-click a cell in the Values area, and then click Value Field Settings.

2. On the Summarize By tab, select Average as the type of calculation.

3. Click the Show Values As tab, and from the drop-down list for Show Values As, select % Of.

4. You want to compare the results from one region to another, so for the Base field, select Region.

5. You want to compare the results for each region to East, which has the strongest sales, so for the Base item, select East.

6. To reduce the number of decimal places, click Number Format, and format with Percentage, and the number of decimal places you want.

7. Click OK twice, to close the dialog boxes.

The pivot table values change, to show each value as a percent of the East's sales. The column for the East region shows 100%, because it's being compared to itself. The remaining columns show the percent of their average units per sale, compared to the East region's average units per sale (see Figure 3-12).

3	Average of Units	Colun ▾			
4	Row Labels ▾	Central	East	West	Grand Total
5	Jan	138%	100%	138%	
6	Feb	61%	100%	59%	
7	Mar	83%	100%	77%	
8	Apr	122%	100%	81%	
9	Grand Total	94%	100%	82%	

Figure 3-12. *The custom calculation % Of, with Region as a base field*

3.5. Using Custom Calculations: % Difference From

Problem

You have monthly sales figures and forecasts for each product, and you would like to compare actual sales to forecast sales for each product per month.

In your pivot table, Date (grouped by Month) and Product are in the Row Labels area, Status (Actual or Forecast) is in the Column Labels area, and Sum of Units is in the Values area (see Figure 3-13). The example shown is from the `ProductSales.xlsx` workbook.

3	Sum of Units	Colum ▾		
4	Row Labels ▾	Actual	Forecast	Grand Total
5	⊟ Jan	2613	2960	5573
6	A703	823	967	1790
7	B306	398	702	1100
8	C589	1299	886	2185
9	D726	93	405	498
10	⊟ Feb	2686	2185	4871
11	A703	1065	693	1758

Figure 3-13. *Actual and Forecast values per month*

Solution

Use the % Difference From custom calculation to compare the Actual to Forecast items in the Status field. You can leave the original copy of the Sum of Units field, so you can see the Units quantity, as well as the % Difference From calculation.

1. Add another copy of the Units field to the Values area, where it will become Sum of Units2. Select a cell that contains the Sum of Units2 label, and then type a more descriptive name, for example, **% Diff**.

2. Right-click one of the % Diff cells in the Values area, and click Value Field Settings.

3. Click the Show Values As tab, and from the drop-down list for Show Values As, select % Difference From.

4. You want to compare the Status field values, so for the Base field, select Status.

5. The Actual values will be compared to the Forecast values, so for the Base item, select Forecast.

6. To reduce the number of decimal places, click the Number Format button, and format with Percentage, and the number of decimal places you want.

7. Click OK twice, to close the dialog boxes.

8. In the PivotTable Field List, move the Status field below the Σ Values field in the Column Labels area. This changes the order of the columns, so the Units are together, and the % Diff columns are together (see Figure 3-14).

		Colum ▾			
3					
4		**Units**		**% Diff**	
5	**Row Labels** ▾	**Actual**	**Forecast**	**Actual**	**Forecast**
6	⊟ Jan	2613	2960	-12%	
7	A703	823	967	-15%	
8	B306	398	702	-43%	
9	C589	1299	886	47%	
10	D726	93	405	-77%	

Figure 3-14. *The % Difference between Actual and Forecast*

The Forecast column is empty in the % Diff field, because it won't be compared to itself. The Actual column shows the % Difference From calculation from the forecast in units sold, for each product for each month.

3.6. Using Custom Calculations: Running Total

Problem

You have monthly sales figures for each product, and the sales manager has asked for a running total of units sold by month. In your pivot table, Date (grouped by Month) is in the Row Labels area, Product is in the Column Labels area, and Sum of Units is in the Values area (see Figure 3-15). Status is in the Report Filter area, with Actual selected. The example shown is from the ProductSales.xlsx workbook.

1	Status	Actual ▾				
2						
3	Sum of Unit	Colum ▾				
4	Row Labe ▾	A703	B306	C589	D726	Grand Total
5	Jan	823	398	1299	93	2613
6	Feb	1065	622	133	866	2686
7	Mar	738	380	879	192	2189
8	Apr	1301	171	807	171	2450
9	**Grand Total**	**3927**	**1571**	**3118**	**1322**	**9938**

Figure 3-15. *Actual product sales per month*

Solution

Use a running total in a custom calculation to accumulate the sales amounts per product, down through the list of months.

1. Right-click a cell in the Values area, and then click Value Field Settings.

2. Click the Show Values As tab, and from the drop-down list for Show Values As, select Running Total In.

3. You want to see the running total by month, so for the Base field, select Date, and then click OK. No base item is required for a running total calculation.

■**Caution** If you select a base field that isn't in the Row or Column Labels area, all the results will show an #N/A error. Also, if an error exists in any month's results, it will carry down through the remaining months.

With Date as the base field, each Product column shows a running total for the year, by month (see Figure 3-16). The Grand Total column shows the overall running total.

	Status	Actual 🔽				
1						
2						
3	**Sum of Unit Colum** 🔽					
4	**Row Labe** 🔽	**A703**	**B306**	**C589**	**D726**	**Grand Total**
5	Jan	823	398	1299	93	2613
6	Feb	1888	1020	1432	959	5299
7	Mar	2626	1400	2311	1151	7488
8	Apr	3927	1571	3118	1322	9938
9	**Grand Total**					

Figure 3-16. *Running total by month per product*

Notes

If dates in a pivot table are grouped by year and month, the running total will stop at the end of each year, and then begin again at the start of the next year. There is no setting you can adjust to change this behavior.

In the sample file `ProductYear.xlsx`, product sales dates range from October 2008 to March 2009, and they are grouped by year and month in the pivot table. Product is in the Column Labels area, Years and Date are in the Row Labels area, and Units is in the Values area.

If you calculate a running total with Date as the base field:

- The subtotals for Years are automatically hidden when the running total is applied.

- The total for each product accumulates from October to December of 2008, and begins again in January 2009.

If you calculate a running total with Years as the base field:

- The subtotals for Years display the running total for each product, from one year to the next.

- The months display the sales per month, not a running total.

To create a running total that continues from December 2008 to January 2009, you can follow these steps to create a field in the source data, and then use it as the base for the running total:

1. Add a column to the source data, with the heading YearMonth.

2. Enter a formula to return the year and month of the date in each row. For example, use this formula if the date is in Column A:

    ```
    =TEXT(A2, "yyyy-mm")
    ```

3. Refresh the pivot table, add the YearMonth field to the Row Labels area, and then remove the Date and Year fields.

4. Create a running total with YearMonth as the base field.

3.7. Using Custom Calculations: % of Row

You have monthly sales figures for each Sales Manager, and you would like to see what percent of their total sales came from each product category. In your pivot table, Sales Manager is in the Row Labels area, Category is in the Column Labels area, and Sum of Units is in the Values area (see the table at the left in Figure 3-17). The example shown is from the ManagerSales.xlsx workbook.

Solution

Because the category sales for each manager are listed across a row, you can use the % of Row custom calculation to show the percent per category for each Sales Manager's sales.

1. Right-click a cell in the Values area, and then click Value Field Settings.

2. Click the Show Values As tab, and from the drop-down list for Show Values As, select % of Row, and then click OK.

■**Note** There's no option to select a base field or base item with this custom calculation.

In the row for each Sales Manager, you can see the percent of the total sold in each category (see the table at the right in Figure 3-17).

■**Tip** You can hide the Grand Total for Rows, because it will always equal 100 percent.

Units Sold (Thousands)

Sum of Units	Colı ▾			
Row Label ▾	Bars	Cookies	Crackers	Grand Total
Boston	23	29	26	79
Lee	16	23	25	64
Parent	22	28	29	79
Grand Total	**61**	**80**	**80**	**221**

Units Sold (% of Row)

Sum of Units	Colı ▾			
Row Labels ▾	Bars	Cookies	Crackers	Grand Total
Boston	29%	37%	33%	100%
Lee	26%	35%	39%	100%
Parent	28%	36%	36%	100%
Grand Total	**28%**	**36%**	**36%**	**100%**

Figure 3-17. *The % of Row custom calculation shows category sales percentages.*

3.8. Using Custom Calculations: % of Column

Problem

You have monthly sales figures for each product Category, and you would like to see what percent of their total sales were attributed to each sales manager. In your pivot table, Sales Manager is in the Row Labels area, Category is in the Column Labels area, and Units is in the Values area (see the table at the left in Figure 3-18). The example shown is from the ManagerSales.xlsx workbook.

Solution

Because the sales in each category are listed down a column, you can use the % of Column custom calculation to show the percent of sales from each Sales Manager.

1. Right-click a cell in the Values area, and then click Value Field Settings.

2. Click the Show Values As tab, and from the drop-down list for Show Values As, select % of Column, and then click OK.

In the column for each Category, you can see the percent of the total for each sales manager (see the table at the right in Figure 3-18).

Units Sold (Thousands)

Sum of Unit	Colı ▾			
Row Lab ▾	Bars	Cookies	Crackers	Grand Total
Boston	23	29	26	79
Lee	16	23	25	64
Parent	22	28	29	79
Grand Total	**61**	**80**	**80**	**221**

Units Sold (% of Column)

Sum of Unit:	Colu ▾			
Row Lab ▾	Bars	Cookies	Crackers	Grand Total
Boston	38%	37%	33%	36%
Lee	27%	28%	31%	29%
Parent	36%	35%	36%	36%
Grand Total	**100%**	**100%**	**100%**	**100%**

Figure 3-18. *The % of Column custom calculation shows sales manager percentages.*

Notes

Unfortunately, there's no % of Subtotal custom calculation option, but you can modify the pivot table layout to achieve a similar result, using % of Row or % of Column.

For example, if Category and SalesMgr are both in the Row labels area, there's no custom calculation that shows what percent of Bar sales were by Parent. With that layout, if you use the % of Column custom calculation, it shows the percent of the grand total for each sales manager for each product.

Change the layout so Category is in the Columns area, as shown in the table at the right in Figure 3-18, and apply a % of Column custom calculation, to see the percent sold by each manager in each category.

3.9. Using Custom Calculations: % of Total

Problem

You have monthly insurance policy counts for your regional offices. You'd like to see what percentage of the existing policies are in each region, for auto policies and property policies. In your pivot table, Region is in the Row Labels area, PolicyType is in the Column Labels area, and the Sum of Policies field is in the Values area. Status is in the Report Filters area, and Existing is selected (see the table at the left in Figure 3-19). The example shown is from the Policies.xlsx workbook.

Solution

To see the percent that each policy type per region contributes to the overall total, you can use the % of Total custom calculation.

1. Right-click a cell in the Values area, and then click Value Field Settings.

2. Click the Show Values As tab, and from the drop-down list for Show Values As, select % of Total, and then click OK.

In each cell, you can see the percent of the total sold in each region for each policy type (see the table at the right in Figure 3-19). The grand total column shows the percent of total policies in each region, and the grand total row shows the percent of policies in each policy type.

Policies (Thousands)

Status	Existing ⇩

Sum of Policies	Colum ⇩		
Row Labels ⇩	**Auto**	**Prop**	**Grand Total**
Central	36	35	71
East	26	22	48
West	33	31	64
Grand Total	**94**	**89**	**183**

Policies (% of Total)

Status	Existing ⇩

Sum of Policies	Colum ⇩		
Row Labels ⇩	**Auto**	**Prop**	**Grand Total**
Central	20%	19%	39%
East	14%	12%	26%
West	18%	17%	35%
Grand Total	**52%**	**48%**	**100%**

Figure 3-19. *The % of Total custom calculation shows percentage policy type by region.*

3.10. Using Custom Calculations: Index

Problem

You have monthly insurance policy counts for your regional offices. You'd like to compare canceled policies in each region, for both auto policies and property policies. In your pivot table, Region is in the Row Labels area, PolicyType is in the Column Labels area, and Sum of Policies is in the Values area. Status is in the Report Filters area, and Cancel has been selected (see the table at the left in Figure 3-20). The example shown is from the Policies.xlsx workbook.

Solution

Use the Index option to show the relative weight of each cell when compared to its row total, its column total, and the grand total.

1. Right-click a cell in the Values area, and then click Value Field Settings.

2. Click the Show Values As tab, and from the drop-down list for Show Values As, select Index.

3. To reduce the number of decimal places, click Number Format, and format with Number, and the number of decimal places you want.

4. Click OK twice, to close the dialog boxes.

In each cell, you can see its index (see the table at the right in Figure 3-20).

Policies (Thousands)

Status	Cance .T

Sum of Policies	Colu ▾		
Row Labels ▾	Auto	Prop	Grand Total
Central	38	37	75
East	22	25	47
West	31	31	62
Grand Total	**91**	**93**	**185**

Policies (Index)

Status	Cance .T

Sum of Policies	Colur ▾		
Row Labels ▾	Auto	Prop	Grand Total
Central	1.02	0.98	1.00
East	0.94	1.05	1.00
West	1.02	0.98	1.00
Grand Total	**1.00**	**1.00**	**1.00**

Figure 3-20. *The Index custom calculation shows an index of the canceled policy type by Region.*

How It Works

Using the Index custom calculation gives you a picture of each value's importance in its row and column context. If all values in the pivot table were equal, each value would have an index of 1. If an index is less than 1, it's of less importance in its row and column, and if an index is greater than 1, it's of greater importance in its row and column.

The index formula is

```
((value in cell) × (Grand Total of Grand Totals)) /
((Grand Row Total) × (Grand Column Total))
```

Two cells with a similar number of canceled policies may have a different index. A value of 1000 has a higher index if it's the highest value in its row and column, but the same value would have a lower index if it's the lowest value in its row and column.

For example, in the West region, the values for Auto and Prop are almost equal, but the index for the Auto is 1.02 and Prop is 0.98.

Because the grand total is higher for the Prop column, the Grand Column Total in the Index formula is larger. The West Prop amount is divided by this larger number, and its resulting index is smaller.

3.11. Using Formulas: Calculated Field vs. Calculated Item

In addition to the built-in summary functions and custom calculations, you can write your own formulas in a pivot table to create calculated fields and calculated items.

■**Note** Formulas are available only in non-OLAP-based pivot tables.

Problem

You want to add custom formulas to your pivot table, but you're not sure when to use a calculated field and when to use a calculated item. The example shown is from the OrderStatus.xlsx workbook.

Solution

You can create *calculated item*s in a field to perform calculations on other items in that field. For example, if your pivot table contains an Order Status field, you could create a calculated item named Sold, that sums the orders with a status of Shipped, Pending, or Backorder, but doesn't include Canceled orders.

You can create *calculated fields* to perform calculations on other fields in the pivot table. For example, you may have agreed to pay sales representatives a 3 percent bonus on any products for which they sold more than 100 units. The calculated field would display the bonus amount using values in the Units and Total fields.

■**Caution** If you create a calculated item in a field, you will be unable to move the field to the Report Filters area and you will be unable to add multiple copies of a field to the Values area.

How It Works

A calculated item becomes an item in a pivot field. Its calculation can use the sum of other items in the same field. A calculated field becomes a new field in the pivot table, and its calculation can use the sum of other fields.

Calculated items and calculated fields are calculated differently. For calculated items, the individual records in the source data are calculated, and then the results are summed. For example, if you create a Tax item that multiplies the Shipped Total by 7 percent, the value in each record is multiplied by 7 percent, and then the individual tax amounts are summed for the Grand Total.

For calculated fields, the individual amounts are summed, and then the calculation is performed on the total amount.

Note You can't create formulas that refer to the pivot table totals or subtotals. Also, the calculated item and calculated field formulas can't refer to worksheet cells by address or by name.

3.12. Using Formulas: Adding Items With a Calculated Item

Problem

Your pivot table contains an Order Status field in the Row Labels area, and you'd like to create a Sold item that sums the orders with a status of Shipped, Pending, or Backorder, but doesn't include Canceled orders. The example shown is from the OrderStatus.xlsx workbook.

Solution

Follow these steps to create a calculated item that adds the Shipped, Pending, and Backorder items.

1. In the pivot table, select a cell in the Row Labels area that contains an Order Status item. For example, select cell A5, that contains the Backorder item. This step is necessary; otherwise, the Calculated Item command won't be available.

2. On the Ribbon's Options tab, in the Tools group, click Formulas, and then click Calculated Item.

3. Type a name for the Calculated Item, for example, **Sold**, and then press the Tab key to move to the Formula box.

4. In the Fields list, select Order Status, and in the Items list, double-click Shipped, and then type a plus sign (+).

5. Double-click Pending, type a plus sign, and then double-click Backorder. The complete formula is =Shipped+Pending+Backorder.

Note If the formula includes spaces after the plus signs, you can remove the spaces or leave them in the formula. They do not affect the formula result.

---

6. Click OK, to save the calculated item, and to close the dialog box.

7. In the pivot table, hide the Shipped, Pending, and Backorder items to see the correct Grand Totals (see Figure 3-21).

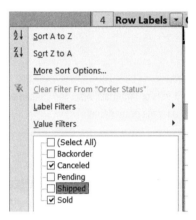

Figure 3-21. *Hide items after you create a Calculated Item.*

3.13. Using Formulas: Modifying a Calculated Item

Problem

You created a calculated item named Sold, in the Order Status field, that sums the orders with a status of Shipped, Pending, or Backorder. You want to change the formula, so it doesn't include the Backorder items. The example shown is from the OrderStatus.xlsx workbook.

Solution

You can go back into the Insert Calculated Item dialog box and modify the calculated item.

1. In the pivot table, select a cell in the Row Labels area that contains an Order Status item. For example, select the cell containing the Canceled item. This step is necessary; otherwise, the Calculated Item command won't be available.

2. On the Ribbon's Options tab, in the Tools group, click Formulas, and then click Calculated Item.

3. From the Name drop-down list, select Sold, which is the name of the calculated item you want to modify.

4. In the Formula box, change the formula, to remove the +Backorder. The revised formula is =Shipped+Pending.

5. Click Modify, to save the change, and then click OK to close the dialog box.

3.14. Using Formulas: Removing a Calculated Item

Problem

You created a calculated item, named Sold, in the Order Status field, that sums the orders with a status of Shipped, Pending, or Backorder. You no longer need the calculation in the pivot table, and you want to remove it. The example shown is from the `OrderStatus.xlsx` workbook.

Solution

You can temporarily hide a calculated item, and then show it again later, or you can permanently remove the calculated item from the pivot table.

To temporarily remove a calculated item, follow these steps:

1. Click the drop-down arrow in the calculated item's Row Labels cell.

2. Remove the check mark from the calculated item, and then click OK.

Tip The calculated item is removed from the pivot table layout, but it remains in the pivot field's list of items. To add the item to the layout later, click the arrow on the Row Labels cell, and then add a check mark to the item in the pivot field's list of items.

To permanently remove a calculated item, follow these steps:

1. In the pivot table, select a cell in the Row Labels area that contains an Order Status item. For example, select the cell containing the Sold item. This step is necessary; otherwise, the Calculated Item command won't be available.

2. In the Tools group, click Formulas, and then click Calculated Item.

3. From the Name drop-down list, select the name of the calculated item you want to delete.

4. Click the Delete button, and then click OK to close the dialog box.

3.15. Using Formulas: Using Index Numbers in a Calculated Item

Problem

You download a new data source file for your pivot table every month, so the dates in the source data change frequently. You'd like to create a calculated item in which you refer to the items in the OrderDate field by number in the formulas, instead of by name. For example, instead of creating a calculated item that sums August 1 and August 15, it would sum the first OrderDate and the fifteenth OrderDate. The example shown is from the `DateCalc.xlsx` workbook.

Solution

You can use an index number in the calculated item's formula, to refer to field items. For example, to sum the data for the first date in the OrderDate field and the fifteenth date, create a calculated item in the OrderDate field, with the following formula:

```
= OrderDate[1]+OrderDate[15]
```

■Caution If you move the calculated item into one of the referenced positions, you create a circular reference.

You can also refer to items by their position relative to the calculated item. For example, you could create a calculated item named DateCalc, with the following formula:

```
= OrderDate[+3]-OrderDate[+2]
```

■Caution If you use a negative number in the relative position, the number is automatically changed to a positive number, and the formula will not produce the expected results.

When DateCalc is in the Row Labels area, it calculates the difference between the value for the OrderDate that is three rows below and the OrderDate that is two rows below. In Figure 3-22, DateCalc has been moved to the top of the list of OrderDates. To move the item, right-click DateCalc, click Move, and then click Move "DateCalc" to Beginning.

3	Sum of Units	Colum ▾			
4	Row Labels ▾	Central	East	West	Grand Total
5	DateCalc	-60	48	34	22
6	2008-08-01	36	95	50	181
7	2008-08-02	60	27	56	143
8	2008-08-03		75	90	165
9	2008-08-04	2	74	60	136

Figure 3-22. *The DateCalc calculated item refers to the dates by relative position.*

3.16. Using Formulas: Modifying a Calculated Item Formula in Cell

Problem

In your pivot table a calculated item, named DateCalc, is in the OrderDate field. It calculates the difference between the value for the OrderDate that is three rows below the calculated item and the OrderDate that is two rows below. You'd like to change the calculated item's formula for one region, because it has missing data on one of the OrderDates. The example shown is from the `DateCalc.xlsx` workbook.

Solution

You can modify the formula for an individual cell that contains a calculated item. For example, in the DateCalc calculated item, the index number was used to calculate the difference between two of the dates:

`=OrderDate[+3]-OrderDate[+2]`

If one of the columns has a blank cell for the date that is offset by 3, you can modify the formula to refer to the date that is offset by 4:

`=OrderDate[+4]-OrderDate[+2]`

To make the change, select the cell, and modify the formula in the formula bar (see Figure 3-23).

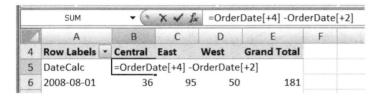

Figure 3-23. *The calculated item's formula is modified for one cell.*

■**Caution** The Undo feature is not available after making this change, and the original formula will not be restored when the pivot table is updated. The modified cell's formula will not be changed if the calculated item's formula is changed.

3.17. Using Formulas: Creating a Calculated Field

Problem

In your pivot table, Rep and Product are in the Row Labels area. In the Values area, the Total field shows the total sales for each sales representative per product, and the Units field summarizes the number of units sold. You'd like to calculate a 3 percent bonus payable if a sales representative has sold more than 100 units of any product. The example shown is from the `OrderStatus.xlsx` workbook.

Solution

To calculate the bonus, you can create a calculated field. In a calculated field's formula, you can refer to other fields in the pivot table. In this example, you'll test the Units field, to see if more than 100 units were sold, and multiply by the Total field.

1. Select any cell in the pivot table, and on the Ribbon, under the PivotTable Tools tab, click the Options tab.

2. In the Tools group, click Formulas, and then click Calculated Field.

3. Type a name for the calculated field, for example, **Bonus**.

4. In the Formula box, type =IF(Units>100,Total*3%,0).

5. Click OK to save the calculated field, and to close the dialog box. The Bonus field appears in the Values area of the pivot table, and in the field list in the PivotTable Field List (see Figure 3-24).

3		Values	
4	Row Labels ▾	Sum of Units	Sum of Bonus
5	⊟Andrews	367	89.20
6	Binder	150	22.46
7	Desk	6	0.00

Figure 3-24. *The calculated field appears in the Values area.*

■**Note** You can't change the summary function for a calculated field. Sum is the only function available for these fields.

3.18. Using Formulas: Modifying a Calculated Field

Problem

You created a calculated field, and you'd like to change it. For example, in Section 3.17, a bonus of 3 percent was calculated. Your company has increased the bonus to 5 percent, and you need to calculate the new amounts. The example shown is from the OrderStatus.xlsx workbook.

Solution

You can go back into the Insert Calculated Field dialog box, and modify the settings.

1. In the pivot table, select any cell, and on the Ribbon, under the PivotTable Tools tab, click the Options tab.

2. In the Tools group, click Formulas, and then click Calculated Field.

3. From the Name drop-down list, select the name of the calculated field you want to modify. In this example, the calculated field is named Bonus.

4. In the Formula box, change the formula. To increase the bonus percent, change the 3 percent to 5 percent.

5. Click Modify, and then click OK to close the dialog box.

3.19. Using Formulas: Removing a Calculated Field

Problem

You created a calculated field, and now you'd like to remove it from the pivot table layout. In this example, the calculated field is named Bonus. The example shown is from the OrderStatus.xlsx workbook.

Solution

You can temporarily hide a calculated field, and then show it again later, or you can permanently remove the calculated field from the pivot table.

To temporarily remove a calculated field, follow these steps:

1. In the pivot table, right-click a cell in the calculated field.

2. Click Remove "Sum of Bonus."

■**Tip** The calculated field is removed from the pivot table layout, but remains in the PivotTable Field List. To add the field to the layout later, add a check mark to the field in the PivotTable Field List.

To permanently remove a calculated field, follow these steps:

1. In the pivot table, select any cell, and on the Ribbon, under the PivotTable Tools tab, click the Options tab.

2. In the Tools group, click Formulas, and then click Calculated Field.

3. From the Name drop-down list, select the name of the calculated field you want to delete. In this example, the calculated field named Bonus is selected.

4. Click Delete, and then click OK to close the dialog box.

3.20. Using Formulas: Determining the Type of Formula

Problem

Your pivot table is complex, with many fields in the Row and Column Labels areas, and several fields in the Values area. You can't tell if a formula is a calculated item or a calculated field.

Solution

Calculated items are listed with other items in the Row or Column Labels areas of the pivot table. Calculated fields appear with the other value fields in the pivot table. Like other value fields, a calculated field's name may be preceded by Sum of.

Another way to identify calculated fields is to check in the PivotTable Field List. If the name appears there, it's a calculated field. Calculated items are not listed.

Also, you can create a list of all the formulas in a pivot table. See Section 3.26 for instructions.

3.21. Using Formulas: Adding a Calculated Item to a Field with Grouped Items

Problem

You want to add a calculated item in a field, but some items are grouped, and you get an error message. For example, if you have manually grouped some of the items in a product field, and then try to create a calculated item in that field, you may see a confusing error message (see Figure 3-25). The example shown is from the GroupError.xlsx workbook.

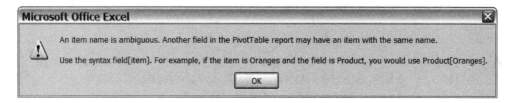

Figure 3-25. *An error message appears when items are grouped.*

Solution

Where duplicate names exist, due to grouping, use the syntax shown in the error message. For example, to calculate a bonus for Desk sales, use the formula =Product[Desk]*.05.

3.22. Using Formulas: Calculating the Difference Between Amounts

Problem

In your pivot table, you have a Forecast amount and an Actual amount. You'd like to calculate the percent difference between Actual and Forecast for each product, but you can't get the calculation to work. The example shown is from the ProductSales.xlsx workbook.

Solution

If Forecast and Actual are separate fields in the source data, you can create a calculated field to calculate the percent difference. Use a formula such as =(Actual/Forecast)-1.

In the ProductSales.xlsx workbook, Forecast and Actual are items in the same field, so you can use the % Difference From custom calculation. In Figure 3-26, Forecast and Actual are items in the Status field, and Sum of Units in the Values area shows the amount for each item. A second copy of the Units field was added to the Values area, and set to show the % Difference From, as described in Section 3.5. For this calculation, Status is the base field, and Forecast is the base item.

Colu ▾				
	Units		% Diff	
Row Labels ▾	Actual	Forecast	Actual	Forecast
A703	3927	3058	28%	
B306	1571	1947	-19%	
C589	3118	2530	23%	
D726	1322	2257	-41%	
Grand Total	9938	9792	1%	

Figure 3-26. *Calculating the difference between amounts*

3.23. Using Formulas: Correcting the Grand Total for a Calculated Field

Problem

You have a calculated field that calculates a bonus based on each product's orders:

```
=IF(Units>100,Total*5%,0)
```

You assume the grand total would be a sum of the bonus amounts, but it performs the same bonus calculation in the grand total row, creating the wrong total. The example shown is from the OrderStatus.xlsx workbook.

Workaround

The grand total for a calculated field performs the same calculation that's defined in the calculated field. As a workaround, you could use formulas outside the pivot table to extract the line totals, and then sum those amounts (see Figure 3-27).

Finally, hide the pivot table column that contains the Bonus calculations, so only the column with the correct Grand Total is visible.

Rep	Andrews ▾		

	Values		
Row Labe ▾	Units	Bonus	Bonus
Binder	150	37.43	37.43
Desk	6	0.00	0.00
Pen	56	0.00	0.00
Pencil	155	23.17	23.17
Grand Total	367	148.67	60.60

Figure 3-27. *The pivot table Grand Total is incorrect for the calculated field.*

Or, if the pivot table layout won't change, you could hide the Grand Total row, and then create formulas below the pivot table to total the columns.

3.24. Using Formulas: Calculated Field—Count of Unique Items

Problem

In your pivot table, you want a count of unique products that have been ordered, but the Values area only shows a count of orders. Some products appear in several orders, so the count of orders doesn't tell you how many unique products were ordered. The example shown is from the ProdCount.xlsx workbook.

Workaround

A pivot table won't calculate a unique count. You could add a column to the source data, and then add that field to the pivot table. For example, add a column in the source data, with the heading ProdCount. To count unique products in Column E, enter the following formula in row 2 of the ProdCount column:

```
=IF(COUNTIF($E$1:E2,E2)=1,1,0)
```

Copy this formula down to the last row of data, and then add the ProdCount field to the pivot table Values area using the Sum function (see Figure 3-28).

Row Labels ▾	Values Units	Count
Binder	1252	1
Desk	29	1
Pen	576	1
Pen Set	830	1
Pencil	926	1
Grand Total	3613	5

Figure 3-28. *Creating a unique count of products*

How It Works

The COUNTIF formula checks the range E1:E2 and counts the instances of the product name entered in cell E2.

For the first occurrence of the name, the count is one. The IF formula checks the result of the COUNTIF formula, and if the count is one, the IF formula returns a one.

For the next occurrence of the product name, the COUNTIF formula would return a two. Because that is not equal to one, the IF formula would return a zero.

When you copy the formula down the column on the worksheet, only the first occurrence of each product returns a one, so the sum of this column is the number of unique products.

In the formula, the reference to cell E1 is absolute ($E$1), so that reference does not change as the formula is copied down the column in the source data. The other references, to E2, are relative, and change in each row, to refer to the cells in that row. The formula always starts its count in cell E1, and counts down to the row that contains the formula.

3.25. Using Formulas: Correcting Results in a Calculated Field

Problem

In your source data, you have columns for cost and units, but the results are incorrect when you use a calculated field in the pivot table to multiply cost by units. The example shown is from the OrderStatus.xlsx workbook.

Solution

When you use a calculated field in the pivot table, the result is the Sum of Cost multiplied by Sum of Units, and the result is inflated, except where the total number of units in a row is one.

Instead of using a calculated field, calculate the total cost (cost × units) for each row in the source data table. Then, add that field to the pivot table's Values area to get the correct totals.

3.26. Using Formulas: Listing All Formulas

Problem

You're documenting your workbook, and you would like to create a list of all the formulas for calculated fields and calculated items you created in the pivot table.

Solution

1. Select any cell in the pivot table, and then on the Ribbon, click the Options tab.

2. In the Tools group, click Formulas, and then click List Formulas.

A new sheet is inserted in the workbook, with a list of calculated items and a list of calculated fields.

3.27. Using Formulas: Accidentally Creating a Calculated Item

Problem

Your pivot table contains a calculated item named Formula1, but you didn't create one and aren't sure how it got there. You'd like to delete the calculated item, and prevent it from happening again. The example shown is from the CalcItem.xlsx workbook.

Solution

It's possible to accidentally create a calculated item if you select a cell that contains a Row or Column label, and drag the fill handle, at the bottom right of the selected cell. Follow these steps to remove the formula:

1. Select the cell that contains the label for the Formula1 calculated item.

2. On the Ribbon, under the PivotTable Tools tab, click the Options tab.

3. In the Tools group, click Formulas, and then click Calculated Item.

4. From the drop-down list of formulas, select the formula you want to delete.

5. Click the Delete button, and then click the Close button.

3.28. Using Formulas: Solve Order

Problem

In your pivot table, there are two calculated items:

```
CancelRate: = Cancel/(Cancel+Existing)
All: East+West
```

In the pivot table, grand totals are hidden and the calculated items are shown (see the table at the left in Figure 3-29). The example shown is from the SolveOrder.xlsx workbook. However, the CancelRate for All is incorrect. It's a sum of the CancelRate for the individual regions (3.3%+2.5%), instead of a calculation of the CancelRate (3.2/(3.2+111.5)), based on the All totals.

You'd prefer to have the CancelRate for All be calculated like the CancelRate for the individual regions.

Original Solve Order

Sum of Policie: Colu ↴			
Row Labels ↴	East	West	All
Cancel	1.6	1.6	3.2
Existing	47.6	63.8	111.5
CancelRate	3.3%	2.5%	**5.8%**

Revised Solve Order

Sum of Polici(Colun ↴			
Row Labels ↴	East	West	All
Cancel	1.6	1.6	3.2
Existing	47.6	63.8	111.5
CancelRate	3.3%	2.5%	**2.8%**

Figure 3-29. *The pivot table, with two calculated items*

Solution

You can change the Solve Order for the calculated items to get the result you want:

1. Select a cell in the pivot table, and then on the Ribbon, click the Options tab.

2. In the Tools group, click Formulas, and then click Solve Order.

3. Select the All formula, and then click the Move Up button. Click Close.

The All CancelRate is adjusted and shows the All cancel ratio, instead of the sum of region ratios (see the table at the right in Figure 3-29).

■**Note** When you change the Solve Order, it affects all calculated items in the pivot table.

How It Works

Calculated items are added to the Solve Order list in the order in which they're created. For any result affected by two or more calculated items, the last calculation listed is the one that determines its value.

In this example, the CancelRate calculated item was created first, and then the All calculated item. The bottom-right cell in the pivot table is affected by both calculated items.

In the original Solve Order, the All calculated item is last in the Solve Order, so the bottom-right cell shows the result of that formula: East+West.

In the revised Solve Order, the CancelRate calculated item is last in the Solve Order, so the bottom-right cell shows the result of that formula: Cancel/(Cancel+Existing).

CHAPTER 4

Formatting a Pivot Table

New formatting features were introduced for pivot tables in Excel 2007, including PivotTable Styles, Document Themes, Conditional Formatting, and Report Layouts, which add many exciting options for enhancing the look of your pivot tables. Questions about these new features are addressed in this chapter. Common problems with pivot table formatting include loss of formatting when the pivot table is changed or refreshed, showing or hiding subtotals and grand totals, and retaining formats applied in the source data.

Unless otherwise noted, the problems in this chapter are based on data in the sample file named Regions.xlsx.

4.1. Using PivotTable Styles: Applying a Predefined Format

Problem

You create several pivot tables each week. Each pivot table has default formatting applied, and you spend time changing the colors and borders to match your company's specifications. You'd like a quick way to format your pivot table, so it easily coordinates with your company's other documents. This example is based on the Regions.xlsx workbook.

Solution

Instead of manually formatting a pivot table, you can apply one of the built-in PivotTable styles, also called *quick styles*. Quick styles may affect the color and font formatting, and they may add borders and row or column shading. Some styles include horizontal borders or shading, which can make the rows easier to follow in a wide pivot table. Some styles have dramatic or dark colors that may be best suited for presentations or online viewing, rather than printing.

Follow these steps to apply a PivotTable style:

1. Select a cell in the pivot table, and on the Ribbon, click the Design tab. In the PivotTable Styles group, you can see one of the styles is selected, and it has a border around it. This is the style currently applied to your pivot table.

2. Point to one of the PivotTable styles, and the pivot table on the worksheet will show a preview of that style. Also, the style's name should appear below the Ribbon, in a ScreenTip (see Figure 4-1), unless you turned off the Screen Tips feature.

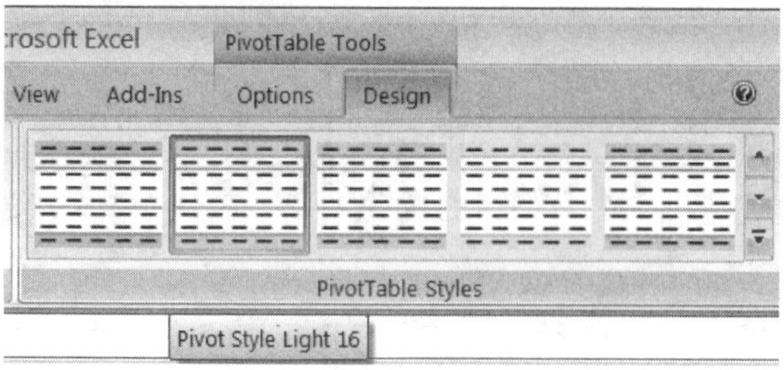

Figure 4-1. *PivotTable styles*

■**Tip** If the preview doesn't show, you may have this feature turned off in the Excel Options. To turn the feature on, click the Microsoft Office Button, click Excel Options, and in the Popular features, add a check mark to Enable Live Preview.

---

3. To see other rows of PivotTable styles, click the up or down arrow at the right end of the PivotTable Styles group, or to open the full gallery of PivotTable styles, click the More button, at the right end of the PivotTable Styles group (shown in Figure 4-1). In the gallery, you can drag the scroll bar up and down to see the PivotTable styles, which are grouped as Light, Medium, and Dark.

■**Tip** If you change your mind, and don't want to apply a style, press Esc on the keyboard, or click outside the Style gallery, and it will close without applying a style.

---

4. When you find a PivotTable style you like, click it, to apply that style to your pivot table.

■**Tip** To apply the selected style and remove any formatting manually applied to the pivot table, right-click the style, and then click Apply and Clear Formatting (this does not remove conditional formatting). If you don't use this option, the manual formatting is retained.

How It Works

When you select one of the PivotTable styles, it applies specific cell formatting to different parts of the pivot table. For example, all the row subtotals may be changed to bold Calibri font, with blue fill color in the cell. If you change the pivot table layout, the formatting is retained and adjusts to the new layout.

You can quickly modify the appearance of a built-in style by using the PivotTable Style Options. With these, you turn on or off the special formatting for the headers, rows, and columns. The Row Headers and Column Headers options apply or remove special fonts and fill colors in the headers. The Banded Rows and Banded Columns apply or remove the shading from rows and columns.

1. Select a cell in the pivot table, and on the Ribbon, click the Design tab.

2. In the PivotTable Style Options group, add or remove the check marks from the style options (see Figure 4-2).

Figure 4-2. *PivotTable Style Options*

4.2. Using PivotTable Styles: Removing a PivotTable Style

Problem

You applied a PivotTable style to a pivot table, and you would like to remove it. You would prefer to have a pivot table with no fill color or header formatting. This example is based on the Regions.xlsx workbook.

Solution

In the PivotTable Styles gallery, you can apply a special style that removes the existing style, or you can use a command to clear the existing style. Follow these steps to clear a PivotTable style:

1. Select a cell in the pivot table, and on the Ribbon, click the Design tab.

2. In the PivotTable Styles gallery, the first style, at the top left of the Light styles, is named None (see Figure 4-3). Click this style, and the existing style is removed. A thin border remains around sections of the pivot table, and the gridlines, if displayed, are not visible within the pivot table.

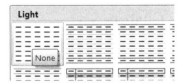

Figure 4-3. *PivotTable style named None*

■Note When no PivotTable style is applied, the preview function won't work when you point to a different style in the PivotTable Styles gallery.

A different way to remove the PivotTable style is to click Clear, at the bottom left of the PivotTable Styles gallery (see Figure 4-4).

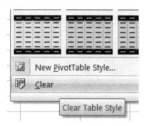

Figure 4-4. *Clear a PivotTable style.*

4.3. Using PivotTable Styles: Changing the Default Style

Problem

You prefer one of the Dark PivotTable styles, and you apply it to almost every pivot table you create. You'd like to change the default PivotTable style, to save time when you create new pivot tables. This example is based on the `Regions.xlsx` workbook.

Solution

You can change the default PivotTable style to one you prefer. Follow these steps to change the default:

1. Select a cell in the pivot table, and then on the Ribbon, click the Design tab.

2. In the PivotTable Styles gallery, right-click the style you want to set as the default, and in the context menu, click Set As Default.

This technique sets the default PivotTable style for the active workbook. If you want to make this the default style for new workbooks, save the workbook as a template. Then, base new workbooks on this template, and your default PivotTable style will be available.

4.4. Using PivotTable Styles: Creating a Custom Style

Problem

None of the existing PivotTable styles has the exact formatting you need. You'd like to create your own PivotTable style, with colors, borders, and fonts that match your company's document specifications. This example is based on the `Regions.xlsx` workbook.

Solution

You can create a custom PivotTable style with the formatting you require. If you find a Pivot-Table style close to what you need, you can duplicate that style, and modify the duplicate.

Follow these steps to create a custom style, based on an existing style:

1. Select a cell in the pivot table, and then on the Ribbon, click the Design tab.

2. In the PivotTable Styles gallery, right-click the style you want to duplicate.

3. In the context menu, click Duplicate. In this example, Pivot Style Medium 8 was duplicated.

■**Note** If you don't want to duplicate any style, click New PivotTable Style, at the bottom of the PivotTable Styles gallery, and then follow the next steps to name and modify the new style.

---

4. In the Modify PivotTable Quick Style dialog box, type a name for the new PivotTable style (see Figure 4-5). In this example, the name is **My Gray Style**.

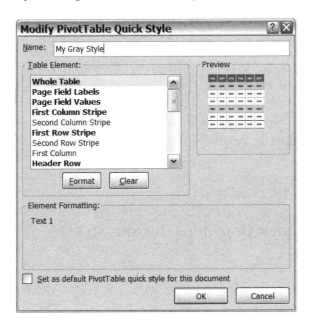

Figure 4-5. *Modify PivotTable Quick Style dialog box*

■**Tip** Click a formatted Table Element, to view a description of its formatting in the Element Formatting section of the Modify PivotTable Quick Style dialog box.

---

5. In the Table Element list, elements in bold font have formatting applied. You can modify these, or clear their formatting. You can also select unformatted elements and format them to meet your requirements. To modify an element's formatting, click it to select it, and then click the Format button.

6. In the Format Cells dialog box, select the Font, Border, and Fill settings you want for the selected element.

7. Click OK, to return to the Modify PivotTable Quick Style dialog box, where the formatted element is listed with a bold font.

8. Repeat Steps 5 to 7, if required, to format other elements.

9. If you want your custom style to be the default PivotTable style, add a check mark to Set As Default PivotTable Quick Style For This Document.

10. Click OK, to close the Modify PivotTable Quick Style dialog box.

■**Note** The new PivotTable style is not automatically applied to the active pivot table.

The custom PivotTable Style you created is added to a Custom section of the PivotTable Styles gallery (see Figure 4-6). You can click the custom style there, to apply it to the active pivot table.

Figure 4-6. *The Custom PivotTable styles on the Ribbon*

4.5. Using PivotTable Styles: Copying a Custom Style to a Different Workbook

Problem

You created several custom PivotTable Styles in a workbook, and you would like to copy those styles to other workbooks. You can't find any command that will let you copy the styles from one workbook to another. This example is based on the Custom.xlsx and Regions.xlsx workbooks.

Solution

To copy a custom PivotTable style to another workbook, you can apply that custom style to a pivot table, and then temporarily copy that pivot table to a different workbook. Follow these steps to copy from the Custom.xlsx workbook to the Regions.xlsx workbook:

1. Select all the cells in a pivot table that has the custom style applied, and then on the Ribbon's Home tab, click Copy.

2. Switch to the workbook where you want the copy of the custom style, and then paste the pivot table.

3. Delete the pasted copy of the pivot table.

The custom PivotTable style now appears in the PivotTable Styles gallery, and it can be applied to any pivot table in the workbook.

4.6. Using Themes: Impacting PivotTable Styles

Problem

You selected a different Document Theme in your workbook, and it changed the appearance of the worksheets and the styles in the PivotTable Styles gallery. You don't understand how Themes work, or why they affect the PivotTable styles. This example is based on the Themes.xlsx workbook.

Solution

Each *Document Theme* is a collection of colors, fonts, and visual effects you can share between Excel and other Office applications. You can use the existing themes, create new themes, or modify the built-in themes.

To see what theme is currently applied, and what its settings are, you can view the Theme information on the Ribbon. Activate a worksheet that contains a pivot table, so you can see the effect of theme changes.

1. On the Ribbon, click the Page Layout tab.

2. In the Themes group, point to the Themes command, and the tooltip then shows the name of the current theme.

3. To view the color palette for the current theme, in the Themes group, click Colors, to open the color list. The current theme's colors are surrounded by a thin border, to show they are selected. If you point to a different theme's colors, you can see the preview colors in your pivot table change.

4. A theme has two fonts: one for headings and one for body text. To view the fonts associated with the current theme, in the Themes group, click the Fonts command, to open the list of fonts. The current theme's fonts are selected, and show the Headings font and the Body font. If you point to a different theme's fonts, you can see the preview fonts in your pivot table change.

5. Finally, a theme also has effects that are used in charts and shapes, so if you create a PivotChart, its appearance will be affected by the current theme's effects. To view the effects associated with the current theme, in the Themes group, click the Effects command, to open the list of effects. The current theme's effects are selected, and they show the line thickness, fill type, and beveling that would be used for charts and shapes.

If you apply a different theme in your workbook, or modify the current theme, your pivot table's appearance and PivotTable styles may be affected. The theme colors and fonts will override the settings in the PivotTable styles, and they could affect the way the pivot table appears.

To apply a different theme, follow these steps:

1. On the Ribbon, click the Page Layout tab.

2. In the Themes group, click Themes, and then in the Themes gallery, click the theme you want to apply.

The colors and fonts in your file will change, and your pivot table and Excel Table may be wider or narrower, if the fonts are much different. In the Themes group on the Page Layout tab, the icons have changed, to reflect the colors, fonts, and effects of the current theme. In the PivotTable Styles gallery, the styles use the colors from the new theme. Even the font in the row and column buttons changes to the Body font for the current theme.

4.7. Using the Enable Selection Option

Problem

In your pivot table, the Region and City fields are in the Row Labels area. You want to use a different font size for the Region subtotals, and you'd like to select and format all the subtotals at the same time, instead of formatting each one separately. This example is based on the Regions.xlsx workbook.

Solution

If the subtotals are at the bottom of the group, in either the Row Labels area or the Column Labels area, you can select them all, and then format them together. To select them, you may have to activate the Enable Selection option.

1. Select a cell in the pivot table, and on the Ribbon, click the Options tab.

2. In the Actions group, click Select, and then check to see if Enable Selection is activated (see Figure 4-7).

Figure 4-7. *The Enable Selection option turned on*

3. If Enable Selection isn't activated, click it to activate the feature. If it is activated, click the worksheet, to close the menu without making a selection.

4. To select subtotals for a Row Labels field, point to the left edge of a cell that contains a subtotal label, and when the pointer changes to a black arrow shape (see Figure 4-8), click to select all the subtotals for that field.

6	New York	4,254	3,577
7	Boston	4,653	8,356
8	→ East Total	**8,907**	**13,734**
9	⊟ West		

Figure 4-8. *The black arrow pointer at the left of the subtotal in Row 8*

5. If the subtotals are for a Column Labels field, point to the top edge of a cell that contains a subtotal label, and when the pointer changes to a black arrow shape, click to select all the subtotals for that field.

6. Format the selected subtotals, using the commands on the Ribbon's Home tab.

4.8. Losing Formatting When Refreshing the Pivot Table

Problem

You manually adjusted the column widths and applied formatting to the cells in your pivot table. However, your pivot table formatting is lost when you refresh the pivot table or change the pivot table layout. Even changing the report filter causes the formatting to be lost. This example is based on the LoseFormat.xlsx workbook.

Solution

Most formatting can be preserved if you change the Format options in the PivotTable Options dialog box.

1. Right-click a cell in the pivot table, and then choose PivotTable Options.

2. On the Layout & Format tab, in the Format options, remove the check mark from Autofit Column Widths on Update. This prevents the column width from changing, if you have manually adjusted it.

3. Add a check mark to Preserve Cell Formatting on Update, and then click OK.

Then, when you apply formatting, do the following:

1. Ensure that Enable Selection is turned on (as shown in Figure 4-7).

2. Unless you want to format a single cell, use the pivot table selection technique to select the elements you want to format (point to the top or left edge of the element, and then click when the black arrow appears).

4.9. Hiding Error Values on Worksheet

Problem

Errors, such as #N/A, are in the Excel Table on which the pivot table is based, and you'd like to hide them in the pivot table. This example is based on the Errors.xlsx workbook.

Solution

By default, error values are displayed in a pivot table. You can hide the errors by changing the PivotTable Options, so blank cells appear instead of the errors:

1. Right-click a cell in the pivot table, and in the context menu, click PivotTable Options.

2. In the PivotTable Options dialog box, click the Layout & Format tab.

3. In the Format section, add a check mark to For Error Values Show (see Figure 4-9).

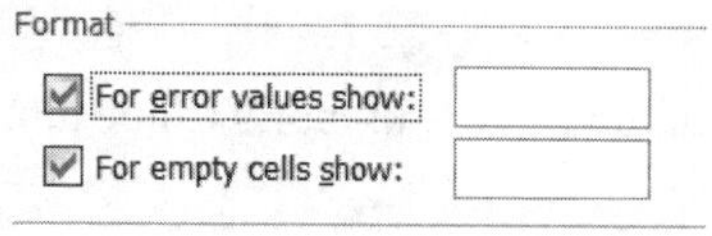

Figure 4-9. *Format option for error values*

4. Leave the text box blank, and the errors will be replaced with blank cells, and then click OK to close the dialog box. If you prefer, you could type other characters, such as a hyphen, in the text box, and the error values will be replaced by that character.

■**Note** This setting only affects cells in the Values area of the pivot table. If error values appear in the Row Labels, Column Labels, or Report Filter areas, they won't be replaced.

4.10. Showing Zero in Empty Values Cells

Problem

Some cells in the Values area are empty, and you'd prefer they contain a zero or a couple of dashes. This example is based on the Regions.xlsx workbook.

Solution

You can change the PivotTable Options and display any number or character, in a Values cell where there is no data:

1. Right-click a cell in the pivot table, and in the context menu, click PivotTable Options.

2. On the Layout & Format tab, add a check mark to For Empty Cells, Show and, in the text box, type a zero (see Figure 4-10). Click OK to close the dialog box.

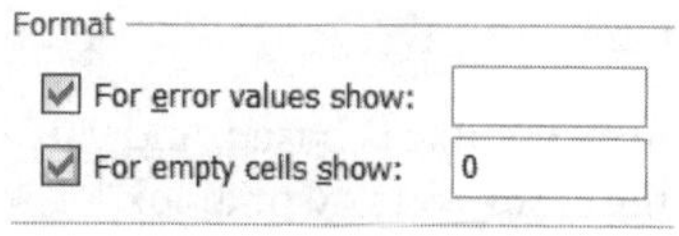

Figure 4-10. *Format option for empty cells*

4.11. Hiding Buttons and Labels

Problem

You're sending your pivot table to a colleague, and you want to hide some of the buttons and filter drop-downs in the pivot table before you send it. Your colleague isn't too familiar with pivot tables, and you want to make it look as simple and uncluttered as possible. This example is based on the `Regions.xlsx` workbook.

Solution

You can change the Pivot Table Options to hide some of the buttons and captions in the pivot table. Follow these steps to hide some of the features:

1. Right-click a cell in the pivot table and, in the context menu, click PivotTable Options.

2. On the Display tab, remove the check mark from Show Expand/Collapse Buttons. This hides the buttons to the left of the outer Row Labels and Column Labels.

3. Also remove the check mark from Display Field Captions and Filter Drop Downs. This hides the filter buttons, as well as the Row Labels and Column Labels captions.

4. Click OK to close the PivotTable Options dialog box.

4.12. Applying Conditional Formatting: Using a Color Scale

Problem

You've created a pivot table report to send to the store managers. Your pivot table is a dense block of numbers, with the Product field in the Row Labels area, the Store field in the Column Labels area, and the TotalPrice field in the Values area. You'd like to color the Values cells, to highlight the highest and lowest values.

Instead of reading all the numbers, the store managers could quickly identify the products and stores with the strongest sales because cells that contain those values would be colored green. The products and stores with the weakest sales would have values in red cells—a signal for trouble! The reasons for those low sales could be investigated. This example is based on the `Stores.xlsx` workbook.

Solution

You can use conditional formatting to add visual impact to the data in a pivot table, just as with other cells in the workbook. To quickly format the cells in a pivot table, you can use one of the built-in color scales.

Follow these instructions to add a conditional formatting color scale to a pivot table with a single block of cells to format.

1. In the pivot table Values area, select the cells you want to color. In the sample file, select cells B5:E15.

Caution Do not include the Grand Total rows or columns, or they will be colored as the highest values.

---

2. On the Ribbon, click the Home tab, and in the Styles group, click Conditional Formatting.

3. In the list of conditional formatting options, click Color Scales, and then click the first option—Green-Yellow-Red Color Scale.

Tip In the Color Scales menu, point to any of the color scale options to see a preview of the formatting on the selected cells.

How It Works

In a three-color scale, the cells with the lowest, median, and highest values are a solid color, and cells with values in between have a graduated color. In the Green-Yellow-Red color scale, the cell with the highest value is solid green, the cell with the median value is solid yellow, and the cell with the lowest value is solid red.

Two-color scales, which use one color for the cell with the highest number, and a second color for the cell with the lowest number, are also available. Cells with values between the highest and lowest are shaded in a graduated color scale.

Note Cells with no data will not be formatted.

4.13. Applying Conditional Formatting: Using an Icon Set

Problem

Your pivot table has a list of sales totals for each product, and instead of numbers, you'd like to show traffic lights, to indicate the high, low, and middle results. This can create a simple report you can share with employees, without disclosing all the numbers. This example is based on the Products.xlsx workbook.

Solution

You can use conditional formatting icon sets to illustrate the data. These small pictures use shapes and colors to mark the values. There is a wide variety of icon sets, including traffic lights, with red for low, yellow for middle, and green for high results.

1. In the pivot table, select the cells where you want to add icons. In the sample file, select cells B4:B14.

2. On the Ribbon, click the Home tab, and in the Styles group, click Conditional Formatting.

3. In the list of conditional formatting options, click Icon Sets, and then click one of the traffic light options. For example, click the 3 Traffic Lights (Unrimmed) option.

■**Tip** Point to any of the icon-set options to see a preview of the formatting on the selected cells.

The icon set is added to the cell, to the left of the numbers. To remove the numbers from the cells, so only the icons are visible, you can adjust the settings for the conditional formatting you applied. Follow these instructions to remove the numbers from the cells:

1. In the pivot table, select the cells that contain the icon set, and on the Ribbon, click the Home tab, and then in the Styles group, click Conditional Formatting.

2. In the list of conditional formatting options, click Icon Sets, and then click More Rules, at the bottom of the list of Icon Sets.

3. In the New Formatting Rule dialog box, the current settings for the icon set are displayed. At the bottom right, add a check mark to Show Icon Only, and then click OK (see Figure 4-11). You can use the Alignment options on the Ribbon's Home tab to center the icons in the cells.

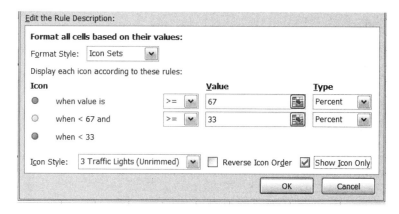

Figure 4-11. *Show Icon Only*

Tip In the New Formatting Rule dialog box, you can also adjust the settings for the icons, to control which percent of values have one of the icons. You can also check the Reverse Icon Order option, to change the order in which the icons are applied. This option is useful if high numbers indicate a poor result, and you want them red, instead of green.

4.14. Applying Conditional Formatting: Using Bottom 10 Items

Problem

You're preparing a report for a sales meeting, and you'd like to highlight only the bottom two results in a list of product sales. You don't want to use a color scale that will color all the selected cells, because you want the discussion to focus on only the lowest results. This example is based on the Bottom.xlsx workbook.

Solution

To highlight just the lowest results, you can use the Bottom 10 Items conditional formatting option. The other options in the Top/Bottom Rules list work similarly, and you can select these to highlight the top or bottom items or percent, or cells with above or below average values.

Follow these instructions to highlight the bottom two results in the selected cells, using a custom format:

1. In the pivot table, select the cells you want to format, and on the Ribbon, click the Home tab, and then in the Styles group, click Conditional Formatting.

2. In the list of conditional formatting options, click Top/Bottom Rules, and then click Bottom 10 Items. The Bottom 10 Items dialog box opens, with ten as the setting in the scroll box at the left. The default formatting option, Light Red Fill with Dark Red Text, is selected in the drop-down list at the right. The selected cells show a preview of this formatting, and you can change either of the settings to meet your requirements.

3. In the scroll box, change the number of items to two.

   You can select a formatting option from the drop-down list or create a custom format.

4. Click the drop-down arrow to open the formatting list, and then click Custom Format, to open the Format Cells dialog box.

5. In the Format Cells dialog box, select the Number, Font, Border, and Fill options you want for the highlighted cells.

■**Note** Some formatting options, such as font size or thick borders, are unavailable, because conditional formatting doesn't allow settings that could affect the cell size.

---

6. Click OK, to close the Format Cells dialog box, and then click OK to close the Bottom 10 Items dialog box.

■**Note** In the case of a tie, more than the specified number of cells may be formatted.

4.15. Applying Conditional Formatting: Formatting Cells Between Two Values

Problem

The sales manager wants to run a promotion at stores with sales between 500 and 1000. In your pivot table report, you'd like any cell that contains a value in this range to be colored green, to stand out from the other amounts. Next week, the target values may change, so you'd like it to be easy to change the formatting criteria. This example is based on the Between.xlsx workbook.

Solution

To highlight cells within a specific range of values, you can use the Highlight Cell Rules conditional formatting option. To make this formatting more flexible, you can type the minimum and maximum amounts on the worksheet, and refer to those cells in the conditional formatting.

1. In an empty cell in the workbook, type the minimum amount for the conditional formatting, and in another cell, type the maximum amount. In the sample workbook, the values are typed in cells E1 and F1.

2. In the pivot table, select the cells you want to format, and on the Ribbon, click the Home tab, and then in the Styles group, click Conditional Formatting.

3. In the list of conditional formatting options, click Highlight Cells Rules, and then click Between.

4. Delete the default value in the minimum box, and click the cell that contains the minimum value you typed. Delete the default value in the maximum box, and click the cell that contains the minimum value you typed on the worksheet (see Figure 4-12).

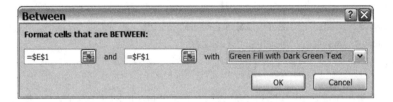

Figure 4-12. *Refer to worksheet cells in the Between dialog box.*

5. In the formatting list, select one of the formatting options, or create a Custom Format.

6. Click OK to close the Between dialog box.

The cells with a value between the minimum and maximum values are now colored green. When the criteria change, you can type new values in the minimum and maximum cells on the worksheet, and the formatted cells will reflect the revised criteria.

4.16. Applying Conditional Formatting: Formatting Labels in a Date Period

Problem

Your pivot table contains several years of sales forecast data, with a date field in the Row Labels area. When you open the workbook, you would like the Row Labels for the current month to be highlighted. This can make it easier to find the data, in a long list of dates. This example is based on the Forecast.xlsx workbook.

Solution

You can use conditional formatting to highlight cells in the Row Labels area. Follow these steps to highlight Row Labels where the date is in the current month.

1. In the pivot table, select the Row Labels with dates you want to format.

2. On the Ribbon, click the Home tab, and then in the Styles group, click Conditional Formatting.

3. In the list of conditional formatting options, click Highlight Cells Rules, and then click A Date Occurring.

4. In the date range drop-down, select This Month, and then click the arrow to open the formatting drop-down list.

5. Select one of the formatting options, or create a Custom Format, and then click OK to close the A Date Occurring dialog box.

The dates from the current month are highlighted, and will stand out in the report when you open the workbook. Because the conditional formatting (This Month) is dynamic, the highlight changes each month when you open the workbook.

4.17. Applying Conditional Formatting: Using Data Bars

Problem

You've created a pivot table to summarize sales for the past two years. The Date field is in the Row Labels area, grouped by Month, and the Sales field is in the Values area. The pivot table will be used in a slide presentation, and you'd like to make it easy to visually compare the total sales for each month. This example is based on the DataBars.xlsx workbook.

Solution

In a list of values, you can use conditional formatting to add data bars to the value cells. This can make it easy to visually compare the list of numbers, to see which months have the smallest numbers, and which months have the largest. Follow these instructions to add data bars to the pivot table.

■**Tip** Color scales, icon sets, and data bars can all be applied simultaneously to the cells. However, using more than one of the conditional formatting options may add confusion to the pivot table, rather than help illustrate the data, and using a single type is best in most cases.

---

1. In the pivot table, select the value cells you want to format. Don't include the Grand Total value, because you only want to compare the individual months. In the sample file, select cells B4:B9.

2. On the Ribbon, click the Home tab, and then in the Styles group, click Conditional Formatting.

3. In the list of conditional formatting options, click Data Bars, and then click one of the Data Bar options. The Data Bar options are identical, except for the color.

■**Tip** If you find it difficult to see where the bars end, because of the graduated coloring in the data bars, you can apply a dark fill color to the cells, and then change the font to a light color.

How It Works

The conditional formatting data bars aren't exactly like using a bar chart. The data bars are not zero-based; the shortest data bar represents the lowest value in the formatted data, and the longest bar represents the highest value in the formatted data.

   If the lowest value is zero, and the highest value is 50, the data bars might look the same as the data bars for data with values that ranged from 500 to 3000, or values from -3000 to -500 (see Figure 4-13). Even if the lowest value is zero, or a negative number, it is represented by a small data bar.

	A	B	C	D	E
1	0		500		-3000
2	10		1000		-2500
3	20		1500		-2000
4	30		2000		-1500
5	40		2500		-1000
6	50		3000		-500

Figure 4-13. *Data bars appear the same for different sets of values.*

In this example, the lowest month is June, with 621 sales, and the highest month is January, with 1277 (see Figure 4-14). Although the lowest number is approximately one half of the highest number, its bar appears to be about one tenth the length of the longest bar. This exaggerates the difference between the values.

Row Lak ⊽	Sum of Sales
Jan	1277
Feb	1003
Mar	1105
Apr	952
May	770
Jun	621
Grand Tot:	**5728**

Figure 4-14. *Data bars and numbers*

You can modify the conditional formatting, to fix the scale of the data bars.

1. In the pivot table, select the cells that contain the formatted value cells.

2. On the Ribbon, click the Home tab, and in the Styles group, click Conditional Formatting, and then click Manage Rules.

3. The Conditional Formatting Rules Manager dialog box opens, where you can see the Data Bar rule, and any other conditional formatting rules in the pivot table. In the list of rules, click your Data Bar rule.

4. Click the Edit Rule button, to open the Edit Formatting Rule dialog box.

The first section of the Edit Formatting Rule dialog box shows where the rule is applied. The second section shows the type of rule that was applied. In the third section, Edit the Rule Description, you can see the current settings for the Data Bar rule, and this is where you edit the rule. No changes are required in the first or second section.

You want to ensure the amounts are accurately represented in the data bars, so you change the settings for the Shortest Bar. Instead of using the lowest value in the range of cells, you use zero as the setting for the Shortest Bar.

1. Click the arrow for the Type drop-down list, under Shortest Bar (see Figure 4-15).

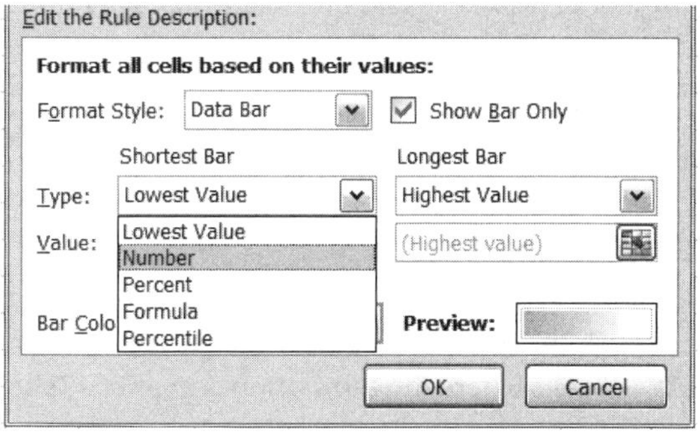

Figure 4-15. *Type options for Shortest Bar*

2. Click Number, and a zero automatically appears in the Value box, for the Shortest Bar. This is the setting you want, so leave the Value as zero.

3. Click OK twice, to close the dialog boxes.

The data bars now use a scale from zero to the highest number, to show a more accurate representation of the numbers.

4.18. Applying Conditional Formatting: Changing the Data Range

Problem

In your pivot table, Date is in the Row Labels area, Territory is in the Column Labels area, and Sales is in the Values area. You applied Above Average conditional formatting to the Values cells, and it is working as expected. The sales manager has asked for a last-minute change to the pivot table layout, and he would like you to show the product sales for each date.

You added the Product field to the Column Labels area, and moved Territory to the Row Labels area, above the Date field. Now the Grand Totals column is formatted, as well as the Values cells. The sales meeting will start soon, and you need to fix the problem. This example is based on the `Territory.xlsx` workbook.

Solution

When you select a block of cells in the pivot table, and then apply conditional formatting, the formatting rule is applied to those cells. If you change the pivot table layout, the formatting rule may adjust correctly and continue to format the cells as intended. However, after some layout changes, the rule may be applied to the wrong cells, especially if additional fields are added to the layout. Follow these instructions to change the conditional formatting range for a rule.

1. Select a cell in the pivot table, and on the Ribbon, click the Home tab.

2. In the Styles group, click Conditional Formatting, and then click Manage Rules. The Conditional Formatting Rules Manager dialog box opens, where you can see the rules that exist for the active pivot table. For each rule, the list shows where the conditional formatting is applied. You can change this setting, to ensure the conditional formatting continues to work as expected, if the pivot table layout changes.

3. In the list of rules, click the Above Average rule.

4. Click the Edit Rule button, to open the Edit Formatting Rule dialog box. In the Apply Rule To section at the top, there are three options, and the Selected Cells option is currently selected. The current range of cells where the formatting is applied is shown (see Figure 4-16).

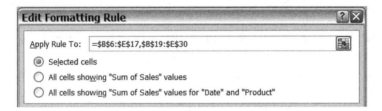

Figure 4-16. *Apply Rule To options in the Edit Formatting Rule dialog box*

- The Selected cells option works in many cases, but when you rearrange the pivot table, the conditional formatting may not adjust correctly. In your pivot table, incorrect cells may be formatted because they are within the range of cells to which the rule is applied.

- In this example, the second option, All Cells Showing "Sum of Sales" Values, might also include too many cells, such as subtotals, and Grand Totals.

- The third option, All Cells Showing "Sum of Sales" Values for "Date" and "Product," is the best option for this pivot table. It restricts the formatting to cells where the Date and Product values appear, and it excludes the subtotals and the Grand Totals.

5. Select the third option, All Cells Showing "Sum of Sales" Values for "Date" and "Product."

6. Click OK, twice, to close the two dialog boxes.

The conditional formatting is now applied correctly, to the individual value cells. The Grand Total cells are not formatted, and their values are not included in the average calculation. You can send the modified report to the sales manager, and go for a well-earned lunch break before the meeting starts.

4.19. Applying Conditional Formatting: Changing the Order of Rules

Problem

In your pivot table, you created a conditional formatting rule to color the top three sales amounts, using bold font and green fill color. You also created a conditional formatting rule to color the above-average sales, using yellow fill color. Now, the top three sales amounts have bold font, but the cells are yellow, instead of green. This example is based on the Order.xlsx workbook.

Solution

Conditional formatting rules are applied in a specified order, and if a cell meets the criteria for multiple conflicting rules, it uses the formatting from the last rule. You can control the rules order, and move rules up or down in the list. Follow these instructions to change the rules order, so the Top 3 rule is applied last.

1. Select a cell in the pivot table, and on the Ribbon, click the Home tab.

2. In the Styles group, click Conditional Formatting, and then click Manage Rules.

The Conditional Formatting Rules Manager dialog box opens, where you can see the two rules you created (see Figure 4-17).

Figure 4-17. *Two rules in the Conditional Formatting Rules Manager dialog box*

When you create a new rule, it goes to the top of the rules list, and has precedence over the other rules. If a formatting conflict occurs, the formatting for the rule with precedence is applied.

You created the Top 3 rule first, so it's at the bottom of the list. When you created the Above Average rule, it was added to the top of the list, taking precedence over the Top 3 rule. Because the Top 3 cells are also Above Average, they are affected by both rules, and the Above Average rule, which has precedence, is applied last, so the cells are colored yellow. No conflict is in the font formatting, however, so the bold formatting remains visible.

You can change the order of the rules, so the Top 3 rule has precedence, and then the green fill color is applied to the Top 3 cells.

1. In the list of rules, click the Top 3 rule.

2. Click the Move Up button (to the right of the Delete Rule button), to move the Top 3 rule above the Above Average rule.

3. Click OK, to close the Conditional Formatting Rules Manager dialog box.

Because you changed the order of the rules, the Top 3 rule now has precedence, and the Top 3 cells are colored green, with bold font.

4.20. Removing Conditional Formatting

Problem

You applied conditional formatting to the cells in your pivot table, and now the sales manager has asked you to remove it. You'd like to remove the conditional formatting, without affecting any of the other formatting in the pivot table. This example is based on the Order.xlsx workbook.

Solution

After applying conditional formatting, you can remove it if it's no longer required. You can choose to remove it from the selected cells, the entire sheet, or the active pivot table. Follow these steps to remove all the conditional formatting from the active pivot table:

1. Select a cell in the pivot table, and on the Ribbon, click the Home tab.

2. In the Styles group, click Conditional Formatting.

3. Click Clear Rules, and then click Clear Rules from This PivotTable.

■**Note** If you want to remove conditional formatting from only specific cells, select those cells, and then use the Clear Rules from Selected Cells command.

4.21. Creating Custom Number Formats in the Source Data

Problem

The lab sent you a workbook with test results, and you created a pivot table to summarize the data by week. Some numbers in the data have a symbol—for example, <0.1—and those numbers aren't showing up in the pivot table. This example is based on the TestResults.xlsx workbook.

Solution

If symbols such as < (less than) and > (greater than) are typed in the source data, they change the numbers into text. In the pivot table, text is displayed as zero in the Values area.

You could create a custom number format, and then apply that format to the source data, instead of using typed symbols, and the values would be totaled correctly in the pivot table.

1. In the source data, enter the actual values, instead of <0.1.

2. Select the cells you want to format, right-click one of the selected cells, and in the context menu, click Format Cells.

3. On the Number tab, select the Custom category.

4. In the Type box, type **[<0.1] <0.1";General** (see Figure 4-18). The custom number format has two sections, separated by a semicolon. In the first section, **[<0.1]** is the condition to use to test the numbers. In this case, numbers less than 0.1 receive special formatting. The text in quotation marks, **<0.1"**, is the formatting the qualifying numbers receive. In the second section, **General** specifies how any other numbers will be formatted.

Figure 4-18. *Enter a Custom Format Type.*

5. Click OK, to close the dialog box.

6. To have this format appear in the pivot table, you can apply the custom number format to the values.

4.22. Changing the Report Layout

Problem

You'd like to change the pivot table layout so it looks like a pivot table from earlier versions of Excel, with each Row Label field in a separate column. You prefer this format, and you'd like to see the Row Label field names at the top of each column. This example is based on the RegionFood.xlsx workbook.

Solution

Instead of the default Compact Form, you can apply a different Report Layout, and the pivot table will have the same structure it had in earlier versions of Excel.

1. Select a cell in the pivot table, and on the Ribbon, click the Design tab.

2. In the Layout group, click Report Layout, and then click either Show in Outline Form or Show in Tabular Form.

How It Works

In Outline Form, each Row Label item is on a separate row, and each Row Label field is in a separate column. The labels for the outer fields are always above the labels for the related inner fields, and the subtotals can be at the top or the bottom of the group.

In Tabular Form, each Row Label field is in a separate column. The labels for the outer fields are on the same row as the first label for the related inner fields, and the subtotals can only be shown at the bottom of the group (see Figure 4-19).

Note Your pivot table may have different borders or fill color, depending on the PivotTable style you applied. To hide some lines within the pivot table in Tabular layout, turn off Gridlines, on the Ribbon's View tab.

Outline Form

Region	City	Orders
East		3031
	Boston	1029
	New York	1186
	Philadelphia	816
West		1165
	Los Angeles	724
	San Diego	441
Grand Total		4196

Tabular Form

Region	City	Orders
East	Boston	1029
	New York	1186
	Philadelphia	816
East Total		3031
West	Los Angeles	724
	San Diego	441
West Total		1165
Grand Total		4196

Figure 4-19. *Comparing Outline Form (left) and Tabular Form (right)*

4.23. Increasing the Row Labels Indentation

Problem

Your pivot table is in the default Compact Form report layout. When you add fields to the Row Labels area, each additional field is indented from the field above it. You would like to slightly increase the indentation, to make the labels easier to read. This example is based on the Regions.xlsx workbook.

Solution

You can change a pivot table option, to increase the number of characters in the indentation.

1. Right-click a cell in the pivot table, and then click PivotTable Options.

2. On the Layout & Format tab, in the Layout section, increase the number of characters in the setting—When in Compact Form Indent Row Labels 1 Character(s). You can set the indent for up to 127 characters, but with that setting, it's not really a compact form!

3. Click OK, to close the dialog box.

4.24. Repeating Row Labels

Problem

When you apply the Outline Form or Tabular Form layout to your pivot table, the Row Labels only appear in the first row for each Region. You would like a label to appear in each row, so you can export the pivot table data for use with other programs (see Figure 4-20). This example is based on the RegionFood.xlsx workbook.

Row Labels in first row only

Region	▾	City	▾	Orders
East		Boston		1029
		New York		1186
		Philadelphia		816
East Total				**3031**
West		Los Angeles		724
		San Diego		441
West Total				**1165**
Grand Total				**4196**

Repeating Row Labels

Region	City	Orders
East	Boston	1029
East	New York	1186
East	Philadelphia	816
East Total		**3031**
West	Los Angeles	724
West	San Diego	441
West Total		**1165**
Grand Total		**4196**

Figure 4-20. *Row Labels in first row only (left) and repeating (right)*

Workaround

The row labels show only once in a pivot table, and there's no setting you can change to force them to repeat. If you need to export a copy of the pivot table with a heading in each row, you can make a copy of the pivot table and repeat the headings there.

In the following steps, you copy the pivot table, select the blank cells, and then create a formula to copy the value from the row above. Finally, you can change the formulas to values.

1. With the pivot table in Tabular Form Layout, select all the cells in the pivot table, and on the Ribbon's Home tab, click Copy.

2. Right-click the cell where you want to paste the copy, and in the context menu, click Paste Special, then click Values, and then click OK.

3. In the copied pivot table, select the cells that contain the Row Labels, and the blank cells below them, where you want the labels repeated.

4. On the Ribbon, click the Home tab, and in the Editing group, click Find & Select, and then click Go To Special.

5. Select Blanks, and then click OK.

6. Type an equal sign, and then press the up arrow on the keyboard—this enters a reference to the cell above.

7. Press Ctrl+Enter—this enters the formula in all selected cells.

If you plan to sort the data, follow these steps to change the formulas to values. This prevents the formula results from changing if the cells move.

1. In the copied pivot table, select all the row labels, and then copy them.

2. On the Ribbon, click the Home tab, click the lower section of the Paste command, and then click Paste Values.

■**Caution** Use Paste Special Values with caution if other cells are in the range that contain formulas.

4.25. Separating Field Items with Blank Rows

Problem

To make the pivot table easier to read, you'd like each outer row field item to be followed by a blank row. When you try to insert rows in the pivot table, you get an error message that says you cannot insert rows. This example is based on the Regions.xlsx workbook.

Solution

In any of the Report Layouts, you can format the outer row fields, so each item has a blank row after it. All the outer row fields will be affected by this setting.

1. Select a cell in the pivot table, and on the Ribbon, click the Design tab.

2. In the Layout group, click Blank Rows, and then click Insert Blank Line After Each Item.

■**Tip** You can't enter text in the blank row, but you can manually format the row—for example, add a fill color to visually separate the items, or you can format the blank rows as part of a PivotTable Style.

4.26. Centering Field Labels Vertically

Problem

Your pivot table is in the Tabular Form layout, and you'd like to center the field labels vertically for the outer fields in the Row Labels area of the pivot table. This example is based on the Regions.xlsx workbook.

Solution

1. Right-click a cell in the pivot table, and then choose PivotTable Options.

2. On the Layout & Format tab, in the Layout section, add a check mark to Merge and Center Cells with Labels.

3. Click OK, to close the dialog box.

This setting automatically centers the Row Labels vertically and horizontally. The subtotals for the Row Labels, and the Grand Total row label are also centered vertically and horizontally.

4.27. Changing Alignment for Merged Labels

Problem

Your pivot table is in Tabular Form layout, and you turned on the Merge and Center Cells with Labels option in the PivotTable Options dialog box. All the row labels are vertically and horizontally center-aligned, but you'd prefer them to be left-aligned. When you select a label cell and try to change the alignment, you get an error message. This example is based on the `Regions.xlsx` workbook.

Solution

Ensure that Enable Selection is turned on, and click at the top of a column of Row Labels, to select all the labels for that field. Click the Align Text Left button on the Home tab of the Ribbon, to change the alignment for all the selected labels.

■**Note** When the pivot table is refreshed or changed, the merged labels return to center alignment and have to be reformatted.

4.28. Displaying Line Breaks in Pivot Table Cells

Problem

Some fields in your source data have line breaks (Alt+Enter). In the pivot table, these appear as a small square and question mark, instead of a line break. This example is based on the `LineBreak.xlsx` workbook.

Solution

In the pivot table, format the cells with Wrap Text, to show the line break character:

1. In the pivot table, select the labels you want to have line breaks. In the sample file, select the City Row Labels.

2. On the Ribbon, click the Home tab, and in the Alignment group, click Wrap Text.

4.29. Freezing Heading Rows

Problem

Your pivot table is quite large and you want to keep the row and column headings visible as you work. This example is based on the `Long.xlsx` workbook.

Solution

You can freeze the cells at the top and left of the window, to keep those cells always in view.

1. Select the cell below and to the right of the cells you want to freeze. For example, to freeze rows 1:5, and columns A:B, select cell C6. The selected cell can be inside your pivot table.

2. On the Ribbon, click the View tab, and in the Window group, click Freeze Panes, and then click Freeze Panes.

4.30. Applying Number Formatting to Report Filter Fields

Problem

You want to change the date format of a field in the Report Filter area. When you right-click the date field label in the Report Filter area, and choose Field Settings, the Number Format button isn't visible in the Field Settings dialog box. This example is based on the `FilterFormat.xlsx` workbook.

Solution

If a numeric field in the source data contains blank cells, or cells with text, then the Number Format button won't be displayed in the Field Settings dialog box for the pivot table field, except in the Values area. Fill the blank cells in the source data and remove any text, then refresh the pivot table, and then you'll be able to format the pivot table field.

4.31. Displaying Hyperlinks

Problem

Hyperlinks are in your source data, but when you add these fields to the pivot table, the hyperlinks don't appear. This example is based on the `Hyperlinks.xlsx` file.

Workaround

The pivot table can't show hyperlinks from the source data, and you can't add hyperlinks to the pivot table. You could add a formula outside the pivot table, to create a hyperlink:

```
=IF(LEFT(A4,3)="www",HYPERLINK("http://"&A4),"")
```

but these formulas could be lost if the pivot table layout changes.

4.32. Changing Subtotal Label Text

Problem

The Product field is the Row Labels area of your pivot table. You want to change the text in some of the Product subtotal labels to make them more descriptive, but when you type a new label, all the Product subtotal labels change to the same text. This example is based on the Labels.xlsx workbook.

Solution

If you select a cell that contains a subtotal label and type a new label that doesn't contain the item name, each item subtotal in the field displays that same text in its label. For example, if you change a subtotal label from Bran Total to Grain Subtotal, every Product will have Grain Subtotal as its subtotal label.

However, if you include the item name in the revised label, then each item subtotal retains its unique identifier. For example, you can change the bran subtotal label from Bran Total to Subtotal—Bran. The subtotal for all other products shows the product name, preceded by Subtotal.

■**Caution** These changes will not be undone if you reset the pivot table captions. You can type the original version of the subtotal text if you want to restore it.

4.33. Formatting Date Field Subtotal Labels

Problem

In your pivot table, the OrderDate field is in the Row Labels area. You selected the date cells, and formatted them as dd-mmm-yy. When you added the Product field to the Row Labels area, the OrderDate subtotals used the mmm-yy date format, like the dates in the source data table. You want the subtotals to use the dd-mmm-yy format. This example is based on the Subtotals.xlsx workbook.

Solution

When you format fields in the Row Labels area, change the formatting in the Field Settings dialog box instead of selecting cells and changing the format.

1. Right-click one of the date field labels, and in the context menu, click Field Settings.

2. Click the Number Format button, and select the date formatting option you want.

3. Click OK twice, to close the dialog boxes.

4.34. Changing the Grand Total Label Text

Problem

One field is in the pivot table's Values area, and you would like to change the text in the Grand Total labels. This example is based on the `Labels.xlsx` workbook.

Solution

You can change all or part of the Row Grand Total text or the Column Grand Total text by typing over the cell or editing in the cell or formula bar.

■**Note** If you change the label for either of these Grand Totals, the other automatically displays the revised text.

You can't change the Row Grand Total text if multiple Values fields are arranged horizontally. You can't change the Column Grand Total text if multiple Values fields are arranged vertically.

CHAPTER 5

▪▪▪

Grouping and Totaling Pivot Table Data

When you add date fields to a pivot table, you can show the dates individually, or group them into larger units, such as years, quarters, or months. This adds flexibility to the pivot table, and enables you to do things like comparing the results from one year to another, or creating a running total by quarter.

You can also group numeric fields, when you add them to the Row Labels or Column Labels area of the pivot table. By using this feature, you can group the numbers into larger chunks, such as groups of 10 or 25. If comparing test scores, or results by age, you can look at larger segments of the population, instead of individual scores or ages.

It's also possible to manually group text items in the Row Labels and Column Labels areas, so you can group cities into a region, or employees into teams, and summarize the data for the group.

Most of the time, grouping goes smoothly, but you may hit snags, or see error messages when you try to group the data in your pivot table. This chapter addresses those problems, and provides solutions or workarounds for the issues you might encounter.

This chapter also covers problems that may arise when summarizing pivot table results in subtotals and grand totals, and when summarizing fields in the Values area.

Except where noted, the problems in this chapter are based on the `Stores.xlsx` sample workbook.

5.1. Grouping: Error Message When Grouping Dates

Problem

You created a pivot table with Category in the Column Labels area, Quantity in the Values area, and OrderDate in the Row Labels area. The sales manager would like the dates grouped by month, instead of seeing quantities for the individual dates.

This seemed like a simple request, but you get an error message, "Cannot group that selection" (see Figure 5-1), when you right-click a date cell, and then click Group. This problem is based on the `GroupError.xlsx` sample workbook.

Figure 5-1. *This is the error message you see when items in a field can't be grouped.*

Solution

This error occurs if there are cells that contain text, instead of dates, in the source data's OrderDate field. For example, you may have entered text, such as N/A, if a date was not available when the data was being entered. To correct the problem, you can do the following:

1. If any of the rows contain text, such as N/A, delete the text, or replace it with a date.

▇**Caution** A blank cell does not cause problems with grouping, but use the Delete key to remove the text. Don't type a space character.

---

2. Refresh the pivot table, and try to group the items in the date field.

3. If you're still unable to group the dates, remove the date field from the pivot table layout, refresh the pivot table, and then add the date field to the pivot table again.

▇**Tip** In the PivotTable Options dialog box, on the Data tab, if Number of Items to Retain Per Field is set to None, you should be able to group the date field without following Step 3.

5.2. Grouping: Error Message When Grouping Numbers

Problem

The logistics manager has asked for a report on the quantities per order. You created a report with Quantity in the Row Labels area, Category in the Column Labels area, and OrderDate in the Values area, as Count of OrderDate. To simplify the report, you would like to show the quantities in groups of ten, such as 1–10, and 11–20, and show the number of orders in each grouping.

However, you get an error message that says, "Cannot group that selection," when you try to group the numbers. You checked the source data, and no text entries are in the Quantity field. This problem is based on the GroupErrorNum.xlsx sample workbook.

Solution

Sometimes, entries that look like numbers are not recognized as real numbers by Excel. The numbers may have been copied or imported from another program, and they are text values instead of real numbers.

A quick way to test if the numbers are being recognized is to select two or more cells that contain numbers. Then, look in the status bar, at the bottom of the Excel window, to see if the numbers show a Sum (see Figure 5-2). If only the Count is displayed in the status bar, the numbers are stored as text.

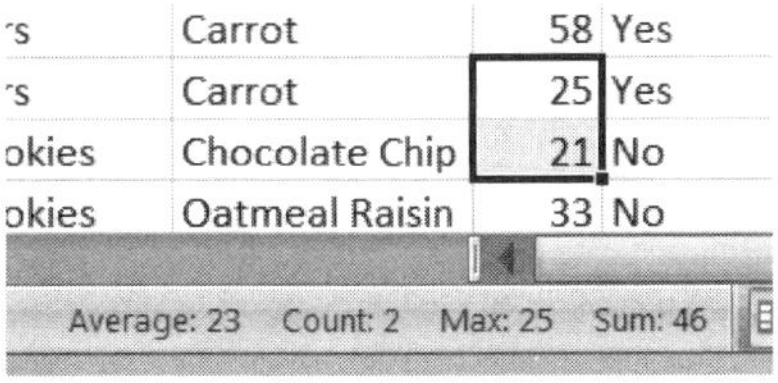

Figure 5-2. *The sum of selected cells shows in the status bar.*

To correct the problem, you can do the following:

1. In the source data, convert the text to numbers, using one of the techniques described in the following "How It Works" section.

2. After converting the text to numbers, refresh the pivot table, and then try to group the numbers in the pivot table.

3. If you're still unable to group the numbers, remove the number field from the pivot table layout, refresh the pivot table, and then add the number field to the pivot table again.

Tip In the PivotTable Options dialog box, on the Data tab, if Number of Items to Retain Per Field is set to None, you should be able to group the numbers without following Step 3.

How It Works

You can convert text "numbers" to real numbers in several ways. For example, you can use the Paste Special command.

1. Select a blank cell in the workbook, and then copy it.

2. In the source data, select the cells that contain the text "numbers."

3. On the Ribbon, click the Home tab, and in the Clipboard group, click the lower section of the Paste command, and then click Paste Special (see Figure 5-3).

Figure 5-3. *Paste Special command on the Ribbon*

4. In the Paste Special dialog box, in the Operation section, select Add, and then click OK.

Another method for converting text numbers to real numbers is to use the Text to Columns feature.

1. Select the cells that contain the numbers you want to convert.

2. On the Ribbon's Data tab, in the Data Tools group, click Text to Columns.

3. In the Convert Text to Columns Wizard, in Step 1, click Finish.

5.3. Grouping the Items in a Report Filter

Problem

You added the OrderDate field to the Report Filter area, and a long list of dates is in the drop-down list. The sales manager frequently asks for a report for a specific month, so you would like to group the dates by month, to make it easier to filter the report.

However, when you select the cell that contains the OrderDate drop-down list, the Group Field command on the Ribbon's Options tab isn't available. This problem is based on the Stores.xlsx sample workbook.

Workaround

You can't group the items in a field located in the Report Filter area. Temporarily move the OrderDate field to the Row Labels or Column Labels area and group the dates, and then move the OrderDate field back to the Report Filter area.

5.4. Grouping: Error Message About Calculated Items

Problem

You're trying to group the dates in the OrderDate field, and you're getting an error message that says, "You cannot add a calculated item to a grouped field" (see Figure 5-4). The Order-Date field doesn't have any calculated items.

The only field with a calculated item is the Category field, and it's not in the pivot table layout. This problem is based on the GroupErrorCalc.xlsx sample workbook.

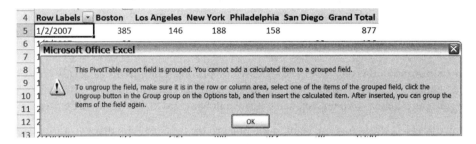

Figure 5-4. *Error message about calculated items*

Workaround

Although the OrderDate field has no calculated items, another field in the pivot table has a calculated item, and that's preventing the grouping. Even though the other field is not visible in the pivot table, it can still prevent the grouping.

■**Tip** When troubleshooting pivot table problems, it may help if you know what formulas are in the pivot table. To create a list of calculated items and calculated fields, select a cell in the pivot table, and on the Ribbon's Options tab, click Formulas, and then click List Formulas.

You can use one of the following workarounds:

- Delete the calculated item in the Category field, and then group the dates in the Order-Date field.

- Add a new field in the source data, with a formula to do the calculation, instead of using a calculated item in the pivot table. Then, add the new field to the pivot table, and delete the calculated item.

- Add a new field with formulas in the source data to create date groups. For example, add a new column with the heading "YearMonth" and use the following formula to show the year and month, for a date in cell A2:

  `=TEXT(A2,"yyyy-mm")`

  Then, refresh the pivot table, and add the YearMonth field to the Row Labels area, instead of using the OrderDate field.

5.5. Grouping Text Items

Problem

Three new stores opened last year and the sales manager asked you for a report that compares quantities sold in the new stores to sales in the older stores. You added the Store field to the Row Labels area of your pivot table, and you'd like to divide the stores into Old and New groups. The three lowest numbers are the older stores, and the three highest are the newer stores.

However, when you select a label in the Store field, the Group Field command on the Ribbon's Options tab isn't available, so you aren't sure how to create the groups. This problem is based on the Stores.xlsx sample workbook.

Solution

The Group Field command is only available for date and number fields in the Row Labels or Column Labels area of the pivot table. Because the store numbers are entered as text, and that's how you want them to remain, you can use the following method to group the stores.

1. Manually select the stores you want in the first group. To select nonadjacent stores, hold the Ctrl key, and then click the store numbers. In the sample file, select stores 3000, 3036, and 3062.

2. On the Ribbon's Options tab, click Group Selection (see Figure 5-5).

Figure 5-5. *Group Selection command*

This creates a group named Group1, with the selected stores listed under that heading (see Figure 5-6). For each of the remaining stores, a heading is created, with its store number.

3	Row Labels ▾	Sum of Quantity
4	⊟ **Group1**	
5	3000	14,157
6	3036	3,981
7	3062	11,224
8	⊟ **3082**	
9	3082	10,344

Figure 5-6. *Group1 created in the Row Labels area*

3. Select the Group1 heading, and then type a name for the group, such as **Old**.

4. Select the remaining stores, and click the Group Selection command to group them. Name the second group as **New**.

■**Tip** To select the remaining stores, drag down through the list of store numbers in the Row Labels area. You can include the store number headings that were created.

As an alternative to grouping the stores in the pivot table, you could add a StoreType field to the source data, and then enter **Old** or **New** for each record. Add the StoreType field as the first field in the Row Labels area and the stores will appear under the correct Store-Type heading.

5.6. Grouping Dates by Month

Problem

Your pivot table is based on two years of sales data. When you group the order dates in your pivot table by month, the January data from both years is lumped together. You'd like to keep the data from different years separated, so you can compare the monthly data between years. This problem is based on the GroupMonth.xlsx sample workbook.

Solution

When you group the dates, select both Year and Month in the Group By list. With this type of grouping, data from each year is grouped, and within each year, the data for each month is grouped.

A Years field is automatically added to the PivotTable Field List, and you can move it to a different area of the pivot table. For example, you could move Years to the Report Filter area, and leave the OrderDate field, showing Months, in the Row Labels area.

5.7. Grouping Dates Using the Starting Date

Problem

You want to group the order dates into four-week periods that coincide with your sales calendar. You successfully group the dates, but the date ranges are a couple of days off, starting midweek instead of on a Monday. This problem is based on the GroupStart.xlsx sample workbook.

Solution

When you group the dates, select to group by days, and set the number of days to 28. As a starting date, Excel automatically selects the first date in your source data, but you can enter a different date, to get the starting date you need.

For example, if the default starting date is Thursday, January 3, 2008, you could enter December 31, 2007 as the starting date for your grouping (see Figure 5-7). This forces all the groupings to start on a Monday, and it matches the company's sales periods.

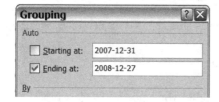

Figure 5-7. *Changing the starting date*

5.8. Grouping Dates by Fiscal Quarter

Problem

You added the OrderDate field to the Row Labels area of your pivot table, and you were able to group the dates by year and quarter. However, you want to group the dates by your company's fiscal quarter, which starts in July, instead of using the calendar quarter available in the Grouping dialog box. This problem is based on the GroupQtr.xlsx sample workbook.

Workaround

There's no built-in option to group by fiscal quarter. In the source data, you can add a column with a formula that calculates the fiscal quarter, and then add that field to the pivot table. For example, if your fiscal year starts in July, use the following formula to calculate the fiscal quarter:

```
=CHOOSE(MONTH(A2),3,3,3,4,4,4,1,1,1,2,2,2)
```

In the Choose formula, the first argument, Month(A2), returns the month of the date in cell A2. It uses that number to select the appropriate fiscal quarter number from the numbers that follow. For example, if the month is April, the month number is 4. In the Choose formula, the fourth number is 4, so that is the fiscal quarter in which April falls.

In another column, you can also calculate the fiscal year. For example, if fiscal year 2009 starts in July 2008:

```
=YEAR(A2)+(MONTH(A2)>=7)
```

Refresh the pivot table, and then ungroup and remove the OrderDate field. Add the fiscal year and fiscal quarter fields to the Row Labels area.

5.9. Grouping Dates by Week

Problem

You added the OrderDate field to the Row Labels area, and you want to group dates by week, but that option isn't available in the Grouping dialog box. You could create a formula in the source data, to calculate the week number, but you'd prefer to group the dates in the pivot table. This problem is based on the GroupWeek.xlsx sample workbook.

Solution

In the Grouping dialog box, select Days, and set the Number of Days to seven (see Figure 5-8). You can also change the starting date, so the first day is a Sunday or Monday, or whatever weekday you would prefer for your grouping.

Figure 5-8. *Group dates by week in the Grouping dialog box.*

This creates groups in the Row Labels area, with the dates formatted using the short date setting defined in the Windows Control Panel, Regional and Language Options dialog box (see Figure 5-9).

3	Row Labels	Sum of Quantity
4	2007-01-01 - 2007-01-07	1003
5	2007-01-08 - 2007-01-14	1013
6	2007-01-15 - 2007-01-21	1208

Figure 5-9. *Row labels grouped by week*

■**Note** The date format may not be exactly the same as the short date format you defined in the Regional and Language Options dialog box, but the year, month, and date should be in the same order, and the date separator you specified should be used. However, if the defined short date format includes a text month name, that is replaced by numbers in the grouped dates.

5.10. Grouping Dates by Months and Weeks

Problem

You wanted to show sales data by week, so you grouped the OrderDate field in seven-day intervals. This successfully grouped the days by week, and the date ranges were displayed in the pivot table.

Later, the sales manager asked you to add month to the date grouping, to summarize the data by month, and by week. When you selected Month in the Grouping dialog box, the days became ungrouped, but you'd like to use months and weeks together when grouping. This problem is based on the GroupWeekNumxlsx sample workbook.

Workaround

In the pivot table, there's no way to group by both weeks and months. You could create a column in the source data, and then calculate one of the grouping levels there. Then, you could add that field to the pivot table.

For example, add a column in the source data, with the heading **WeekNum**, and use the following formula to calculate the week number: =WEEKNUM(A2).

With the OrderDate field in the Row Labels area, group the dates by years and months. In the Row Labels area, add the WeekNum field below the OrderDate field, to summarize the data by month and week number (see Figure 5-10).

■**Note** If a week starts in one month and ends in another, then it appears under each month.

4	Row Labels ▼	East	West	Grand Total
5	⊟ 2006			
6	⊟ Jan	4881	1180	6061
7	1	1649	367	2016
8	3	1893	539	2432
9	5	1339	274	1613
10	⊟ Feb	4385	936	5321
11	5	419		419

Figure 5-10. *Row labels grouped by month and week number*

5.11. Grouping Dates in One Pivot Table Affects Another Pivot Table

Problem

You have two pivot tables based on the same Excel Table. In one pivot table, the order dates are grouped by month, and in the other, you'd like to group the dates by quarters. However, when you change the grouping in one pivot table, the same grouping appears in the other pivot table. You'd like to change one pivot table without affecting the other pivot table. This problem is based on the GroupTwoTables.xlsx sample workbook.

Solution

Because the two pivot tables use the same pivot cache, the grouped items are the same in both tables. If you need different groups in the pivot tables, you can create a named range based on the Excel Table, and use that name as the source for the second pivot table.

For example, on Sheet1 is an Excel Table named Sales_Data. Follow these steps to create a new range named SalesDataNew.

1. On the Ribbon's Formulas tab, in the Defined Names group, click Define Name.

2. In the New Name dialog box, type **SalesDataNew** in the Name box.

3. In the Refers To box, type an OFFSET formula, that refers to the OrderDate header cell in the Sales_Data table, and offsets zero rows and zero columns from that cell (see Figure 5-11).

```
=OFFSET(Sales_Data[[#Headers],[OrderDate]],0,0,
COUNTA(Sales_Data[OrderDate])+2,COUNTA(Sheet1!$1:$1))
```

The COUNTA functions count the number of rows in the Sales_Data table and the cells with data in Row 1 on Sheet1. The size of the new range is based on those counts. Two extra rows (+2) are added to the size of the range, to make it slightly different from the original table's range.

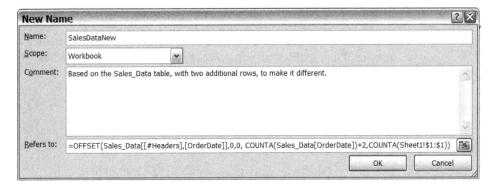

Figure 5-11. *Create a new named range.*

4. Click OK, to close the New Name dialog box.

5. Select a cell in the second pivot table, and on the Ribbon's Options tab, click Change Data Source.

6. In the Change PivotTable Data Source dialog box, change the Table/Range to Sales-DataNew, and then click OK.

7. In the second pivot table, change the grouping for the OrderDates to Quarters. Because a blank row was intentionally included in the SalesDataNew range, a (blank) item appears in the list of order dates. You can hide that item in the OrderDate filter list.

Because you based the second pivot table on the new range, you created a second pivot cache, and grouping the dates or numbers in one pivot table does not affect the other pivot table.

5.12. Grouping Dates Outside the Range

Problem

When you group by date, and set a start or end date, Excel automatically creates groups for all dates before the start date and after the end date, even though those dates don't exist in the data (see Figure 5-12). You'd like to prevent this from happening. This problem is based on the Stores.xlsx sample workbook.

Figure 5-12. *Groups are created for dates outside the range.*

Workaround

There's no setting you can change to prevent this from happening. However, because no records are in this date range, the groups before and after the date range won't normally appear in the pivot table. The only place you can see these groups is in the filter list.

If you change the field setting for the date field, to show items with no data, these items would be listed with the other dates. In this situation, you can uncheck these groups in the date field's filter list to prevent them from appearing in the pivot table.

5.13. Summarizing Formatted Dates

Problem

In your source data, you formatted the order dates to show as year and month (yyyy-mm). When you add the OrderDate field to the Row Labels area of your pivot table, several instances of each year-month occur instead of just one (see the table at the left in Figure 5-13). You want all the orders for each month summarized under one row label. This problem is based on the DateFormat.xlsx sample workbook.

2	Formatted Dates		Calculated Dates	
3	Row Labels ▾	Orders	Row Labels ▾	Orders
4	2007-01	3	2007-01	38
5	2007-01	1	2007-02	28
6	2007-01	4	2007-03	42
7	2007-01	11	2007-04	34
8	2007-01	9	2007-05	47
9	2007-01	10	2007-06	33

Figure 5-13. *Individual dates appear in the OrderDate field in the pivot table at the left; the YrMth field summarizes data in the pivot table at the right.*

Solution

Formatting the source data doesn't change the underlying dates, so each date is listed separately in the pivot table Row Labels area. If you click a date in the Row Labels, you see the underlying date in the formula bar. Because the dates are different, each date is listed individually.

Instead of formatting, you can use the pivot table's grouping feature to combine the data by month and year.

1. Right-click an OrderDate row label, and then in the context menu, click Group.

2. In the Grouping dialog box, in the By list, select Months and Years, and then click OK.

You may not want to group the dates, however, so you can use calculated items in the pivot table, or for other reasons. Another option is to add a new column to the source data, and use a formula there to convert the dates to text. With OrderDates in Column A, with headings in Row 1, follow these steps.

1. Add a blank column to the source data table, with the heading YrMth.

2. In the cell below the heading, type the formula =**TEXT(A2,"yyyy-mm")**.

3. Copy this formula down to the last row of data. If your data is in an Excel Table, the formula should copy down automatically.

4. Refresh the pivot table, and then add the YrMth field to the pivot table Row Labels area. Then, remove the OrderDate field (see the table at the right in Figure 5-13).

5.14. Creating Multiple Values for a Field

Problem

You added the Quantity field to the Values area, where it is displayed as Sum of Quantity. You'd like to keep the Sum of Quantity in the pivot table, but you'd also like to show the average quantity per order. This problem is based on the Stores.xlsx sample workbook.

Solution

You can add a field to the pivot table multiple times; for example, you could add the Quantity field to the Row Labels area, and then add it to the Values area, as Count of Quantity. You can also add multiple copies of a field to the Values area, by following these steps:

Note You cannot add a field more than once if any field has calculated items.

---

1. In the PivotTable Field List, drag the Quantity field from the Field section to the Values area. This creates a field named Sum of Quantity2 in the Values area of the PivotTable Field List, and in the pivot table.

2. In the pivot table, right-click a value in the Sum of Quantity2 column, click Summarize Data By, and then click Average. Format the values as a number with the number of decimal places you prefer.

3. To make the heading easier to read, select the heading cell for the Average of Quantity2 field, and then type a shorter heading, such as Avg Qty. You can use any heading that isn't the name of a field from the source data.

5.15. Displaying Multiple Value Fields Vertically

Problem

You have two fields in the Values area of your pivot table, and each field is listed in a separate column (see the table at the left in Figure 5-14), with headings shown horizontally, in the Column Labels area. The report is getting too wide, and you would prefer the values be listed vertically, in one column. This problem is based on the Stores.xlsx sample workbook.

Values in Column Labels area

	Column			
	East		West	
Row Labe	Qty Sold	Avg Qty	Qty Sold	Avg Qty
Bars	15369	53	6569	55
Cookies	15951	60	6881	57
Grand Total	**31320**	**56**	**13450**	**56**

Values in Row Labels area

	Colum	
Row Labels	East	West
Bars		
Qty Sold	15369	6569
Avg Qty	53	55
Cookies		
Qty Sold	15951	6881
Avg Qty	60	57
Total Qty Sold	**31320**	**13450**
Total Avg Qty	**56**	**56**

Figure 5-14. *Value fields displayed horizontally (at left), and vertically (at right)*

Solution

By default, the Values are added to the Column Labels area, but you can move them to the Row Labels area. This changes the Values from being displayed horizontally in the pivot table, to a vertical list, in the Row Labels area.

To move the Values fields, in the PivotTable Field List, drag the ∑ Values from the Column Labels area to the Row Labels area, below the existing fields. The Values headings move to the Row Labels area, and the values are displayed in a single column (see the table at the right in Figure 5-14).

5.16. Displaying Subtotals at the Bottom of a Group

Problem

You added the Region and City fields to the Row Labels area, and the subtotals are automatically shown at the top of each group of items. Instead, you'd like the subtotals to appear at the bottom of each group. This problem is based on the Stores.xlsx sample workbook.

Solution

In the default report layout, Compact Form, subtotals are at the top, and you can move them to the bottom of the group. To move the subtotals, follow these steps.

1. Select a cell in the pivot table, and on the Ribbon, click the Design tab.

2. In the Layout group, click Subtotals, and then click Show All Subtotals at Bottom of Group.

■Note Although you can display subtotals at the top or bottom, you can't change the Grand Total position in the pivot table. If displayed, the Row Grand Total is always at the bottom of the pivot table, and the Column Grand Total is always at the right.

How It Works

The position of the subtotals is also affected by the Report Layout applied to the pivot table. To change the Report Layout, follow these steps:

1. Select a cell in the pivot table.

2. On the Ribbon's Design tab, in the Layout group, click Report Layout, and then click one of the layout options.

In Compact Form and Outline Form, you can show the subtotals at the top or bottom of the group. The labels for the outer Row fields are always above the labels for the related inner fields, even when the subtotals are at the bottom of the group.

In Tabular Form, the labels for the outer Row fields are on the same row as the first label for the related inner fields, and the subtotals can only be shown at the bottom of the group (see Figure 5-15).

Compact Form			**Outline Form**				**Tabular Form**		
Row Labels ▾	**Orders**		**Region** ▾	**City** ▾	**Orders**		**Region** ▾	**City** ▾	**Orders**
⊟ **East**			⊟ **East**				⊟ **East**	New York	293
New York	293			New York	293			Boston	249
Boston	249			Boston	249			Philadelphia	175
Philadelphia	175			Philadelphia	175		**East Total**		717
East Total	717		**East Total**		717		⊟ **West**	Los Angeles	181
⊟ **West**			⊟ **West**					San Diego	102
Los Angeles	181			Los Angeles	181		**West Total**		283
San Diego	102			San Diego	102		**Grand Total**		1000
West Total	283		**West Total**		283				
Grand Total	1000		**Grand Total**		1000				

Figure 5-15. *Subtotals at the bottom of the group in different report layouts*

■**Note** Column fields are not affected by the setting for Subtotals, which always appear at the bottom of the group.

5.17. Preventing Subtotals from Appearing

Problem

When you add more fields to the Row Labels or Column Labels area, some of the fields get subtotals. You'd like to stop these subtotals from appearing automatically. This problem is based on the Stores.xlsx sample workbook.

Solution

You can change a setting to remove all subtotals, and to stop new subtotals from automatically appearing for outer Row Labels and Column Labels.

1. Select a cell in the pivot table, and on the Ribbon, click the Design tab.

2. In the Layout group, click Subtotals, and then click Do Not Show Subtotals.

This change turns off the subtotals for all fields in the pivot table. Whether the subtotals are turned on or off, you can also turn subtotals on or off for an individual row label.

1. Right-click a row label for which you want to change the subtotal setting.

2. In the context menu, click Subtotal "*Field Name*". For example, to turn off the subtotals for the Region field, click Subtotal "Region" (see Figure 5-16).

Figure 5-16. *Turn Subtotal on or off for an individual row label.*

Using this command toggles the Subtotal setting—if the Subtotal setting was on, it is turned off. The subtotal for the selected field appears in the position that was last specified for the pivot table. For example, if subtotals were at the top of the group, and then you turned off subtotals, the field's subtotals appear at the top of its group.

5.18. Creating Multiple Subtotals

Problem

Region and City fields are in the Row Labels area in your pivot table. Two fields are in the Values area: *Sum of Quantity* (Qty) shows the total quantity for each city, and *Count of OrderDate* is displayed with the heading Orders. A subtotal row exists for each region, which shows the total quantity and total order count for each region. You'd like another row of subtotals for each region, to show the average quantity and order count. This problem is based on the SubtotalsMulti.xlsx sample workbook.

Solution

You can change the field settings for the Region field and it will show more subtotal rows:

1. Right-click one of the Region row labels, and in the context menu, click Field Settings.

2. In the Field Settings dialog box, click the Subtotals & Filters tab, and then in the Subtotals section, click Custom.

■**Note** When you select Custom, the Automatic subtotal is removed.

---

3. In the list of functions, click each function you want to use as a subtotal, and then click OK. In this example, click Sum and Average.

4. Format the subtotal values with the number of decimal places you prefer.

■**Note** When you select multiple Custom subtotals, the subtotals are displayed at the bottom of the group, even if you set the option to show subtotals at the top of the group.

How It Works

When multiple fields are in the Row Labels area or the Column Labels area, the last field in the list is the inner field, and all the other fields are outer fields. In the pivot table, each outer field automatically displays subtotals, unless you turned off that feature.

By default, the subtotals are set as Automatic, and they use the same summary function as each field in the Values area (see Figure 5-17, in the table at the left).

Automatic Subtotals at Top of Group				Custom Subtotals — Sum and Average			
	Values				**Values**		
Row Labels ▾	**Qty**	**Orders**		**Row Labels** ▾	**Qty**	**Orders**	
⊟ **East**	**159614**	**3031**		⊟ **East**			
Boston	56516	1029		Boston	56516	1029	
New York	53938	1186		New York	53938	1186	
Philadelphia	49160	816		Philadelphia	49160	816	
⊟ **West**	**59126**	**1165**		**East Sum**	**159614**	**119599321**	
Los Angeles	40712	724		**East Average**	**53**	**39459**	
San Diego	18414	441		⊟ **West**			
Grand Total	**218740**	**4196**		Los Angeles	40712	724	
				San Diego	18414	441	
				West Sum	**59126**	**45987529**	
				West Average	**51**	**39474**	
				Grand Total	**218740**	**4196**	

Figure 5-17. *Automatic Subtotals (left) and Custom Subtotals (right)*

When you use Custom subtotals, all fields in the Values area use the same custom subtotal function (see Figure 5-17, the table at the right). This is not a problem if all the Value fields use the Sum function, but if other summary functions are used, the results may not be satisfactory. For example, in the example show at the right in Figure 5-17, the OrderDate field was used to create a count of records. The count looks correct for each city, but the subtotal rows use the date's numeric value, and the sum and average are based on those numbers, not on the count of records.

If you use Custom Subtotals, be cautious if you're using summary functions other than Sum in the Values fields.

5.19. Showing Subtotals for Inner Row Labels

Problem

In your pivot table, Region and City are in the Row Labels area. You created custom subtotals for the Region field, to show the Sum and the Count. You want to show Sum and Count subtotals for the City field, too, but subtotals aren't showing for the City field. This problem is based on the SubtotalsInner.xlsx sample workbook.

Solution

When added to the pivot table, the innermost fields in the Row Labels and Column Labels areas don't automatically display subtotals. You can format them to show subtotals.

1. Right-click one of the row labels for the City field, and in the context menu, click Field Settings.

2. On the Subtotals & filters tab, in the Subtotals section, select Custom.

3. In the list of functions, click each function you want to use as a subtotal, and then click OK. In the sample file, click the Sum and Count functions.

■Note All the subtotals for the innermost field appear after the last item, listed in the sort order for the innermost field.

5.20. Simulating an Additional Grand Total

Problem

In your pivot table, Category is in the Row Labels area, Region is in the Column Labels area, and Quantity is in the Values area, as Sum of Quantity. The Grand Total shows the Sum of Quantity, and you'd like to show another Grand Total, with the Average of Quantity for each Region. When you try to change the summary function for the Grand Total, it changes the function for all the Values. This problem is based on the GrandAdd.xlsx sample workbook.

Workaround

You can't change the summary function for the Grand Total row or column. To simulate an additional grand total, you could use one of the following techniques:

*   Add another copy of the Quantity field to the Values area, and set its summary function to Average.

*   Create a copy of the pivot table, and remove the Category field from the Row Labels area, to show just the heading rows and grand total. Then, change the grand total, so it summarizes by Average (see Figure 5-18).

	East	West	Grand Total
Average of Quantity	53	55	54

Figure 5-18. *A copy of the pivot table shows heading and grand total only.*

*   If you don't want another field in the Values area, and you just want the average at the bottom of the pivot table, you can use the following technique:

    a. Add a new column in the source data with the heading **Avg**.

    b. In the new column, enter the same value for all record, such as a 1 or a space character, or leave all the cells blank.

c. Refresh the pivot table, and then add the Avg field as the first field in the Row Labels area.

d. You can type a new caption for the Avg field's item. For example, if you left the cells in the source data blank, replace the (blank) caption with a space character, or **All Categories**.

e. Right-click the Avg row label, and in the context menu, click Field Settings.

f. In the Field Settings dialog box, select the Subtotals & Filters tab.

g. In the Subtotals section, select Custom, select the Average function, and then click OK.

h. On the Ribbon, click the Design tab.

i. In the Layout group, click Subtotals, and then click Show All Subtotals at Bottom of Group.

The pivot table shows each Region's average quantity just above the Grand Total row (see Figure 5-19).

Sum of Quantit Colur ▾			
Row Labels ▾	East	West	Grand Total
⊟			
Bars	15369	6569	21938
Cookies	15951	6881	22832
Crackers	3918	1468	5386
Snacks	2821	753	3574
Average	**53**	**55**	**54**
Grand Total	**38059**	**15671**	**53730**

Figure 5-19. *Region Averages created with a special subtotal*

5.21. Hiding Specific Grand Totals

Problem

In the Values area of your pivot table, you have Sum of Quantity and Quantity as % of Row. You'd like to hide the Grand Total for % of Row, because every row is 100%. You don't want to remove the grand total for Sum of Quantity. This problem is based on the GrandHide.xlsx sample workbook.

Workaround

You can't hide specific grand totals within the pivot table. However, you could use one of the following workarounds:

- Manually hide the worksheet column that contains the % of Row totals.

- Change the font and fill color to white for the % of Row grand total. The column appears empty, and the results stay hidden, even if you change the pivot table layout.

5.22. Totaling Hours in a Time Field

Problem

In your source data, you record the hours you worked on different projects. In the pivot table, you want the total hours per project, but the results are shown as time rather than total hours. For example, you worked for 25 hours on Project C: 10 hours+10 hours+5 hours. However, in the pivot table the sum of 10:00+10:00+5:00 is shown as 1:00 A.M. instead of 25:00 hours. This problem is based on the TotalHours.xlsx sample workbook.

Solution

In the pivot table, format the cells that contain total times with the number format [h]:mm:ss, and they'll total correctly. To apply this format, do the following:

1. Right-click a value cell in the TimeSpent field.

2. Click Number Format.

3. In the Format Cells dialog box, in the Category list, click Time.

4. In the Type list, click 37:30:55, and then click OK.

■**Note** With some regional settings, the 37:30:55 time format is not listed. You can create a custom format [h]:mm:ss;@. This time format totals the hours, instead of calculating the time from the hours.

5.23. Displaying Hundredths of Seconds

Problem

In your source data there are times, with a custom format of m:ss.00. The times show correctly in the worksheet—for example, 5:15.25—but they are rounded in the pivot table, with all the hundredths showing as zero—for example, 5:15.00. This problem is based on the Time100th.xlsx sample workbook.

Workaround

To correctly display the times in the pivot table, you can use the following workaround:

1. In the source data, add a column, **TimeCalc**, with a formula that refers to the time column—for example, =B2.

2. Format this column as General instead of Time.

3. Add the TimeCalc field to the pivot table, replacing the original time field, and format it with the custom number format of m:ss.00.

■ ■ ■

CHAPTER 6

Modifying a Pivot Table

In this chapter, you'll find solutions for problems you encounter as you make changes to your pivot tables. One of the greatest benefits of using pivot tables is this: after you create a pivot table, you can easily modify it. You can move the fields to a different area of the pivot table, add or remove fields, show or hide items, and make other changes to the layout.

You may encounter problems as you change the layout, with fields that don't behave as expected, or features that are unavailable after you move a field. You may want to alter the labels or values in the pivot table, and have unexpected results when you try to make the changes. Except where noted, the problems in this chapter are based on the Sales_06.xlsx sample workbook.

6.1. Using Report Filters: Shifting Up When Adding Report Filters

Problem

In cell A1, above your pivot table's Report Filter, you entered heading text for the worksheet. In the PivotTable Field List, you dragged another field to the Report Filters area, below the existing Report Filter. When you release the mouse button, you get a warning about replacing the contents of the destination cells (see Figure 6-1). If you click OK, the Report Filters move up and remove the heading in cell A1.

You'd prefer the Report Filters move down when they're added, so they don't delete the worksheet heading you created. This problem is based on the RptFilters.xlsx sample workbook.

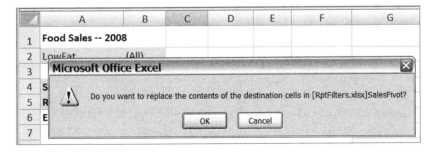

Figure 6-1. *Adding a Report Filter deletes text in cells above the pivot table.*

Workaround

When you add fields to the Report Filters area, Excel tries to keep the main section of the pivot table in its current position. Existing Report Filters are pushed up to prevent the main section from moving down. There isn't a setting you can change to prevent this, but one of the following workarounds may help:

- Instead of arranging the Report Filters vertically, change them to a horizontal layout, as described in the following section.

- If you have headings on the worksheet, above the pivot table, leave a few blank rows between them and the pivot table. If necessary, insert blank rows before adding fields to the Report Filters area.

- If the heading information is only required for printing, move the heading text to the Header, where it won't be affected by changes to the pivot table layout. To insert a Header, on the Ribbon, click the Insert tab, and then click Header & Footer in the Text group.

6.2. Using Report Filters: Arranging Fields Horizontally

Problem

You have added several fields to the Report Filters area, and they're pushing the pivot table down on the worksheet. You'd like to arrange the report filters horizontally, but when you select a report filter cell on the worksheet, and drag it to the right, you get a lengthy message that says you cannot move a part of a PivotTable report. This problem is based on the `Horizontal.xlsx` sample workbook.

Solution

By default, the Report Filters are arranged vertically above the body of the pivot table. You can arrange the Report Filters horizontally by changing the PivotTable Options:

1. Right-click a cell in the pivot table, and then click PivotTable Options.

2. On the Layout & Format tab, click the arrow in the drop-down list beside Display Fields in Report Filter Area, and then click Over, Then Down (see Figure 6-2).

Figure 6-2. *Set the Layout options for report filters.*

3. Because you selected Over, Then Down, the following drop-down list is labeled "Report Filter Fields per Row." Select three as the number of report filters you want across each row, before the next row of report filters starts.

4. Click OK to close the PivotTable Options dialog box.

How It Works

If your pivot table has many report filters, you can arrange the filters to make the most efficient use of the worksheet space. The report filters should be easily accessible, not spread out too far across the worksheet. Avoid a long column of filters above the pivot table, pushing the pivot table body far down the worksheet.

By using the Display Fields in Report Filter Area option, you can find the best balance of height and width for the report filter layout. The report filters can be arranged in a single column, a single row, columns of a set number of filters, or rows of a set number of filters. For column arrangements, use the Down, Then Over option, and for row arrangements, use the Over, Then Down option.

Down, Then Over

When a pivot table is created, the Down, Then Over option is selected by default, and the Report Filter Fields per Column setting is zero. With these settings, the report filters are displayed vertically, in a single column, with no limit to the number of filters in the column. The zero acts as a "No Limit" setting.

To limit the number of report filters in each column, change the setting from zero to another number. For example, if you select 2, the report filters are limited to two per column (see Figure 6-3). Once the column limit is reached, the filters move over, to start a new column.

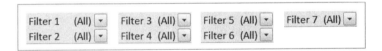

Figure 6-3. *Report filters arranged Down, Then Over, two per column*

Over, Then Down

If you select the Over, Then Down option, the report filters are arranged in a row. In the Report Filter Fields per Row option, select the number of report filters you want across each row, before the next row of report filters starts. For example, if you select two, the report filters are limited to two per row (see Figure 6-4). Once the row limit is reached, the filters move down, to start a new row.

■**Note** If the Report Filter Fields per Row option is set at zero, the filters are arranged in a single row.

Figure 6-4. *Report filters arranged Over, Then Down, two per row*

6.3. Using Values Fields: Changing Content in the Values Area

Problem

You use a pivot table to keep track of product samples from each category that were sent to each sales region. You'd like to enter the sample quantities in the Values area of the pivot table, instead of creating records in the source data. When you try to type in a cell in the Values area, you see the error message "Cannot change this part of a PivotTable report."

In the pivot table, the Region field is in the Row Labels area, Category is in the Column Labels area, and Quantity is in the Values area. This problem is based on the ChangeValues.xlsx sample workbook.

Workaround

You can't type in cells in the Values area, with the exception of cells that contain calculated items. For this example, you could create a calculated item with the name Samples, and a formula of =0. Follow these steps to create a calculated item in the Category field:

1. Select one of the label cells for the Category field. If you don't select one of these cells, you won't be able to create the calculated item.

2. On the Ribbon's Options tab, in the Tools group, click Formulas, and then click Calculated Item.

3. Type **Sample** as the name for the calculated item.

4. Leave the default formula of =0, and then click OK.

In the pivot table, select one of the calculated item cells and type the number of samples you sent to that region (see Figure 6-5).

kers	Snacks	Samples	Grand Total
1448	1072	25	14631
1130	1261	32	14548
2578	2333	25	29179

Figure 6-5. *Type a number in a calculated item's cell.*

Caution If you clear a calculated item's cell, you won't be able to make any further changes to that cell. Type a zero instead of pressing the Delete key, and you will be able to edit the cell again later.

For other cells in the Values area, unless the PivotTable settings are changed programmatically, you can't make any changes to the PivotTable values. Even if you programmatically change a setting to allow edits to the pivot table values, the original values are restored when the pivot table is changed or refreshed.

6.4. Using Values Fields: Renaming Fields

Problem

When you add the Quantity field to the pivot table Values area, it's automatically given the custom name Sum of Quantity. You'd like to change the custom name to Quantity, so it's easier to read and makes the column narrower. When you select the cell and type Quantity, you get an error message: "PivotTable field name already exists." This problem is based on the Rename.xlsx sample workbook.

Solution

If you try to create a custom name that's the same as a field name in the source data, you see the error message "PivotTable field name already exists." In this example, because one of the fields in the source data is named Quantity, you can't use Quantity as a custom name in the pivot table.

However, you can avoid this problem, by adding a space character to the end of the custom name (see Figure 6-6), and it will be accepted.

3	Row Labels ▼	Quantity
4	Bars	12531
5	Cookies	11712
6	Crackers	2578

Figure 6-6. *Add a space character at the end of a custom name.*

Tip Adding a space character is a subtle change to the custom name, and would not be noticed by most users. To help those who'll maintain the pivot table after you're promoted, create an Admin_Notes sheet in the workbook. There, you can document custom name changes, calculated items, calculated fields, and other helpful details.

6.5. Using Values Fields: Arranging Vertically

Problem

You added two fields to the Values area, and the Values fields are listed horizontally with the Column Labels fields. You want the Values fields arranged vertically, under the Row Labels. This will make the report narrower, and you'll be able to print it vertically on the page. This problem is based on the Values.xlsx sample workbook.

Solution

To arrange the Values fields vertically, drag the $\sum$ Values field in the PivotTable Field List, from the Column Labels area to the Row Labels area (see Figure 6-7).

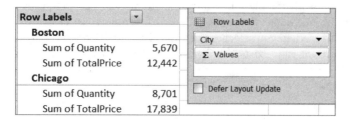

Figure 6-7. *Move the $\sum$ Values field to the Row Labels area.*

6.6. Using Values Fields: Fixing Source Data Number Fields

Problem

Your source data contains a column of numbers that shows the quantity for each order. You added the Quantity field to the Values area, and the sums show zero, instead of the correct totals. This problem is based on the FixNumbers.xlsx sample workbook.

Solution

Perhaps that column in the source data was formatted as text, before the quantities were entered, so the numbers in the Quantity column are really text. When added to the Values area, text cells total zero. To convert text "numbers" to real numbers, you can use one of the techniques described in Section 5.2.

6.7. Using Values Fields: Showing Text in the Values Area

Problem

When you add the Region field to the Values area, it appears as Count of Region, instead of showing the region names from the source data. You'd like to show the region names, so you can create a summary report showing the region for each store. This problem is based on the ValueText.xlsx sample workbook.

Workaround

You can't display text fields as text in the Values area. You could add the Region field to the Row Labels area, where the names will be displayed, and then use another field in the Values area to show a count of the occurrences. It won't create the exact layout you wanted, but it would display the region and store information.

In this example, there are only two region names, so a custom number format could be used to display the regions. Follow these steps to display the region names in the Values area:

1. In the source data, add a new column with the heading RegNum. Enter a region number of 1 or 2 in this column—1 for East region orders and 2 for North region orders.

2. Refresh the pivot table, and add the RegNum field to the Values area, and then summarize by Max.

3. To apply a custom number format to display the region names, right-click a cell in the Values area in the pivot table, and in the context menu, click Number Format.

4. In the Category list, select the Custom category.

5. In the Type box, enter [=1]"East";[=2]"North";General.

6. Click OK.

Notes

You can also display a limited amount of text in the Values area by setting the pivot table's options to show text instead of empty cells:

1. Right-click a cell in the pivot table, and then choose PivotTable Options.

2. On the Layout & Format tab, add a check mark to the For Empty Cells Show option, and in the text box, type **N/A** (see Figure 6-8), and then click OK.

Figure 6-8. *Specifying text to display in empty cells*

6.8. Using Pivot Fields: Adding Comments to Pivot Table Cells

Problem

You'd like to add comments to some of the pivot table cells, so users understand what the fields mean, or to explain why certain values are so low. When you add the comments, they don't display when you point to the cell in the pivot table. This problem is based on the NoteLink.xlsx sample workbook.

Workaround

You can add comments to cells in the pivot table, but the comments are attached to the worksheet cell, rather than to the pivot item's cell. If you change the pivot table layout, the comments won't move with the item, and they may create confusion for users instead of helping them.

As another deterrent to using comments in the pivot table, if contextual tooltips are enabled for the pivot table, the tooltips, instead of the comment, appear when a user points to a pivot table cell. If you decide to add comments, you need to turn off the tooltips, and deprive users of that feature. To turn off the tooltips, follow these steps:

1. Right-click a cell in the pivot table, and then click PivotTable Options.

2. In the PivotTable Options dialog box, on the Display tab, remove the check mark from Show Contextual Tooltips (see Figure 6-9), and then click OK. Users can now see the comment when they point to a cell, but they can no longer see the contextual tooltips that show information about the pivot table.

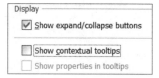

Figure 6-9. *Turning off the Show Contextual Tooltips option*

Instead of inserting comments in the pivot table, you could add a column to the source data, and enter brief comments there. A user who has a question about the data in the pivot table could use the Show Details feature to extract the source data and read any notes entered.

Another way to add documentation or comments to the pivot table would be to insert a new worksheet with the name Notes. To help users navigate between the pivot table worksheet and the Notes sheet, add a hyperlink in a frozen section at the top of each sheet. Follow these instructions to create the links:

1. On the pivot table's worksheet, in cell D1, type **Notes**.

2. Select cell D1, and on the Ribbon's Insert tab, in the Links group, click Hyperlink.

3. In the Link To list at the left, click Place in This Document.

4. In the list of places in the document, click Notes, and then click OK. This creates a hyperlink to cell A1 in the Notes sheet.

5. Click the hyperlink in cell D1, and the Notes sheet is then activated, with cell A1 selected.

6. Add a link in Row 1 on the Notes sheet, to return to the pivot table worksheet.

7. To freeze the top row, on the Ribbon's View tab, in the Window group, click Freeze Panes, and then click Freeze Top Row.

6.9. Using Pivot Fields: Collapsing Row Labels

Problem

In your pivot table, Region, Category, and Store fields are in the Row Labels area. If you collapse the East region, the North region is not affected. However, when you collapse the Bars category in the East region, the Bars category in both regions is collapsed (see Figure 6-10). You only want to collapse Bars in the East region. This problem is based on the `Collapse.xlsx` sample workbook.

4	Row Labels	Sum of Quantity
5	⊟ East	56,605
6	⊞ Bars	25,017
7	⊟ Cookies	31,588
8	3000	24,747
9	3036	6,841
10	⊟ North	86,119
11	⊞ Bars	41,591
12	⊟ Cookies	44,528
13	3055	27,701
14	3166	16,827
15	Grand Total	142,724

Figure 6-10. *Collapsing Row Labels*

Workaround

Collapse and Expand affect all occurrences of a Row Label. Because there's only one instance of the East region, in the outermost field, it is the only item that's collapsed. However, there are multiple instances of the Bars category, and they all are collapsed. You can't change this feature to expand or collapse the selected Row Label only.

As a temporary workaround, you could manually hide the worksheet rows that contain the items.

6.10. Using Pivot Fields: Collapsing All Items in the Selected Field

Problem

In your pivot table, Region, Category, and Store fields are in the Row Labels area. To hide the details for a Region or Category item, you can click the Collapse/Expand indicator, at the left of the region or category label. Occasionally, you want to see the region totals only, without the category and store detail, and you'd like to collapse all the regions at once, instead of collapsing each region individually. This problem is based on the Collapse.xlsx sample workbook.

Solution

Instead of using the Collapse/Expand indicators, use a command on the context menu, as described in the following steps:

1. Right-click a Row Label for one of the Regions.

2. In the context menu, click Expand/Collapse, and then click Collapse Entire Field.

6.11. Using Pivot Fields: Changing Field Names in the Source Data

Problem

In the pivot table's source data, you changed a column heading from Qty to Quantity, and when you refreshed the pivot table, the Qty field disappeared from the pivot table layout. This wasn't replaced by the Quantity field, even though it's in the same place in the source data. You had to add the Quantity field to the pivot table layout again, and reapply the number formatting you had previously applied. This problem is based on the `FieldNames.xlsx` sample workbook.

Solution

If possible, leave the column headings in the source data unchanged, and create custom names for the fields in the pivot table. For example, to create a custom name for the Qty field, select a cell in the pivot table that contains the pivot field name, and then type the custom name, Quantity.

6.12. Using Pivot Fields: Clearing Old Items from Filter Lists

Problem

The Product field is in the Row Labels area of your pivot table. You changed a product name in your source data, from Whole Wheat to Whole Grain, but the old name still appears in the Product field's filter list, even though you refreshed the pivot table. You want to clear the old name from the filter list, so it's easier to find the active products in the list. This problem is based on the `OldItems.xlsx` sample workbook.

Solution

Follow these steps to clear the old items from any of the pivot table's filter lists, and to prevent old items from being retained in the future:

1. Right-click a cell in the pivot table, and then click PivotTable Options.

2. In the PivotTable Options dialog box, click the Data tab.

3. From the Number of Items to Retain per Field drop-down list, choose None (see Figure 6-11), and then click OK.

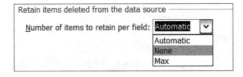

Figure 6-11. *Number of Items to Retain per Field option*

4. Refresh the pivot table, and the old product name disappears from the Product field's filter list.

How It Works

The default setting in a pivot table is to store deleted items in the pivot table's pivot cache, as long as the field is in the pivot table layout. In the Number of Items to Retain per Field, you can select Automatic, None, or Max from the drop-down list of settings. You can also type a specific number of items to retain. For example, if you type **2** as the number to retain, the first two old product names would be retained in the filter list. Any additional old names would be dropped from the filter list.

■**Note** If you remove the field from the pivot table, and refresh the pivot table, the old items are then removed, no matter what setting you made for Number of Items to Retain per Field.

6.13. Using Pivot Fields: Changing (Blank) Row and Column Labels

Problem

In the source data, a few of the sales orders don't have a Store number entered. You want blank cells in the Row Labels area and Column Labels area to contain the text "N/A." In the Pivot-Table Options dialog box, you entered **N/A** as the text to display in empty cells. However, the empty cells appear as (blank) in the Row and Column Labels areas (see Figure 6-12). This problem is based on the `Blanks.xlsx` sample workbook.

4	Row Labels ▾	Bars	Cookies	Crackers	Snacks	Grand Total
5	⊟ Boston	5394	7436	2299	1426	16555
6	3000	5340	7436	2178	1376	16330
7	(blank)	54	N/A	121	50	225
8	⊟ Los Angeles	4962	6507	314	954	12737

Figure 6-12. *(Blank) items in the Row Labels area*

Solution

In the PivotTable Options dialog box, the setting for empty cells affects cells in the Values area, but not the Row or Column Labels areas. You can manually change the (blank) labels in the Row or Column Labels areas by typing over them in the pivot table. You can type any text to replace the (blank) entry, but you can't clear the cell and leave it empty:

1. Select one of the Row or Column Labels that contains the text (blank).

2. Type **N/A** in the cell, and then press the Enter key.

■**Note** All other (blank) items in that field will change to display the same text, N/A in this example.

6.14. Using Pivot Items: Showing All Months for Grouped Dates

Problem

In your pivot table, you added the OrderDate field to the Row Labels area, and grouped the dates by months. To keep the report consistent throughout the year, you want to show all 12 month names in your pivot table, even though you only have sales data for the first 3 months. This problem is based on the Months.xlsx sample workbook.

Solution

You can set the OrderDate field to show all possible items:

1. In the pivot table, right-click one of the OrderDate labels, and then click Field Settings.

2. On the Layout & Print tab, add a check mark to the Show Items With No Data option, and then click OK.

If extra date items, such as <2008-01-01, appear in the Row Labels area, use the OrderDate filter list to hide them.

Note If the date field is not grouped, no additional dates are displayed in the pivot table, but all dates in the source data are listed under each subtotal heading.

6.15. Using Pivot Items: Showing All Field Items

Problem

In your pivot table, the Product and Store fields are in the Row Labels area. Some stores haven't ordered every product, but you'd like to see a complete list of stores under each product. That can make it easier to identify which stores have not ordered one of the products.

A new store has just opened, and you'd also like it included in the list. This problem is based on the Stores.xlsx sample workbook.

Solution

To ensure that all the stores appear below each product, you can set the Store field to show all items:

1. In the pivot table, right-click one of the Store labels, and then click Field Settings.

2. On the Layout & Print tab, add a check mark to the Show Items With No Data option, and then click OK.

However, the new store won't be included automatically in the list of stores. To have a new store appear in the pivot table, before any orders are processed, add at least one record to the data source with the store's name in the Store field. After real records are added for the store, you can delete the dummy record.

6.16. Using Pivot Items: Hiding Items with No Data

Problem

In your pivot table, Region and City fields are in the Row Labels area. You created a calculated item (NewCat) in the Category field, and every City now appears under each Region (see Figure 6-13). You only want the City names to appear under the region in which they're located. This problem is based on the NewCat.xlsx sample workbook.

3	Sum of Quantity	Column			
4	Row Labels ▾	Crackers	Snacks	NewCat	Grand Total
5	⊟ East	1236	1072	4930.4	7238.4
6	Boston	496	554	1382.4	2432.4
7	Los Angeles			0	0
8	New York	457	282	2060	2799
9	Philadelphia	283	236	1488	2007
10	San Diego			0	0

Figure 6-13. *All Cities are listed in each Region, due to the NewCat calculated item.*

Workaround

When your pivot table includes a calculated item, all the items are listed for fields that intersect the calculated item. It's irritating, it can slow down a large pivot table, and there's no way to turn off this behavior. The calculated item generates a *Cartesian product,* which is a result where every possible combination of items is created in the NewCat calculation.

In the pivot table shown in Figure 6-13, the NewCat value is calculated for each City, for each Region, and shows a zero result where no data is available.

Tip If possible, avoid the problem by creating calculations in the source data, instead of using calculated items in the pivot table.

You can filter the City field, to hide the rows that have a zero in the Grand Total column, as described in the following steps.

1. Right-click a cell that contains a City row label, and in the context menu, click Filter, and then click Value Filters.

2. In the Value Filter dialog box, from the first drop-down list, select Sum of Quantity, which is the Values field you want to check.

3. In the second drop-down list, select Does Not Equal, and in the third box, type **0** (zero), and then click OK (see Figure 6-14).

Figure 6-14. *Value Filter dialog box*

The rows where the grand total is zero are hidden, and the wayward city names disappear from each region.

6.17. Using Pivot Items: Ignoring Trailing Spaces When Summarizing Data

Problem

When you receive the data for your pivot table, some fields occasionally contain extra space characters at the end of the entry, due to sloppy data entry. In your source data Excel Table, when you apply a filter on the City column, items with differing trailing spaces—such as "Boston" and "Boston "—show as one entry in the column heading's filter list. When you add the City field to the pivot table, "Boston" and "Boston " show up separately, but you'd like them treated as one item. This problem is based on the Spaces.xlsx sample workbook.

Workaround

A pivot table doesn't ignore trailing spaces, the way an Excel Table's filter does. You could add another column to the source table, and use the TRIM worksheet function to remove the extra spaces. For example, do the following if city names are in Column C:

1. Create a new column in the source data, with the heading CityName.

2. In Row 2 of the new column, enter the formula =TRIM(C2).

3. Copy the formula down to the last row of data in the source table. If the source data is stored in an Excel Table, the formula should copy down automatically.

4. Refresh the pivot table, and then add the CityName field to replace the City field in the pivot table.

6.18. Using a Pivot Table: Allowing Drag-and-Drop

Problem

In previous versions of Excel, you were able to drag fields from the PivotTable Field List onto the pivot table layout. In Excel 2007, you can only move the fields within the areas in the Pivot-Table Field List. You'd like to move fields onto the worksheet layout, as you did before. This problem is based on the Sales_06.xlsx sample workbook.

Solution

If you prefer to drag the fields onto the worksheet layout, you can change a pivot table option.

1. Right-click a cell in the pivot table, and then click PivotTable Options.

2. Click the Display tab, and add a check mark to Classic PivotTable Layout.

3. Click OK, to close the PivotTable Options dialog box.

4. Point to a field label, such as Region, in the pivot table layout, and when the pointer changes to a four-headed arrow, drag the field label to a different area (see Figure 6-15). Or, drag fields into the pivot table layout from the PivotTable Field List, or drag field labels out of the pivot table layout.

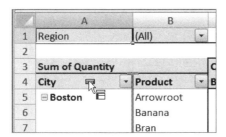

Figure 6-15. *Dragging fields in Classic PivotTable layout*

When you enable the Classic PivotTable layout option, the pivot table's report layout automatically changes to Tabular form. You can use this layout, or the Outline form, with the Classic PivotTable layout. If you change the layout to Compact form, the blue outlines of the pivot table areas are still visible on the worksheet when the pivot table is active. However, you won't be able to drag-and-drop the fields within the pivot table layout on the worksheet.

6.19. Using a Pivot Table: Deleting the Entire Table

Problem

You want to remove the pivot table from your workbook, but you can't delete the entire worksheet because it contains other data. This problem is based on the Sales_06.xlsx sample workbook.

Solution

Follow these instructions, to select the pivot table and delete it:

1. Select a cell in the pivot table, and on the Ribbon, click the Options tab.

2. In the Actions group, click Select, and then click Entire PivotTable.

3. On the keyboard, press the Delete key.

This removes the pivot table, and its PivotTable Style formatting, from the worksheet.

CHAPTER 7

Updating a Pivot Table

Most pivot tables are based on source data that continues to change; new records or fields may be added to the source data, existing records are modified, or the source data file is moved to a new location. You want to ensure that your pivot table contains the latest available data and is correctly connected to the source data.

To reproduce the environment in which they were created, sample files must be stored in a C:_Work folder, for testing. If a different folder is used, the connections will be broken. Create this folder on your computer's C: drive, and then copy all the sample files to it. Depending on your security settings, you may see a security warning when opening some sample files. To work with the file, you can enable the data connections.

Except where noted, the problems in this chapter are based on the `Sales_07.xlsx` sample workbook.

7.1. Using Source Data: Locating the Source Excel Table

Problem

You've been asked to make changes to the pivot table on the ProductSales worksheet, and you'd like to find the Excel Table used as its source data. Several Excel Tables are in the workbook, and you aren't sure which one was used. This problem is based on the `Sales07.xlsx` sample workbook.

Solution

You can locate the Excel Table that contains the source data by following these steps:

1. Select a cell in the pivot table, and on the Ribbon, click the Options tab.

2. In the Data group, click the upper section of the Change Data Source command.

3. In the Change PivotTable Data Source dialog box, you can see the source table or range in the Table/Range box. This may be a table name, such as

   `Sales_East`

   or a worksheet reference, such as

   `Sales_East!$A$1:$O$500`

4. On the worksheet, you can see the source range, surrounded by a moving border.

5. Click OK, or Cancel, to close the dialog box.

How It Works

In most cases, the source range is visible, and surrounded by a moving border. If the source range is not activated, it may be on a hidden worksheet. Follow these steps to unhide the sheet:

1. Right-click any worksheet tab, and then click Unhide.

2. In the Unhide Sheet list, select the sheet you want to make visible, and then click OK.

■**Tip** If the sheet name is not on the list of hidden sheets, it may have been hidden programmatically or removed from the workbook.

If a range name appears in the Table/Range box and the range is not selected, you can check the name definition, to find its location, and to see if there are any problems with the name definition:

1. On the Ribbon, click the Formulas tab, and in the Defined Names group, click Name Manager.

2. In the Name Manager, the Excel Tables and defined names are listed (see Figure 7-1). Select a name in the list, and in the Refers To box, you'll see the worksheet name on which the range is located.

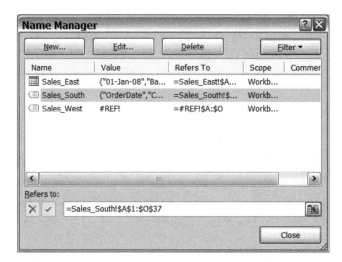

Figure 7-1. *Name Manager dialog box*

Tip If the Refers To formula for a defined name contains #REF! errors, the worksheet, or some of its cells, may have been deleted.

---

3. If errors are in the formula for a defined name, correct them if possible, or delete the problem name, and then select a new source for the pivot table.

Note The formulas for Excel Tables cannot be changed in the Name Manager. Close the Name Manager, and then make the changes on the worksheet where the Excel Table is located. To add rows or columns, drag the resize handle at the bottom right of the last cell in the Excel Table.

7.2. Using Source Data: Automatically Including New Data

Problem

Your pivot table is based on data in the same Excel file, and you frequently add new records to the source data. Each time you add records, you have to change the source range for the pivot table, to include the new rows.

You would like the source data range to automatically expand to include any new rows and columns. This problem is based on the NewData.xlsx sample workbook.

Solution

When creating a pivot table from Excel data, the best solution is to create a formatted Excel Table from the data, as described in Section 1.4. Then, use the name of the Excel Table as the source for the pivot table. The Excel Table automatically adjusts if records are added or deleted, and the pivot table includes the latest data when it's refreshed.

If you don't want to use a formatted Excel Table, you can use a dynamic range as the pivot table's source. The dynamic range automatically expands to include the new rows and columns. Follow these steps to create a dynamic range, in the sample file:

1. On the Orders sheet, select cell A1, which is the top-left cell in the source range. This step isn't necessary, but it helps you by inserting the cell reference in the name definition.

2. On the Ribbon, click the Formulas tab, and then in the Defined Names group, click Define Name, to open the New Name dialog box.

3. In the Name box, type a name for the dynamic range, for example, **PivotSource**.

4. Leave the Scope setting as Workbook, and add a comment (optional), to describe the name or its purpose.

5. In the Refers To box, type an OFFSET formula that references the selected cell

```
=OFFSET(Orders!$A$1,0,0,COUNTA(Orders!$A:$A),COUNTA(Orders!$1:$1))
```

or you can use a nonvolatile formula, which may be more efficient in larger workbooks, where calculation speed is an issue:

```
= Orders!$A$1:INDEX(Orders!$1:$10000,
     COUNTA(Orders!$A:$A),COUNTA(Orders!$1:$1))
```

The formula is set to a limit of 10,000 rows, which can be increased if required.

6. Click the OK button.

■**Caution** These formulas do not work correctly if other items are in Row 1 or Column A of the Orders worksheet. Those items would be included in the count, and would falsely increase the size of the source range, or they could cause an error when the pivot table is refreshed. Blank cells within the data in the row or column being counted would also cause a problem, reducing the size of the source range. Count a column and row where there is always a value.

After you create the named range, change the pivot table's source to the dynamic range:

1. Select a cell in the pivot table, and on the Ribbon, click the Options tab.

2. In the Data group, click Change Data Source.

3. In the Table/Range box, type the name of the dynamic range, **PivotSource** in this example, and then click OK.

■**Tip** While in the Table/Range box, delete the existing table or range. Then, to see a list of defined names, press the F3 key. Click a name in the Paste Name dialog box, to select it, and then click OK.

How It Works

The *OFFSET function* returns a range reference of a specific size, offset from the starting range by a specified number of rows and columns. The function has three required arguments (shown in bold font), and two optional arguments:

```
=OFFSET(reference,rows,columns,height,width)
```

In our example

```
=OFFSET(Orders!$A$1,0,0,COUNTA(Orders!$A:$A),COUNTA(Orders!$1:$1))
```

the returned range starts in cell A1 on the worksheet named Orders. It is offset zero rows and zero columns. The height of the range is determined by counting the cells that contain data in Column A of the Orders worksheet:

```
COUNTA(Orders!$A:$A)
```

▦Note If Column A contains any blank cells within the data range, use a column that does not contain blank cells. Blank cells reduce the count and result in a range that is too small.

The width of the range is determined by counting the cells that contain data in Row 1 of the Orders worksheet:

```
COUNTA(Orders!$1:$1)
```

This creates a dynamic range, because if rows or columns are added, the size of the range in the defined name increases.

The INDEX formula is similar, but it creates a range that starts in Cell A1 on the Orders sheet, and ends at the cell referenced by the INDEX function.

```
= Orders!$A$1:INDEX(Orders!$1:$10000,
    COUNTA(Orders!$A:$A),COUNTA(Orders!$1:$1))
```

7.3. Using Source Data: Automatically Including New Data in an External Data Range

Problem

In your workbook, you imported a text file that contains billing data, on to the BillingData worksheet. This created an external data range that has a connection to the text file. If new billing records are added to the external file, they appear in the external data range when it's refreshed. However, the pivot table is based on the imported data, but when you refresh the pivot table, the new records don't appear.

You can't create a formatted Excel Table from the external data range, or the connection to the external data will be lost.

This problem is based on the `Billing.xlsx` sample workbook. Depending on your security settings, you may see a security warning when opening the sample file. To work with the file, you can enable the data connections.

Solution

When you import external data to an Excel worksheet, using the commands in the Get External Data group on the Data tab of the Ribbon, a named External Data Range is created for the imported data. If you base the pivot table on this named range, it expands automatically as new records are added, and the pivot table contains all the data.

When you created a pivot table from the external data, you may have used a reference to range of cells, such as BillingData!$A$1:$J$19, instead of using the external data range's name. If data is added to the external data file, the new data appears in the Excel workbook, when the external data range is refreshed. However, the pivot table continues to use the original range, and the new data is not included in the pivot table when it's refreshed.

Follow these steps to change the pivot table's data source, so it uses the external data range name:

1. To see the name of the external data range, right-click a cell in the external data range, and then click Data Range Properties. The range name is shown at the top of the External Data Range Properties dialog box. Click OK to close the dialog box.

2. To base the pivot table on this range, select a cell in the pivot table, and then click the Options tab on the Ribbon.

3. In the Data group, click Change Data Source.

4. Type the external data range's sheet name and table name in the Table/Range box. For example, if the sheet name is BillingData and the external data range name is Billing_1:

   `BillingData!Billing_1`

5. Click OK.

7.4. Using Source Data: Moving the Source Excel Table

Problem

Your pivot table is based on a named range in another workbook. Using Windows Explorer, you copied the two workbooks to your laptop, so you could work at home, but when you tried to refresh the pivot table, you got an error message: "Cannot open PivotTable source file...." This problem is based on the SalesData.xlsx and SalesPivot.xlsx sample workbooks.

Solution

You can reconnect the pivot table to the named range, in its new location:

1. Open both files—the file with the pivot table, and the file that contains the source data.

2. Activate the file that contains the pivot table, and then select a cell in the pivot table.

3. On the Ribbon, click the Options tab, and in the Data group, click Change Data Source.

4. While the Change PivotTable Data Source dialog box is open, on the Ribbon, click the View tab. Click Switch Windows, and select the workbook that contains the source data.

5. Select the table that contains the source data, and then click OK.

■**Note** When you copy the files back to your desktop computer, you'll have to follow the same steps to reconnect them.

How It Works

When you create a pivot table that's based on data in another workbook, and that workbook is in a different folder, the folder path is stored as part of the source range. When you copy the files to a different computer, or move the data source file to a different folder, the pivot table can't connect to it.

To prevent this problem, create and save the pivot table file in the same folder as the data source file. Then, you can move the two files to any other location, keeping the two files together, and when refreshing, the pivot table looks for the data source file in its current folder.

7.5. Using Source Data: Changing the Source Excel Table

Problem

Your pivot table is based on an Excel Table in the same workbook as the pivot table. You want to change the source to a table in another workbook. This problem is based on the Central.xlsx and East.xlsx sample workbooks.

Solution

Follow these steps to change the source for the pivot table in the Central.xlsx workbook to the Excel Table in the East.xlsx workbook:

1. Open both workbooks—the file with the pivot table (Central.xlsx), and the file that contains the new source data (East.xlsx).

2. Select a cell in the pivot table, and then on the Ribbon, click the Options tab.

3. In the Data group, click Change Data Source.

4. While the Change PivotTable Data Source is open, on the Ribbon, click the View tab. Click Switch Windows, and then select the workbook that contains the new source data.

5. Select the range for the source data, and the Range reference is created, including the workbook name, for example:

   ```
   [East.xlsx]Sales_East!$A$1:$G$21
   ```

6. If you select an Excel Table or named range in the other workbook, the name won't be shown in the Range reference, so you can modify the reference to include it. For example, if the workbook contains an Excel Table named EastData, you'd type

   ```
   [East.xlsx]Sales_East!EastData
   ```

   For a workbook-level range named PivotRange, you'd remove the square brackets and the sheet reference, and then type

```
East.xlsx!EastData
```

7. Click OK.

■Note The workbook that contains the source data can be open or closed when you're using or refreshing the pivot table. However, if the reference is to an Excel Table, or to a dynamic range in the other workbook, that workbook must be open to refresh the pivot table.

7.6. Using Source Data: Locating the Source Access File

Problem

You inherited a pivot table that's based on a Microsoft Access query. When you click the Change Data Source command, you can see the connection name in the Change PivotTable Data Source dialog box. However, you can't see the name of the Access file, or tell which query was used to create the pivot table. You'd like to find out which database and query were used, so you can make a change to the query. This problem is based on the Shipments.xlsx and Shipments.accdb sample files.

Solution

You can view the connection properties to find the Access file name and path:

1. In the Shipments.xlsx file, select a cell in the pivot table, and then on the Ribbon, click the Data tab.

2. In the Connections group, click Properties.

3. In the Connection Properties dialog box, you can see the Connection name at the top. Click the Definition tab.

4. In the Connection File box, you can see the name and path of the database. In the Command Text box is the name of the Access query.

5. Click Cancel to close the Connection Properties dialog box.

7.7. Using Source Data: Changing the Source Access File

Problem

You created a pivot table from an Access query, and the Access file was moved to a different directory. When you tried to refresh the pivot table, you got the error message "Could not find file 'C:_Work\Shipments.accdb'." When you clicked OK, a dialog box appeared with the heading, "Please Enter Microsoft Office Access Database Engine OLE DB Initialization Information." Just reading that heading makes you tired, and you'd like to find a simple way to reconnect the pivot table to the database. This problem is based on the Shipments.xlsx and Shipments.accdb sample files.

Solution

If the source database has moved, you can change the connection in the workbook:

1. In the Shipments.xlsx file, select a cell in the pivot table, and on the Ribbon, click Data, and then in the Connections group, click Properties.

2. On the Definition tab, click Browse.

3. In the Select Data Source dialog box, locate and select the database you want to use as the source, and then click Open.

4. In the Select Table dialog box, select a table or query, and then click OK.

5. Click OK to close the Connection Properties dialog box.

7.8. Using Source Data: Changing the Source CSV File

Problem

You created a pivot table from a CSV file with the Central region's data, and you want to change the source to a different CSV file, that contains the South region's data.

You tried to change the connection, but the Text Import Wizard opens, instead of connecting to the new file. You've already spent time formatting the pivot table, and you'd rather not start from scratch.

This problem is based on the PivotCSV.xlsx, South.csv, and Central.csv sample files.

Solution

You can edit the existing connection, or create a connection to the new CSV file, and then use that connection for the existing pivot table. To edit the existing connection, you'll type the path and the query information. Creating a connection requires more steps, but you can select the path and query, instead of typing.

Edit the Existing Connection

You can view the connection properties, and then change the information that tells Excel where the source file is and which information to use from that source file. Follow these steps to edit the existing connection:

1. In the PivotCSV.xls file, select a cell in the pivot table.

2. On the Ribbon's Data tab, in the Connections group, click Properties.

3. Click the Definition tab, where you can see the Connection String and Command Text (see Figure 7-2).

Connection string:	DBQ=C:_WORK;DefaultDir=C:_WORK;Driver={Microsoft Text Driver (*.txt; *.csv)};DriverId=27;Extensions=txt,csv,tab,asc;FIL=text;MaxBufferSize= 2048;MaxScanRows=25;PageTimeout=5;SafeTransactions=0;Threads= 3;UID=admin;UserCommitSync=Yes;
	☐ Save password
Command type:	SQL ▼
Command text:	SELECT Central.Date, Central.SalesRep, Central.Region, Central.Item, Central.Cost, Central.Units, Central.Dollars FROM Central.csv Central

Figure 7-2. *Connection string and command text*

4. At the beginning of the connection string is the location of the current connection's file and the default directory, which you can edit if the new file is in a different folder:

    `DBQ=C:\_WORK;DefaultDir=C:\_WORK;`

5. In the command text, change the file name references to the new file name. For example, change Central to South. If you want all the fields from the source file, use the asterisk, instead of listing the fields individually:

    `SELECT South.* FROM South.csv South`

6. Click OK, to close the Connection Properties dialog box.

Create a New Connection

The other option is to create a new connection, and use it as the pivot table's data source. The long list of steps may look daunting, but the entire process should only take a couple of minutes:

1. Select an empty cell in the workbook that contains the pivot table.

2. On the Ribbon's Data tab, in the Get External Data group, click From Other Sources, and then click From Microsoft Query. Depending on your security settings, you may see a security warning.

3. In the Choose Data Source dialog box, on the Databases tab, select <New Data Source>, and then click OK.

4. Name the data source, such as MyCSV_New, and from the drop-down list of drivers, select Microsoft Text Driver (*.txt,*.csv).

5. Click Connect, and leave the check mark for Use Current Directory, because you want to connect to the South.csv file in the C:_Work directory.

6. To connect to a file in a different directory, remove the check mark, click Select Directory, select a different directory, and then click OK.

7. Click OK, to close the ODBC Text Setup dialog box.

8. For the default table, select the South.csv file, and then click OK, twice.

9. In the Query Wizard, select the South.csv file as the table, and then click the arrow button to move all its fields into the query.

10. Click Next, three times, to reach the last step in the Query Wizard, and then click Finish.

11. In the Import Data dialog box, select PivotTable Report, and select a location for this temporary pivot table, and then click OK.

12. Delete the temporary pivot table, which isn't needed now that the connection is established.

13. Select a cell in the original pivot table, and on the Ribbon's Options tab, click Change Data Source, and then click Choose Connection.

14. Select the new connection, Query from MyCSV_New, in the list, click Open, and then click OK.

Note After you delete the temporary pivot table, you must use the new connection before closing the file, or the connection is automatically deleted.

7.9. Refreshing When a File Opens

Problem

Your pivot table is based on a csv file that is updated every evening, and you want to ensure the pivot table is updated as soon as the file that contains the pivot table opens. This problem is based on the `PivotCSV.xlsx` sample file.

Solution

You can set a pivot table option to refresh the pivot table automatically, as the file opens. This setting can be used for pivot tables with an external data source, and for pivot tables based on data in the same Excel file as the pivot table.

1. Right-click a cell in the pivot table, and then click PivotTable Options.

2. On the Data tab, add a check mark to Refresh Data When Opening the File.

3. Click OK to close the PivotTable Options dialog box.

7.10. Preventing a Refresh When a File Opens

Problem

In the Trust Center, you have enabled all data connections, and your pivot table is set to refresh when the file opens. This works well, and ensures that the pivot table is automatically updated each morning, when you open the workbook. However, you occasionally want to open the file without having the pivot table refresh, so you can review the previous day's data before moving forward. This problem is based on the Refresh.xlsx sample workbook.

Workaround

Although you can't override the Refresh Data When Opening the File setting, you can undo the refresh, after the file has opened, and before you perform any other tasks.

Click the arrow on the Undo button, on the Quick Access Toolbar, and then click to undo any of the listed PivotTable Refresh actions (see Figure 7-3).

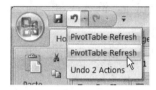

Figure 7-3. *Undo PivotTable Refresh*

■**Tip** To stop a long refresh in progress, press the Esc key as the file opens.

7.11. Refreshing Every 30 Minutes

Problem

The database to which your pivot table is connected is updated frequently throughout the day, and you would like the pivot table to refresh automatically every 30 minutes. However, when you right-click the pivot table and choose PivotTable Options, you only see an option to Refresh Data When Opening the File. This problem is based on the Shipments.xlsx sample workbook.

Solution

The Refresh Every *n* Minutes option is in the Connection Properties dialog box. To change the setting, follow these steps:

1. Select a cell in the pivot table, and then on the Ribbon's Data tab, in the Connections group, click Properties.

2. On the Usage tab, add a check mark to Refresh Every 60 Minutes.

3. Change the number of minutes to 30, and then click OK.

■**Note** This option is only available for pivot tables with an external data source. For pivot tables based on an Excel Table in the same workbook, you can use programming to automatically refresh the pivot table when the source data changes, as described in Chapter 11.

7.12. Refreshing All Pivot Tables in a Workbook

Problem

Several pivot tables are in your workbook, based on different Excel Tables. You want to refresh all of them at the same time, instead of refreshing each pivot table individually. This can save you several minutes each day, if you don't have to go to each worksheet and update the pivot tables one at a time. This problem is based on the Sales07.xlsx sample workbook.

Solution

To refresh all the pivot tables in the active workbook at the same time, on the Ribbon's Data tab, in the Connections group, click the upper section of the Refresh All command (see Figure 7-4).

Figure 7-4. *Refresh All command*

■Note Using the Refresh All command also refreshes all external data ranges in the active workbook, and it affects both visible and hidden worksheets.

7.13. Stopping a Refresh in Progress

Problem

You clicked the Refresh button to update your pivot table. The refresh is taking a long time to run, and you want to stop it, so you can work on something else in the workbook, and then run the refresh later. This problem is based on the Shipments.xlsx sample workbook.

Solution

To stop a long refresh, press the Esc key on the keyboard.

    If a refresh is running as a background query, you can double-click the Refresh indicator on the status bar (see Figure 7-5). In the External Data Refresh Status dialog box, click the Stop Refresh button, and then close the dialog box.

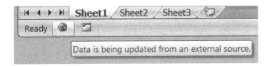

Figure 7-5. *Refresh indicator on the status bar*

■Note When you refresh the pivot table, the entire pivot table is affected. You can't refresh only part of a pivot table, or just add the new data to the pivot cache.

7.14. Creating an OLAP-Based Pivot Table Causes Client Safety Options Error Message

Problem

When you try to create an OLAP-based pivot table, you get the error message "Client Safety options do not allow pass through statements to be issued to the data source." There is no sample file for this problem, but you may encounter this error as you work with your own files.

Solution

This error occurs if you have an OLAP cube in which you opted to rebuild the cube every time the report is opened. To stop the message from appearing when the file opens, you can add a new setting to the Windows Registry.

The steps for this are outlined in the Microsoft Knowledge Base article "You Receive an Error When You Create an OLAP Cube-Based PivotTable in Excel," at `http://support.microsoft.com/default.aspx?id=887297`.

■Caution If you decide to modify the Windows Registry, as described in the Knowledge Base article, follow the instructions carefully, and observe the warnings to back up the Registry before changing it, as well as the security cautions.

7.15. Refreshing a Pivot Table on a Protected Sheet

Problem

You protected the worksheet that contains your pivot table, and under the Allow All Users of This Worksheet To list, you added a check mark to Use Pivot Table Reports. However, when you right-click a cell in the pivot table, the Refresh command is disabled, and you can't refresh the pivot table. This problem is based on the `Protect.xlsx` sample workbook.

Solution

The worksheet must be unprotected before you can refresh the pivot table. You can do this manually or use programming to unprotect the sheet, refresh the pivot table, and then protect the sheet. A programming example is in Chapter 11.

■**Note** If pivot tables on different sheets use the same pivot cache, the worksheets for all the related pivot tables must be unprotected before any of the pivot tables can be refreshed.

7.16. Refreshing When Two Tables Overlap

Problem

You have two pivot tables on the same worksheet, and sometimes when you modify one of the pivot tables, you get an error message "A PivotTable report cannot overlap another PivotTable report." You want to view them side by side, but would like the second pivot table to move to the right if necessary, instead of creating the error message. This problem is based on the Overlap.xlsx sample workbook.

Workaround

If the pivot table being modified will expand, and if it needs space that's occupied by the other pivot table, you'll see that message. There's no setting you can change that will move the other pivot table, to accommodate the first pivot table.

You could store each pivot table on a separate worksheet, and use multiple windows in the workbook to view them simultaneously:

1. To create a new window in the active workbook, on the Ribbon's View tab, in the Window group, click New Window. The title bar shows a number at the end of the file name, to indicate which window is active.

2. To view both windows simultaneously, on the Ribbon's View tab, in the Window group, click Arrange All.

3. Select Tiled, and add a check mark to Windows of Active Workbook, and then click OK.

4. In each window, activate one of the worksheets that contain a pivot table. With this arrangement you can see the pivot tables side by side, but they won't overlap if one of the pivot tables is modified.

7.17. Refreshing Pivot Tables After Queries Have Been Executed

Problem

When you use the Refresh All command on the Ribbon's Data tab, your pivot tables are refreshed before your queries for external data have run. You want to pause the pivot cache refresh until after the queries are executed, to ensure all the current data is displayed in the pivot table. This problem is based on the Refresh.xlsx sample workbook.

Solution

You can change a setting for the external data range's connection:

1. On the Ribbon's Data tab, click Connections.

2. In the list of connections, select the one you want to change, and then click Properties.

3. On the Usage tab, remove the check mark from Enable Background Refresh, click OK, and then click Close.

With the Enable Background Refresh option off, other processes will wait while Excel refreshes the query for the external data source.

7.18. Refreshing Pivot Tables: Defer Layout Update

Problem

You frequently make changes to the pivot table layout, moving several of the fields to a different area, and then adding and removing fields from the layout. The pivot table updates after each change, and this slows things down. You'd prefer to make all the changes, and then update the pivot table. This problem is based on the Sales07.xlsx sample workbook.

Solution

To prevent the updates from occurring as you make the changes, you can change a setting in the PivotTable Field List:

1. Select a cell in the pivot table.

2. In the PivotTable Field List, add a check mark to Defer Layout Update.

3. Make the layout changes to the pivot table, and then click Update (see Figure 7-6).

Figure 7-6. *Defer Layout Update option and Update button*

4. When you finish changing the layout and updating the pivot table, remove the check mark from Defer Layout Update.

■**Note** While the Defer Layout Update option is checked, some features of the pivot table, such as Row Labels filters, are disabled.

CHAPTER 8

■ ■ ■

Pivot Table Security, Limits, and Performance

If other people have access to your pivot table, you may want to disable some of the features, address privacy concerns, monitor access to protected data sources, or prevent users from making some changes. Some pivot table security settings require programming, and are discussed in Chapter 11. Other settings can be made manually, and are explained here.

When a pivot table is based on external data, Excel's security settings can affect your ability to update the pivot table. You can change the security settings, to control the security warnings displayed when you connect to the file. The external data source may have a password you'd like to store in your Excel file, to make it easier to connect.

Pivot tables can summarize large amounts of data, but a few limits exist to what can go into different areas of the pivot table layout. When you're working with very large databases, performance can suffer, and creating or refreshing a pivot table can be extremely slow. This chapter outlines some of the limits and discusses ways to optimize pivot table performance.

8.1. Security: Storing a Database Password

Problem

Your pivot table is based on a query in an Access database that is password protected, and you want to use the pivot table without entering the password. Currently, when you open the Excel file and refresh the pivot table, a Database Password dialog box appears, in which you have to enter the password AjPze$nZ. This password is hard to remember, and there isn't room at the edge of your monitor for another sticky note. This problem is based on the `PivotPwd.xlsx` sample file that is connected to a query in the `HardwarePwd.accdb` database, which is stored in a C:_Work folder. If a different folder is used, the connections will be broken. Depending on your security settings, you may see a security warning when opening some sample files. To work with the file, you can enable the data connections.

Solution

In the Excel file that contains the pivot table, you can change the connection properties, and store the password in the connection string:

1. Open the `PivotPwd.xlsx` file, and refresh the pivot table, entering the password when prompted.

2. Select a cell in the pivot table, and on the Ribbon, click the Data tab.

3. In the Connections group, click Properties.

4. On the Definition tab, add a check mark to Save Password.

5. In the alert message that appears, you are warned that the password is saved without encryption in the Excel file, making your data less secure. To save the password, click Yes. The password is now visible in the connection string (see Figure 8-1).

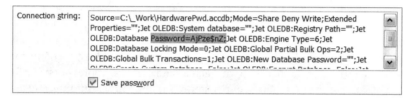

Figure 8-1. *Database password visible in connection string*

6. Click OK, to close the Connection Properties dialog box.

Tip With the database password saved in the connection string, you won't be prompted for the password when you open the file and refresh the pivot table. However, the database password is visible in the connection string, so you should store the Excel file in a secure folder on the network.

8.2. Security: Enabling Data Connections

Problem

You created a workbook with a pivot table connected to an Access database, and when you open the workbook, you see a security warning in the message bar, above the formula bar (see Figure 8-2). When you refresh the pivot table, a security notice is displayed, warning that Microsoft Office has identified a potential security concern.

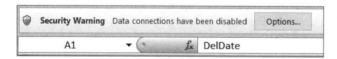

Figure 8-2. *Security warning in the message bar*

You trust the data source, and you would like to work with the pivot table file without seeing the warnings. This problem is based on the `PivotShipment.xlsx` sample file that is connected to a query in the Shipment.accdb database, which is stored in a C:_Work folder. If a different folder is used, the connections will be broken.

Solution

You can change the data connection settings in Excel's Trust Center, to hide the message bar, and to allow data connections. These are application level settings, and they affect all workbooks you open.

1. Click the Microsoft Office button, and then click Excel Options.

2. Click the Trust Center category, and then click Trust Center Settings.

3. To hide the message bar, click the Message Bar category, and then click Never Show Information About Blocked Content.

4. To change the connection settings, click the External Content category.

5. In the Security Settings for Data Connections section, click Enable All Data Connections.

6. Click OK, to close the Trust Center, and then click OK to close Excel Options.

■**Note** If you prefer not to enable all data connections, you could click Prompt User about Data Connections, in the Security Settings for Data Connections section. Then, refresh the pivot table by using a macro that runs automatically when the workbook opens, and the warning will not appear. See Chapter 11 for sample code to refresh a pivot table.

8.3. Protection: Preventing Changes to a Pivot Table

Problem

You want to prevent users from making any changes to the pivot table. They should be able to view the pivot table, but not change the selected items, type over any of the field names, or rearrange the layout. However, you want users to be able to make changes to data and formulas in other areas of the worksheet. This problem is based on the PivotProtect.xlsx sample file.

Solution

If you protect the worksheet without enabling pivot table use, users won't be able to modify the pivot table.

Preparing the Worksheet

When protecting a worksheet, prepare the sheet first by unlocking cells where changes can be made. Then, turn on the worksheet protection.

To prepare the sheet, follow these steps:

1. Select any cells in which users are allowed to make changes. In the sample file, users can make changes to cell E2.

2. On the Ribbon, click the Home tab.

3. In the Cells group, click Format. The Lock Cell command is enabled if the active cell is locked (see Figure 8-3). To unlock the cells, click Lock Cell.

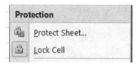

Figure 8-3. *The Lock Cell command is enabled.*

Protecting the Worksheet

After you prepare the worksheet, follow these steps to protect the worksheet:

1. On the Ribbon, click the Review tab, and then in the Changes section, click Protect Sheet.

2. If desired, enter a password. If you don't enter a password, the worksheet will be protected, but it can be unprotected simply by clicking Unprotect Sheet on the Review tab on the Ribbon.

3. Remove the check mark from Use PivotTable Reports, and then check the items you want enabled on the protected worksheet (see Figure 8-4).

Figure 8-4. *Select items to enable on a protected worksheet.*

4. Click OK and confirm the password, if one was entered.

How It Works

When you protect the worksheet, you can allow or disallow Use PivotTable Reports. With either choice, if the worksheet is protected, use of the pivot table is affected.

Not Allowing Use PivotTable Reports

If the worksheet is protected, and Use PivotTable Reports was not selected in the Protect Sheet dialog box, users won't be able to make any changes to the pivot tables on the worksheet. For example, they won't be able to open the drop-down lists on the pivot field buttons, move fields, remove fields, or add fields. The PivotTable Field List will be hidden.

You can create a pivot chart from a pivot table on the protected sheet, but you won't be able to change the pivot chart layout or use the PivotChart filter. You can change the pivot chart formatting, chart type, and chart options. If you allow users to Edit Objects on the protected sheet, a pivot chart can be inserted on the protected sheet. If Edit Objects was not checked, you can create an empty chart on an unprotected sheet, and change its source to the pivot table.

Other pivot tables, based on the same Excel Table as the pivot tables on a protected sheet, will have some features disabled, such as Refresh.

▓Tip If you use worksheet protection to disable the pivot table, many other features of the worksheet are also disabled, such as AutoSum, Spelling, Subtotals, and Creating or refreshing a pivot table. If these features are required on the worksheet, you may prefer to use programming to protect the pivot table, while leaving the worksheet unprotected.

Allowing Use PivotTable Reports

If you enable pivot table use when protecting the worksheet, users can open the drop-down lists on the pivot field buttons, move the fields, remove fields, and add fields. The PivotTable Field List can be shown. Users can work with existing pivot tables, but they can't create a new pivot table on the protected sheet or refresh existing pivot tables.

▓Note When enabling PivotTable report use, you can't control which pivot table features are allowed. If you want to enable some features, such as selecting items from the Pivot field drop-down lists, and disable other features, such as changing the layout, you can use programming, as described in Chapter 11.

Even with the Use PivotTable Reports setting turned on, many commands are disabled if the worksheet is protected, including the following:

- Report Layout

- Refresh

- Group and Ungroup

- PivotTable Options

- Show Report Filter Pages

- Calculated Field

- Calculated Item

- Enable Selection

- PivotTable Styles

■**Tip** To refresh the pivot table, the worksheet owner can temporarily unprotect the worksheet, refresh the pivot table, and then protect the sheet.

8.4. Protection: Disabling Show Report Filter Pages

Problem

To reduce the number of sheets in the workbook, you want to prevent users from using the Show Report Filter Pages feature. Using this feature adds sheets to the workbook, which users forget to delete, and the workbook size is getting too big. This problem is based on the PivotProtect.xlsx sample file.

Solution

You can protect the workbook structure, and users won't be able to add new sheets.

1. On the Ribbon, click the Review tab, and then click Protect Workbook.

2. Add a check mark to Structure, and if desired, enter a password.

3. Click OK to close the dialog box, and if prompted, confirm the password.

With the workbook protected, if users try to use the Show Report Filter Pages feature, they'll see an error message, "Workbook is protected and cannot be changed."

You can also use programming to add a prefix to the sheet names as they are created, and then delete the sheets automatically as the workbook closes. See Chapter 11 for sample code.

8.5. Privacy: Preventing Viewing of Others' Data

Problem

Your pivot table contains sales data for several departments. You deleted the worksheet that contains the source data. Now, you want to send each department a copy of the pivot table with their department selected in the Report Filter, and prevent users from seeing data for departments other than their own. This problem is based on the PivotProtect.xlsx sample file.

Workaround

You can protect the worksheet without allowing pivot table use, to prevent users from selecting a different department in the Report Filter. However, users may be able to circumvent Excel's security features, and remove the worksheet protection. Then, they could select a different department from the Report Filter, or double-click a cell in the Values area, and use the Show Details feature to re-create the source data.

■**Caution** Excel worksheet protection can be easily circumvented. If you don't want users to view the underlying data, don't include the data in the pivot table source.

To protect the data, you could create a separate data source for each department and base its pivot table on that source, with each pivot table in a separate, password-protected workbook. That would provide each department with a fully functioning pivot table, while maintaining each department's privacy.

Or, if users need to see the results, but they do not need to change the pivot table layout, you can create a copy of the pivot table for each department.

1. Select a department name from the report filter.

2. Select the pivot table, right-click a selected cell, and then click Copy.

3. In another workbook, right-click a cell where you would like to create a copy of the pivot table.

4. In the context menu, click Paste Special.

5. Click Values, and then click OK.

6. Format the copied pivot table.

How It Works

In Excel, you can protect a file with a password when saving it. You can also password-protect a workbook's structure and windows, as well as its worksheet contents.

Applying Excel security features can help prevent accidental errors or deletions, but may not thwart a determined malicious attack. A knowledgeable user can circumvent worksheet- and workbook-structure protection by using tools, such as password crackers, that are readily available on the Internet. A strong password on the Excel file, or storing the file in a secure network folder can provide better protection.

The "Security Policies and Settings in the 2007 Office System" article provides detailed coverage of the security settings and privacy options available in Excel, as well as other Office programs: http://technet2.microsoft.com/Office/en-us/library/03d787aa-598d-40a9-87ec-31a8ea80e0371033.mspx?pf=true. The "What's New and What's Changed" section, on Page 14, outlines the Trust Center, message bar, and documentation-protection features that are in the user interface in Excel 2007.

8.6. Understanding Limits: 16,384 Items in the Column Area

Problem

Your Excel Table contains many years of data. When you tried to move the OrderID field to the Column Labels area of your pivot table, you got a warning message that said the field has more than 16,384 items and can't be placed in the column area (see Figure 8-5). This problem is based on the OrdersLimit.xlsx sample file.

Figure 8-5. *Error message when a column has more than 16,384 items*

Solution

As the warning message suggests, you could place the field in the Row Labels or Report Filter area of the pivot table instead of the Column Labels area.

If you place the field in the Row Labels area, you may be able to group the items to create fewer items than the 16,384 limit, and then move the grouped field to the Column Labels area.

8.7. Understanding Limits: Number of Records in the Source Data

Problem

You want to create a pivot table from a database that contains thousands of records in 20 fields, but you don't know if the pivot table would be able to work with that much data. No sample file exists for this problem, but you may encounter this situation in creating a pivot table from your own data.

Solution

There's no fixed maximum on the number of records the source database can contain, but working with a large database can be slow. For large databases, you may be able to create an OLAP cube that presummarizes some of the data and can be used to build a pivot table in Excel.

A whitepaper is available for download on the Microsoft web site, that can guide you, or the person creating your OLAP cube: "Excel 2007 Document: Designing SQL Server 2005 Analysis Services Cubes for Excel 2007 PivotTables" at http://www.microsoft.com/downloads/details.aspx?familyid=2D779CD5-EEB2-43E9-BDFA-641ED89EDB6C.

Although the whitepaper refers to SQL Server 2005 Analysis Services, the information would be useful to anyone creating an OLAP cube, from any source.

How It Works

Although there's no fixed limit to the number of records in the source database, creating a pivot table from a large external database can result in a pivot table that is slow to refresh and update. Also, other limits may affect your work, as shown in Table 8-1.

Table 8-1. *Pivot Table Limits*

Feature	Limit	Note
Number of Row Fields	No fixed limit	The available memory in your computer may limit the number of fields you can add.
Number of Column Fields	No fixed limit	The available memory in your computer may limit the number of fields you can add.
Unique Items per Field	1,048,576	You can't drop a field in the Column Labels area if the field has more than 32,767 unique items. Creating calculated items can cause you to exceed this limit in a pivot table based on a large data source.
Number of Calculated Item Formulas	No fixed limit	The available memory in your computer may limit the number of formulas you can add.
Displayed Column Labels	16,383	There are 16,384 columns in an Excel worksheet, and one is reserved for Row Labels.
Number of Report Filters	256	The available memory in your computer may limit the number of fields you can add.
Length of a Text String	32,767	Text in Row Labels or Column Labels will be truncated after this number of characters.
Number of Value Fields	256	The available memory in your computer may limit the number of fields you can add.

8.8. Improving Performance When Changing Layout

Problem

Your pivot table is based on a large data source, and it responds very slowly when you add fields or move fields to a different area of the pivot table, and you'd like to speed up the process. There is no sample file for this problem, but you may encounter this situation in creating a pivot table from your own data.

Solution

To improve performance, remove any pivot table styles and any other formatting, such as conditional formatting that you applied to the pivot table. In testing on an OLAP-based pivot table, an update took 45 seconds when conditional formatting was applied to the pivot table data, and only 4 seconds without conditional formatting.

In some pivot tables, calculated items can severely impact the speed of updating. If possible, remove any fields that contain calculated items, or delete the calculated items from the fields. In testing on a pivot table with one simple calculated item, an update took 2:13 minutes, and only 2 seconds without a calculated item.

If you plan to add or move more than one field, add a check mark to the Defer Layout Update box in the PivotTable Field List (see Figure 8-6).

Figure 8-6. *Defer Layout Update option*

Then, move or add the fields, and click the Update button, to the right of the Defer Layout Update check box. This reduces the time required, because the fields are all added or moved, and then the pivot table is recalculated once. If this box is not checked, the pivot table is recalculated after each field is added or moved.

When you finish changing the layout, remove the check mark from the Defer Layout Update check box, to restore full functionality to the pivot table. Some features, such as filtering and grouping, are not available when Defer Layout Update is activated.

8.9. Reducing File Size: Excel Data Source

Problem

Your workbook contains a few pivot tables, and it has almost doubled in size, even though you only added a few rows to the Excel Table that's the pivot table source. Every time you add a pivot table, the size goes up a few megabytes. You'd like to make the file smaller. There is no sample file for this problem, but you may encounter this situation in creating a pivot table from your own data.

Solution

To reduce the file size, try one of the following options.

Changing the Pivot Table Layout

The pivot table layout can have a dramatic effect on the file size. If the pivot table layout is large, the used range is larger, and this can increase the file size. If file size is a concern, move most fields to the Report Filter area before closing the workbook to minimize the used range.

Turn off Save Data with Table Layout

To make the file smaller when saving, you can change a pivot table option so the data isn't saved when the workbook is closed:

1. Right-click a cell in the pivot table, and then choose PivotTable Options.

2. On the Data tab, remove the check mark from Save Source Data With File.

3. Click OK to close the PivotTable Options dialog box.

When the data isn't saved with the layout, the file size is smaller because the pivot cache isn't being saved, and it reduces the time required to save the workbook. When you open the workbook, you have to refresh the pivot table to rebuild the pivot cache when you want to use the pivot table. This is slower than refreshing a pivot table with a saved cache.

Storing the Excel Table in a Separate Workbook

The Excel Table on which the pivot tables are based can be stored in a separate workbook. This reduces the size of the workbook that contains the pivot tables. The Excel Table workbook can remain closed when working with the pivot table file, which reduces the amount of memory used.

Save in Excel Workbook Format

If you created the workbook in an older version of Excel, you may be using the workbook in Compatibility mode. Or, if you're sending the workbook to others who are working in an older version of Excel, you may have saved the file in Excel 97–2003 format. Saving the file in this format can make the size much larger.

Remove Shapes and Pictures

If any unnecessary shapes or pictures are in the workbook, remove them. These can increase the file size and slow the performance.

Use an Excel Table As the Source

If your data is stored in Excel, create an Excel Table from the source data, and use that formatted table as the source. To create the table, select a cell in the source data, and on the Ribbon's Insert tab, click Insert Table. Some users include many blank rows in the source data range, to ensure that new data will be included when the pivot table is refreshed. An Excel Table automatically expands to include new data, so you won't need an artificially big source data range, which could increase the file size.

After creating the table, press Ctrl+End, to go to the last cell in the worksheet's used range. Delete any unused rows and columns between this cell and the Excel Table.

CHAPTER 9

Printing and Extracting Pivot Table Data

One of the strengths of pivot tables is the capability to change the layout and analyze data from different perspectives. Sometimes, though, you want a static picture from the pivot table and need to print the data. For the most part, pivot tables print the same as other data on a worksheet, but you can apply a few special settings to a pivot table. Some printing issues, such as printing a copy of the pivot table for each item in the Report Filter field, can be solved by programming, and examples are given in Chapter 11.

After you create a pivot table, you may want to extract some of the summarized data for use in other parts of the workbook. The GetPivotData worksheet function can be used for retrieving specific data from the pivot table. Another way to extract data is to use the Show Details feature, which returns records from the source data for the selected pivot table cell. Finally, the Show Report Filter Pages feature can be used to create copies of the pivot table on newly inserted worksheets.

Except where noted, the `RegionSales_09.xlsx` workbook is used as the sample file for the problems in this chapter.

9.1. Repeating Pivot Table Headings

Problem

Your pivot table spans several printed pages and the report filter, row labels, and column labels only print on the first page. You want the heading rows and labels on every page, so readers can understand the report. In your pivot table, the Product and OrderDate fields are in the Row Labels area, Region is in the Column Labels area, Category is in the Report Filter area, and Sum of TotalPrice is in the Values area. This problem is based on the `RegionSales_09.xlsx` workbook.

Solution

You can set options for the pivot table to make the heading rows and labels appear on every page when you print the pivot table. There are two settings to change:

- The print titles option determines if the heading rows and columns appear at the top and left on each printed page.

- The row labels option determines if row labels are repeated if their items continue on another page.

Setting Print Titles

Before you turn on this option, clear any entries for row and column print titles on the worksheet, as described in the following steps. If either of these boxes contains an entry, the Set Print Titles option won't be applied for the pivot table.

1. On the Ribbon, click the Page Layout tab, and in the Page Setup group, click Print Titles. The Page Setup dialog box opens with the Sheet tab activated.

2. Under Print titles, clear the Rows to Repeat at Top and Columns to Repeat at Left boxes, and then click OK.

3. Right-click a cell in the pivot table, and then click PivotTable Options.

4. On the Printing tab, add a check mark to Set Print Titles, and then click OK.

Repeating Row Labels

You can change a pivot table option so the labels appear on each page. This option has no effect if the pivot table is in the Compact Form layout, so if one of the other report layouts isn't already applied, the first step is to select one of them.

Note This setting will have no effect if the pivot table is in the Tabular Form layout and the option for Merge Labels is turned on.

---

1. Select a cell in the pivot table, and on the Ribbon's Design tab, in the Layout group, click Report Layout.

2. Click Show in Outline Form, or click Show in Tabular Form. The pivot table layout changes to show each field in the Row Labels area in a separate column, instead of all fields in a single column.

3. Right-click a cell in the pivot table, and then choose PivotTable Options.

4. On the Printing tab, add a check mark to Repeat Row Labels on Each Printed Page, and then click OK.

5. Click the Microsoft Office Button, and then point to Print, and click Print Preview, to see the changes to the report setup. Headings repeat on all pages, and the row labels repeat if their items continue on another page. In Figure 9-1, the Banana label is repeated at the top of Page 2.

■**Note** If you zoom in or out in Print Preview, the repeated row labels may disappear temporarily.

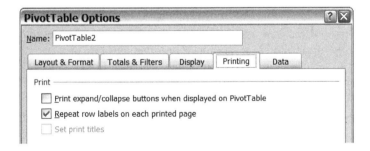

Page 2 of 6				
Category	(All)			
Sum of TotalPrice		**Region**		
Product	**OrderDate**	**East**	**North**	**Grand Total**
Banana	2008-07-01	$111	$313	$424
	2008-08-01	$50	$390	$440

Figure 9-1. *Headings and row labels repeat in print preview.*

How It Works

When you turn on the Set Print Titles option, it adds settings to the Print Titles boxes in the Page Setup dialog box, on the Sheet tab. To see the settings, on the Ribbon's Page Layout tab, in the Page Setup group, click Print Titles.

■**Caution** If you clear the Print Titles settings in the Page Setup dialog box after turning on the Set Print Titles option, you have to turn the Set Print Titles option off, and then turn it back on, for it to take effect.

Only one pivot table per worksheet can have the Set Print Titles option selected. If the setting is turned on in one pivot table, the option is unavailable in the PivotTable Options dialog box for other pivot tables (see Figure 9-2).

Figure 9-2. *The Set Print Titles option is unavailable.*

When the Set Print Titles option is selected, the report filter, row labels, and column labels print on every page. If multiple pivot tables are on the worksheet, or other data, the pivot table headings also print with those.

9.2. Setting the Print Area to Fit the Pivot Table

Problem

Your pivot table frequently changes size, and you have to reset the print area every time you want to print it. You would like the print area to adjust automatically, so you don't waste paper, or print only part of the pivot table. This problem is based on the PrintArea.xlsx workbook.

Solution

Don't set a print area on the sheet with the pivot table, and the entire pivot table will print, no matter what its size, although it may span several printed pages. To remove an existing print area, on the Ribbon's Page Layout tab, in the Page Setup group, click Print Area, and then click Clear Print Area.

If you're setting a print area because other items are on the sheet that you don't want to print, move those items to another sheet, if possible, so you can print the pivot table separately.

If the items must remain on the same sheet as the pivot table, use the following technique to quickly set a print area that encompasses the entire pivot table:

1. Select a cell in the pivot table, and on the Ribbon's Options tab, in the Actions group, click Select, and then click Entire PivotTable.

2. On the Ribbon's Page Layout tab, in the Page Setup group, click Print Area, and then click Set Print Area.

■**Tip** You can add Select Entire PivotTable and Set Print Area buttons to the Quick Access Toolbar.

9.3. Printing the Pivot Table for Each Report Filter Item

Problem

Several stores carry your products, and you were asked to send each store manager a printed copy of the pivot table, customized to show their sales results. You added the Store field to the Report Filter area, and you can select a store in the report filter, to show its totals in the pivot table, and then print the worksheet. However, you'd like to find a more efficient way to print the reports, because you'll have to do this each week. This problem is based on the RegionSales_09.xlsx workbook.

Solution

You can use the Show Report Filter Pages feature to create a worksheet for each item in the Store report filter field. Then, you can group the worksheets and print them:

■**Tip** Before using the Show Report Filter Pages command, select (All) from the Store report filter. If a store is selected, a worksheet will not be created for that store.

1. Select a cell in the pivot table, and on the Ribbon's Options tab, in the PivotTable group, click the arrow for Options, and then click Show Report Filter Pages (see Figure 9-3).

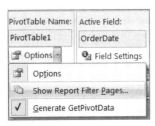

Figure 9-3. *Show Report Filter Pages command*

2. In the Show Report Filter Pages dialog box, select the Store field, and then click OK. A worksheet with a copy of the pivot table is then created for each store, with the store's name on the sheet tab, and that store is selected in the report filter.

3. To select all the worksheets created, click the sheet tab for the first store sheet at the left, and then scroll to see the last store's sheet tab. Hold the Shift key, and click the last store's sheet tab.

■**Caution** While the sheets are grouped, any changes you make to the active sheet are also made to the other sheets in the group.

4. While the sheets are grouped, you can set the Page Setup options, if desired. On the Ribbon's Page Layout tab, in the Page Setup group, click the commands to set the margins, orientation, or other options. To open the Page Setup dialog box, click the dialog launcher at the bottom right of the Page Setup group (see Figure 9-4).

Figure 9-4. *Page Setup dialog launcher*

5. To print the grouped sheets, click the Microsoft Office Button, and then click Print.

6. After printing, you can delete the Store sheets that were created, or close the workbook without saving the changes.

9.4. Printing Field Items: Starting Each Item on a New Page

Problem

Your pivot table has Store and Product in the Row Labels area, and when you print your pivot table, you want each store's data to start on a new page. This enables you to print the entire report, and send each store its own section. This problem is based on the RegionSales_09.xlsx workbook.

Solution

You can change a setting in the Store field, so each item starts on a new page in the printed report:

1. Right-click one of the Store labels in the pivot table, and then click Field Settings.

2. In the Field Settings dialog box, on the Layout & Print tab, add a check mark to Insert Page Break After Each Item.

3. Click OK, to close the dialog box.

Tip When starting each item on a new page, your pivot table may be easier to understand if you set the pivot table print titles, as described in Section 9.1. This repeats the pivot table headings on each page, so they're visible with each store's data.

Notes

Using the Insert Page Break After Each Item setting won't ensure all items for a field fit on one page. It only ensures the next item will start on a new page. For fields with many items, two or more pages may be required.

If several of the fields have a short list of items, your printed report could end up using an excessive amount of paper with this setting. You may prefer to turn the setting off and manually adjust the page breaks in Page Break Preview. On the Ribbon's View tab, in the Workbook Views group, click Page Break Preview. Dashed lines indicate an automatic page break and solid lines are manual page breaks. To move a page break, point to it, and drag up or down on the page.

Note You can't move or delete the page breaks created by the Insert Page Break After Each Item setting.

9.5. Printing in Black and White

Problem

You applied the PivotTable Style Medium 16, which has a blue fill color in the cells, and it has black headings with white text. This style is attractive on the worksheet, but it's difficult to read when you print it on your black and white printer. You'd like to print the worksheet without all the shading, so it's easy to read and uses less toner or printer ink. This problem is based on the RegionSales_09.xlsx workbook.

Solution

You can change a page setup option, so the shading is removed when printing:

1. On the Ribbon's Page Layout tab, click the dialog launcher at the bottom right of the Page Setup group.

2. In the Page Setup dialog box, on the Sheet tab, add a check mark to Black and White.

3. Click OK, to close the dialog box, or click Print Preview, to see the revised coloring. All the text is in black font, and all the fill color is removed from the cells.

9.6. Extracting Underlying Data for a Value Cell

Problem

Your pivot table summarizes discount amounts per store, for each category. The Category field is in the Column Labels area, Store is in the Row Labels area, and Discount is in the Values area, as Sum of Discount. One store shows a very high discount total for the Cookies category, and you'd like to see more detail on those orders. None of the other stores is close to this amount, and you wonder if an error occurred in the data, or if there's another cause for the high amount. This problem is based on the RegionSales_09.xlsx workbook.

Solution

For pivot tables based on non-OLAP source data, you can use the pivot table's Show Details feature to extract the source data. For this example, in the pivot table, simply double-click the cell that contains the high discount total.

The *Show Details* feature extracts the records that contribute to the summarized data, and sends the records to a new sheet in the active workbook. On that sheet, you can examine the records to see if a problem exists.

■**Tip** Instead of double-clicking a cell, you can right-click a cell in the Values area of the pivot table, and then, in the context menu, click Show Details.

If you double-click a cell in the pivot table, you may see an error message that says, "Cannot change this part of a PivotTable report." The Show Details feature may be turned off in the PivotTable Options dialog box. To turn it on, follow these steps:

1. Right-click a cell in the pivot table, and then choose PivotTable Options.

2. On the Data tab, add a check mark to Enable Show Details, and then click OK to close the PivotTable Options dialog box.

How It Works

The Show Details feature uses the information stored in the pivot table's pivot cache to create a new sheet that shows the related records from the original source data. It's a good way to investigate anomalies in the summarized data.

The extracted records are copies of the original records in the source data for the pivot table. They are not connected to the original records or to the pivot table.

Note If you make changes in the exported records, this will have no effect on the pivot table, and the changes will not be reflected in the original records.

If Show Details is used in a pivot table, all columns from the source data are shown, not just the fields currently in the pivot table layout.

A new worksheet is automatically created for the extracted records; you can't change a setting to control where the extracted records are placed.

9.7. Re-creating the Source Data Table

Problem

Someone accidentally deleted the worksheet that contained the source data for your pivot table, and you would like to re-create it. (Yes, you know you should have kept a backup copy!) This problem is based on the SourceData.xlsx workbook.

Solution

You may be able to use the pivot table's Show Details feature to re-create the source data:

1. Ensure that none of the items in the visible fields are hidden. Each report filter field should have (All) selected, and the (Select All) item should be checked in each of the row and column fields. To clear all the filters, on the Ribbon's Options tab, in the Actions group, click Clear, and then click Clear Filters.

Tip You don't need to include all fields in the pivot table to see them in the Show Details output. A pivot table with just one field in the Values area, and nothing in the Row Labels, Column Labels, or Report Filter areas, can output all the source data when the grand total cell is double-clicked.

---

2. On the Ribbon's Design tab, in the Layout group, click Grand Totals, and then click On For Rows and Columns.

3. Double-click the grand total cell at the bottom right of the pivot table.

This should create a new sheet with all the records from the original source data. If the source table contained formulas, then you have to re-create them, as the Show Details feature exports the data only. If the Show Details feature doesn't work, check that the Show Details feature is enabled, as described in Section 9.6.

The original records can't be re-created if the source data was not saved with the file. This option is set in the PivotTable Options dialog box, on the Data tab.

How It Works

The *Show Details feature,* where available, creates a new worksheet with the records from the source data included in the amount shown in the double-clicked cell. The columns are in the same order as those in the source data, and the list is formatted with the default Table style for the workbook.

The records exported in the Show Details process are from the current pivot cache. If you had made changes to the source data, but you hadn't yet updated the pivot table, those changes wouldn't be reflected in the exported records.

To see the name of the new Excel Table, select a cell in the Excel Table. On the Ribbon's Design tab, the Table Name is visible in the Properties group, at the far left. You can change that name to the same name as the Excel Table that originally held the source data, and the pivot cache may automatically connect to the new source data. If not, you can connect to the new source range:

1. Select a cell in the pivot table, and on the Ribbon's Options tab, click Change Data Source. In the Table/Range box, you can see the name of the original source table.

2. Select the new Excel Table, or type the name of the new Excel Table, and then click OK.

▮Tip If your pivot table is based on a named range, you may have to redefine the named range if the original range was deleted.

9.8. Formatting the Extracted Data

Problem

When you use the Show Details feature, the underlying data is exported to a table in a new worksheet. You don't like the blue formatting that's used on the new table, and you have to spend time formatting each set of records you extract. You'd like the table formatted automatically, using a different table style. This problem is based on the RegionSales_09.xlsx workbook.

Solution

The extracted records are formatted with the default Table Style for the workbook. To change to a different default style, follow these steps:

1. Select a cell in one of the Excel Tables in the workbook.

2. On the Ribbon's Design tab, in the Table Styles group, click the More button, to open the Table Styles gallery.

3. Right-click a style you like, and then click Set As Default.

Now, when you use the Show Details feature, the extracted records are stored in an Excel Table that uses the new default table style.

Changing the default table style does not affect the number and date formatting in the extracted records. All the fields in the extracted data use the General number format, or the Short Date format. There's no way to control the format of the data exported during a Show Details operation. After the data is exported, you can format the results.

To manually format the data, use the Format Painter button on the Ribbon's Home tab to copy the formatting from the source Excel Table and apply it to the new table.

9.9. Deleting Sheets Created by Extracted Data

Problem

When you use the Show Details feature, data is exported to a new worksheet. This creates extra work for you, as you have to delete all the created sheets before closing the workbook. You'd like a quick way to delete the sheets, so they don't clutter the workbook. This problem is based on the RegionSales_09.xlsx workbook.

Solution

Save the workbook just before you use the Show Details feature. Then, close the workbook without saving the changes, after viewing the additional sheets created by the Show Details feature. Or, save the workbook with a new name to preserve the original workbook without the extra worksheets.

■**Note** A new worksheet is automatically created for the extracted records; you can't control where the extracted records are placed.

9.10. Using GetPivotData: Automatically Inserting a Formula

Problem

You want to refer to a pivot table cell in one of your worksheet formulas, so you can perform calculations using the summarized data. When you type an equal sign, and then click a cell in the pivot table, Excel inserts a GetPivotData formula:

```
=GETPIVOTDATA("TotalPrice",$A$3,"Product","Arrowroot")
```

When you try to copy the formula down the worksheet, the results are the same in every row. You would prefer a simple cell reference, like =B4. This problem is based on the Insert.xlsx workbook.

Solution

Instead of typing an equal sign, and then clicking a cell in the pivot table, you can type the cell reference yourself. For example, type **=B4** instead of clicking Cell B4 to create the reference.

How It Works

The *GetPivotData worksheet function* extracts data from the pivot table for a specific pivot field and pivot item. By default, a GetPivotData formula is automatically created when you refer to a pivot table cell in a worksheet formula. You can turn this feature on or off.

Although the GetPivotData formula looks complex, and you're more comfortable using a simple cell reference, you may get more reliable results by using the GetPivotData function, especially if you plan to add items to the pivot table source.

If you refer to a cell in the pivot table by using a cell reference, the result is whatever is currently in that cell. Today, Cell B15 might contain the Grand Total for Sum of TotalPrice but, tomorrow, it may contain the Count of Orders for Cookies in the East Region. If you use a GetPivotData formula, it returns the result from the correct location in the table, as long as the referenced fields are still in the pivot table. If the referenced fields aren't visible in the pivot table, then the formula returns an error instead of incorrect data.

■**Tip** To ensure the referenced fields and items remain visible, you could create a pivot table that is a copy of the main pivot table and stored on a hidden sheet. In your GetPivotData formulas, refer to this hidden pivot table. Users can change the layout of the main pivot table, and it won't affect your GetPivotData formula results.

The GetPivotData function requires two arguments:

```
=GETPIVOTDATA(data_field,pivot_table)
```

For example, the formula

```
=GETPIVOTDATA("TotalPrice",$A$3)
```

would return the grand total for the TotalPrice values in the pivot table located at Cell A3.

■**Tip** For non-OLAP-based pivot tables, the data_field argument can be the displayed name, for example, Sum of TotalPrice, or the field name, TotalPrice. For an OLAP-based pivot table, use the name as displayed in the Pivot Field list, for example, Sum of TotalPrice.

Also, you can include up to 126 pairs of pivot fields and pivot items in the GetPivotData function, after the pivot_table argument:

```
=GETPIVOTDATA("TotalPrice",$A$3,field1,item1,...)
```

■**Tip** The field/item pairs can be in any order, following the data_field and pivot_table arguments, but the related field and item must be listed together, with the field name followed by the item name.

Using the optional field/item pairs enables you to extract specific details from the pivot table. For example, adding one field/item pair, as shown here

```
=GETPIVOTDATA("TotalPrice",$A$3,"Product","Arrowroot")
```

would return the total TotalPrice for the Arrowroot product. Product is a pivot field, and Arrowroot is an item in the Product field.

Expanding the previous formula with two field/item pairs, as shown here

```
=GETPIVOTDATA("TotalPrice",$A$3,"Product","Arrowroot","Region","East")
```

would return the total TotalPrice for the Arrowroot product in the East region. Region is a pivot field, and East is an item in the Region field.

■**Note** Because a GetPivotData formula can only display visible data from the pivot table, it's best suited to a pivot table that has the referenced fields in the Row Labels or Column Labels areas, and limited layout changes for the fields used in the GetPivotData formula.

9.11. Using GetPivotData: Turning Off Automatic Insertion of Formulas

Problem

Excel inserts a GetPivotData formula every time you try to link to a cell in the pivot table. You want to turn off this feature, so it's easier to create a simple link to the cells in the pivot table, such as =B4. This problem is based on the Insert.xlsx workbook.

Solution

You can use a command on the Ribbon to toggle this feature on and off:

1. Select a cell in the pivot table, and then click the Ribbon's Options tab.

2. In the PivotTable group, click the arrow on the Options command.

3. Click Generate GetPivotData to toggle this feature on and off (see Figure 9-5).

Figure 9-5. *The Generate GetPivotData command*

9.12. Using GetPivotData: Referencing Pivot Tables in Other Workbooks

Problem

Your GetPivotData formula refers to a pivot table in another workbook. When you open the workbook and update the links, you get a #REF! error in the GetPivotData formulas. This problem is based on the Linked.xlsx workbook, which has references to the Insert.xlsx workbook, stored in the C:_Work folder.

Solution

The GetPivotData function, like some other Excel functions, only returns data for references in the same file, or another open file. To see the results of the GetPivotData formula, open the Insert.xlsx workbook that contains the referenced pivot table.

Or, create the GetPivotData formula in the Insert.xlsx workbook that contains the pivot table, perhaps on a hidden worksheet. Then, in the Linked.xlsx workbook, link to the cell that contains the GetPivotData formula in the Insert.xlsx workbook.

9.13. Using GetPivotData: Using Cell References Instead of Text Strings

Problem

You frequently change the text strings in the GetPivotData formula when you want to see the results for a different product in your pivot table. It's time-consuming to modify the formula, and it's easy to make a mistake as you edit the product names in the formula. This problem is based on the Reference.xlsx workbook.

Solution

You can replace the text strings in the GetPivotData formula with references to cells that contain the text you want to extract. For example, instead of a formula that contains a product name, like this one,

```
=GETPIVOTDATA("TotalPrice",$A$3,"Product","Arrowroot")
```

type the product name in Cell F1, and then change the formula to

```
=GETPIVOTDATA("TotalPrice",$A$3,"Product",F1)
```

Tip Use the Generate GetPivotData feature to create the formula by clicking a cell in the pivot table. Then, in the formula, highlight a text string and its enclosing quotation marks, and click the cell you want to use as a reference for this text.

Type a different product name in the referenced cell, and the formula will show the results for the new name (see Figure 9-6). This is much quicker and easier than adjusting a small part of the formula.

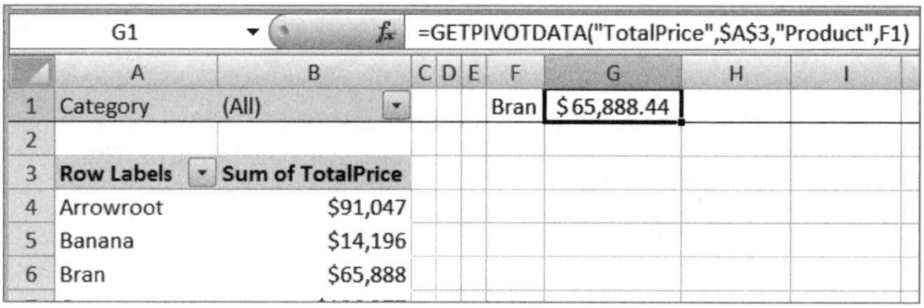

G1		f_x	=GETPIVOTDATA("TotalPrice",$A$3,"Product",F1)					
	A	B	C D E	F	G	H	I
1	Category	(All)		Bran	$65,888.44		
2							
3	Row Labels	Sum of TotalPrice					
4	Arrowroot	$91,047					
5	Banana	$14,196					
6	Bran	$65,888					

Figure 9-6. *Using a cell reference in a GetPivotData formula*

Note The referenced cell should contain only the text, not the double quotes that surround the text in the formula.

9.14. Using GetPivotData: Using Cell References in an OLAP-Based Pivot Table

Problem

You want to replace some of the text strings in the GetPivotData formulas that refer to your OLAP-based pivot table. You're having trouble getting the syntax right, and the formulas are returning #REF! errors. This problem is based on the PivotOLAP.xlsx HardwareSales.cub file.

Solution

Because the OLAP data is in levels, those levels are included in the GetPivotData arguments. When you link to a cell in an OLAP-based pivot table, that starts in Cell A1, the resulting formula may look similar to this:

```
=GETPIVOTDATA("[Measures].[Sum Of Qty]",$A$1,
    "[Region]","[Region].[All].[West]")
```

In the sample file, this would return a value of 7010, which is the Sum of Qty for the West region. If you type **West** in Cell H3, you can replace that part of the formula with a cell reference:

```
=GETPIVOTDATA("[Measures].[Sum Of Qty]",$A$1,
   "[Region]","[Region].[All].[" & H3 & "]")
```

■Note The square brackets in the field and item names mark the start and end of the level names. When replacing text with a cell reference, do not delete the square brackets from the formula, or the formula will return an error.

With West in Cell H3, the formula returns the same result, 7010. Type **East** in Cell H3, and the formula result changes to 10349, which is the Sum of Qty for the East region (see Figure 9-7).

	H4	▾		f_x	=GETPIVOTDATA("[Measures].[Sum Of Qty]",$A$1, "[Region]","[Region].[All].[" & H3 & "]")					
	A	B	C	D	E	F	G	H	I	
3	Row Labels ▾	Sum Of Qty						East		
4	⊞ Central	8585						10349		
5	⊞ Electric	4511								
6	⊞ Hand Tools	4074								
7	⊞ East	10349								
8	⊞ Electric	5448								

Figure 9-7. *Using a cell reference for an OLAP-based pivot table*

9.15. Using GetPivotData: Using Cell References for Value Fields

Problem

In your pivot table, the Quantity and TotalPrice fields are in the Values area, and Product is in the Row Labels area. When you link to a cell in the pivot table, a GetPivotData formula is automatically created, and shows "TotalPrice" as the first argument:

```
=GETPIVOTDATA("TotalPrice",$A$3,"Product","Arrowroot")
```

You'd like to make the formula more flexible, so you type **TotalPrice** in Cell E1, and change the formula to refer to that cell:

```
=GETPIVOTDATA(E1,$A$3,"Product","Arrowroot")
```

The formula returns a #REF! error, even though Cell E1 contains the correctly typed field name, "TotalPrice". This problem is based on the `Insert.xlsx` workbook.

Solution

To use a cell reference for the value field, concatenate an empty string at the start or end of the reference. For example, you could use

```
=GETPIVOTDATA("" & E1,$A$3,"Product","Arrowroot")
```

or

```
=GETPIVOTDATA(E1 & "",$A$3,"Product","Arrowroot")
```

9.16. Using GetPivotData: Extracting Data for Blank Field Items

Problem

In the source data, some of the orders do not have a store number entered. In the pivot table, the Store field is in the Row Labels area, and a (blank) item is listed. You want to extract the total for this item using a GetPivotData formula. This problem is based on the GetPivotData.xlsx workbook.

Solution

In the formula, leave an empty reference where the item name argument would appear. For example, the formula to return the total quantity for store 3000 is

```
=GETPIVOTDATA("Sum of Quantity",$A$3,"Store","3000")
```

and for the (blank) store item

```
=GETPIVOTDATA("Sum of Quantity",$A$3,"Store",)
```

If you're using cell references in the formula, the referenced cell should contain the text (blank). For example, if Cell H2 contains (blank), the following formula will return the total Quantity for the (blank) store item:

```
=GETPIVOTDATA("Sum of Quantity",$A$3,"Store",H2)
```

9.17. Using GetPivotData: Preventing Errors for Missing Items

Problem

In your pivot table, Product is in the Row Labels area, Region is in the Column Labels area, and Quantity is in the Values area. You use a GetPivotData formula to return the total quantity sold for each product. With the OrderDate field in the Report Filter area, you can select an order date and see the quantity sold for the selected date.

Some products may have no sales for the selected date, and they don't appear when the filter is applied. If you refer to these products in a GetPivotData formula, this results in #REF! errors being returned. You would like the formula to return a zero, instead of an error. This problem is based on the Missing.xlsx workbook.

Solution

You can use the IFERROR function to return a zero instead of an error. For example, if the original formula is

```
=GETPIVOTDATA("Quantity",$A$3,"Product","Pretzels")
```

use an IFERROR formula to check for the error:

```
=IFERROR(GETPIVOTDATA("Quantity",$A$3,"Product","Pretzels"),0)
```

You can also return a text message, instead of a zero:

```
=IFERROR(GETPIVOTDATA("Quantity",$A$3,"Product","Pretzels"),"No Pretzels")
```

How It Works

The *IFERROR function* is one of the new worksheet functions introduced in Excel 2007. It requires two arguments: the value to test for an error, and the result to show if the value is an error. In this example, the GetPivotData formula returns the quantity of Pretzels in the pivot table. If Pretzels is not found, the GetPivotData formula returns a #REF! error. Because the GetPivotData formula returns an error, the IFERROR formula returns the text message, "No Pretzels" (see Figure 9-8).

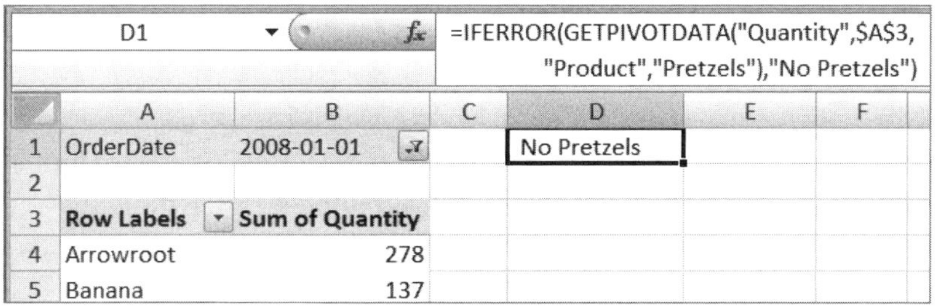

D1	▼	f_x	=IFERROR(GETPIVOTDATA("Quantity",$A$3,		
			"Product","Pretzels"),"No Pretzels")		

	A	B	C	D	E	F
1	OrderDate	2008-01-01		No Pretzels		
2						
3	Row Labels	Sum of Quantity				
4	Arrowroot	278				
5	Banana	137				

Figure 9-8. *Using IFERROR to hide error values*

9.18. Using GetPivotData: Preventing Errors for Custom Subtotals

Problem

In your pivot table, Category and Product are in the Row Labels area, and Quantity is in the Values area. In the Field Settings for the Category field, you selected both Sum and Average as functions for Custom subtotals.

You created a link to the subtotal cell that shows the average for Bars, and a GetPivotData formula was automatically created (see Figure 9-9). This formula looks different than the other GetPivotData formulas on the worksheet, and it returns a #REF! error:

```
=GETPIVOTDATA($A$3,"Category[Bars;Data,Average]")
```

3	Row Labels	Sum of Quantity					
4	⊟ Bars						
5	Banana	2,625					
6	Bran	20,681					
7	Carrot	42,776					
8	Bars Sum	66,082					
9	Bars Average	321	=GETPIVOTDATA($A$3,"Category[Bars;Data,Average]")				
10	⊟ Cookies						

Figure 9-9. *GetPivotData formula for custom subtotal*

You'd like to fix the GetPivotData formula so it returns the correct result. This problem is based on the Subtotals.xlsx workbook.

Solution

When linking to custom subtotals at the bottom of a group, the automatically generated GetPivotData formulas return a #REF! error. This is a bug that has existed in Excel for several versions, but the formula can be easily corrected.

To fix the formula so it calculates correctly, remove the "Data," from the formula. The corrected formula for this example is

```
=GETPIVOTDATA($A$3,"Category[Bars;Average]")
```

How It Works

If subtotals are shown at the top of the group when the GetPivotData formula is created for a custom subtotal, a normal GetPivotData formula is inserted. If subtotals are at the bottom, a GetPivotData formula with a Data reference is created.

■**Note** If there are multiple subtotals for a field, the subtotals cannot be shown at the top of the group.

If you move subtotals to the top, after creating a GetPivotData formula with a Data reference, the formula may return incorrect results in some circumstances. Follow these steps to see an example:

1. Clear the existing pivot table, and create a pivot table layout with Category, Region, and City fields in the Row Labels area, and Quantity in the Values area.

2. On the Ribbon's Design tab, in the Layout group, click Subtotals, and then click Show All Subtotals at Bottom of Group.

3. To create a custom subtotal, right-click a label the Region field, such as East, and then click Field Settings.

4. On the Subtotals & Filters tab, click Custom, click Count, and then click OK. In the pivot table, Bars, for the East region, shows a subtotal of 118.

5. Select a cell outside of the pivot table, type an equal sign, and then click the subtotal cell for Bars East. Press the Enter key to complete the formula. The formula in the cell contains the Data reference and returns a #REF! error:

```
=GETPIVOTDATA($A$3,"Bars Region[East;Data,Count]")
```

6. On the Ribbon's Design tab, change the subtotals to show at the top of the group. The formula now works correctly, and returns 118 as the result.

7. Remove the City field from the Row Labels area. The GetPivotData formula now returns 35314, which is the Sum of Quantity for bars sold in the East, not the count of bars sold in the East region (see Figure 9-10).

	D5	▾	⬭	*fx*	=GETPIVOTDATA($A$3,"Bars Region[East;Data,Count]")			
	A	B	C	D	E	F	G	H
3	**Row Labels** ▾	**Sum of Quantity**						
4	⊟ **Bars**	66082						
5	East	35314		35314				
6	North	30768						
7	⊟ **Cookies**	77246						

Figure 9-10. *GetPivotData formula shows an incorrect result.*

If you plan to use the GetPivotData function with custom subtotals, show the subtotals at the bottom of the group, if possible, or be alert for possible errors.

9.19. Using GetPivotData: Preventing Errors for Date References

Problem

In your pivot table, OrderDate is in the Row Labels area, and Quantity is in the Values area. You created a GetPivotData formula to extract the total quantity for a specific date. Although that date is visible in the pivot table, the formula is returning an error:

```
=GETPIVOTDATA("Quantity",$A$3,"OrderDate","1/1/08")
```

This problem is based on the Dates.xlsx workbook.

Solution

If the date is in the pivot table, but formatted differently, the GetPivotData formula will produce a #REF! error. Instead of entering the date as a text string, you can use either the DATE or DATEVALUE function. For example,

```
=GETPIVOTDATA("Quantity",$A$3,"OrderDate",DATE(2008,1,1))
```

or

```
=GETPIVOTDATA("Quantity",$A$3,"OrderDate",DATEVALUE("1/1/08"))
```

Both functions return a serial number that represents a date. The arguments of the DATE function are Year, Month, and Day. The DATEVALUE function requires a text string as its argument.

Or, you can enter a valid date in a worksheet cell, and then refer to that cell in the GetPivotData formula:

```
=GETPIVOTDATA("Quantity",$A$3,"OrderDate",D3)
```

where Cell D3 contains a valid date, in any format recognized as a date by Excel.

9.20. Using GetPivotData: Referring to a Pivot Table

Problem

Two pivot tables are on your worksheet, with each one summarizing data for a different region. When you create a GetPivotData formula, it includes a reference to a cell in the pivot table as the second argument. In this example, the pivot table is located at Cell A3:

```
=GETPIVOTDATA("TotalPrice",$A$3)
```

You'd like to type a cell address on the worksheet, and have the GetPivotData formula return the total from the pivot table located at that cell. For example, you want to type **H3** in Cell E1, and see the total from the pivot table that starts in Column H.

When you refer to Cell E1 in the formula, it returns a #REF! error. This problem is based on the TwoPivots.xlsx workbook.

Solution

You can use the INDIRECT function in the GetPivotData function to create a range reference based on the text in Cell E1. For example:

```
=GETPIVOTDATA("TotalPrice",INDIRECT(E1))
```

If you type **A3** in Cell E1, the formula returns the total from the first pivot table, and if you type **H3** in Cell E1, the formula returns the total from the second pivot table.

How It Works

The INDIRECT function requires one argument

```
=INDIRECT(ref_text)
```

and returns the range specified by the reference text argument. For example, if Cell E1 contains the text **A3**, the following formula would return the value from Cell A3:

```
=INDIRECT(E1)
```

9.21. Creating Customized Pivot Table Copies

Problem

You'd like to create a separate copy of the pivot table for each store to make it easier for the store managers to focus on their individual sales results. This problem is based on the Region-Sales_09.xlsx workbook.

Solution

The Show Report Filter Pages feature creates a copy of the pivot table on a separate worksheet for each item in the selected report filter field. This is a quick way to create multiple versions of the pivot table for viewing or printing.

Follow these steps to create the copies:

1. Move the Store field to the pivot table Report Filter area, and then select (All) from its filter list.

Note If an individual item is selected in the filter list, instead of (All), a separate worksheet is not created for the selected item.

---

2. Select a cell in the pivot table, and then click the Ribbon's Options tab.

3. At the far left, in the PivotTable group, click the arrow for the Options command, and then click Show Report Filter Pages.

4. In the Show Report Filter Pages window, select the Report Filter field for which you want to create the pages, and then click OK.

Tip If a Report Filter field is the active cell on the worksheet, when the Show Report Filter Pages window opens, that field is selected in the list of Report Filter fields. Otherwise, the first Report Filter field on the worksheet is selected in the list.

How It Works

A copy of the pivot table, on a new worksheet, is created for each item in the field you select in the Show Report Filter Pages window. In this example, a new sheet is created for each store. The new sheet is named the same as the field item, and that item is selected in the Report Filter field.

■**Note** A copy of the pivot table is not created for the (All) item, or the (Multiple Items) selection.

If the pivot table's options are set to preserve cell formatting on update, and to autofit column widths on update, most formatting from the original pivot table should be retained, including the PivotTable style. Conditional formatting will be lost.

Each copy is based on the original pivot table, and uses the same pivot cache, so this technique may have a minimal impact on the file size, if the layout doesn't include too many rows and columns.

Only the pivot table is copied; other data on the same sheet as the original pivot table is not copied, and neither are page settings, such as footers and margins. If you want to include other data, such as formulas in cells adjacent to the pivot table, you can create a copy of the worksheet, instead of using the Show Report Filter Pages command.

When the sheets are created, normal sheet name rules are followed.

- The following characters can't be used in a sheet name:

  : \ / ? * [ ]

- If an item name contains one of those characters, a generic name, for example, Sheet5, is used for that item's sheet.

- The maximum number of characters allowed in a sheet name is 31. Only the first 26 characters of the item name are used.

- If a sheet already exists with the item name, or the first 26 characters of the item's name, a new sheet is created with "(2)" appended to the name.

CHAPTER 10

Pivot Charts

After you create a pivot table, you can create a pivot chart, based on one of the pivot tables in your workbook. A pivot chart can't be created on its own; it must be based on a pivot table. Pivot charts are similar to normal Excel charts, but they have some differences and limitations, as described in this chapter. Except where noted, the problems in this chapter are based on the Sales10.xlsx sample file.

10.1. Planning and Creating a Pivot Chart

Problem

The sales manager is preparing for a budget meeting in the East region, and she asked you to create a pivot chart, to show the sales for each food category at each store.

You created a pivot table on the Region Pivot worksheet, with Store and Category in the Row Labels area, and Quantity in the Values area. Region is in the Report Filters area, with East selected from the drop-down list.

You aren't sure which type of chart will work best, and you're having trouble arranging the fields so the chart looks right. The meeting is tomorrow, and you're running out of time. This problem is based on the Budget.xlsx sample file.

Solution

When you create a pivot chart, it will use the same layout as the pivot table on which it's based.

- Fields in the pivot table's Row Labels area become the fields on the pivot chart's *category axis*—the horizontal axis across the bottom of a column or line chart.

- Fields in the pivot table's Column Labels area become *legend fields* (series) in the pivot chart—the lines or columns.

- Fields in the pivot table's Values area become the values in the pivot chart, and they determine the height of a column, or the position of the point on a line.

- Fields in the pivot table's Report Filters area continue to act as filters in a pivot chart.

When planning a pivot chart, consider how you want the fields arranged in the chart. If no fields are in the Column Labels area, the chart will have only one series, representing the fields in the Row Labels area. In this example, with Store and Category fields in the Row Labels area, a column chart would have one column for each store's sales in each category. All the columns would be the same color.

If you move the Store field to the Column Labels area and create a pivot chart, each store would be a series, with a different colored column for each store. You could compare the sales of each category, to see which store had the best or worst sales.

If, instead, you move the Category field to the Column Labels area and create a pivot chart, each category would be a series, with a different colored column for each category. You could compare the sales at each store, to see which category had the best or worst sales.

In this example, the presentation is to the store managers, who may be interested in how well their stores are performing, compared to the other stores.

1. In the pivot table, move the Store field to the Column Labels area, and leave the Category field in the Row Labels area.

2. To create a pivot chart, select a cell in the pivot table, and on the Ribbon, click the Options tab.

3. In the Tools group, click PivotChart.

4. The Insert Chart dialog box opens, where you can select a chart type and subtype. For this chart, select a Column chart type, and a Clustered Column subtype, and then click OK. A column chart is a good choice if you are comparing sets of numbers, as in this case, where you want to compare the total sales for each category at each store.

This creates a pivot chart on the same worksheet as the pivot table (see Figure 10-1). Each store is represented by a different color column, with the colors and store numbers shown in the chart's legend. The category names appear on the horizontal axis at the bottom of the chart, and you can see which store had the best or worst sales for each category. The height of each bar represents the quantity sold in each store, for each category. Because the pivot table is filtered to show the East region's sales, the pivot chart is also filtered.

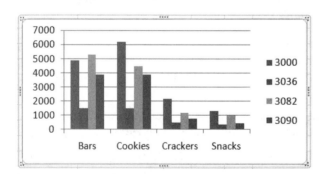

Figure 10-1. *The pivot chart shows sales per category.*

It may take some experimentation, moving the fields to different areas of the pivot chart, but try to create a chart that presents a limited amount of data, in a clean and simple chart layout. To see the different layouts available with the Store, Category, and Quantity fields, try the following:

1. With the pivot chart selected, move Store to the Axis Fields (Categories) area, below Category. This creates one series, with the legend entry of Total. All the columns are blue, and two sets of labels are on the horizontal axis. The category names are the outer labels on the axis, and store numbers are the inner labels. This layout lets you compare the sales for all categories at all stores, but the horizontal axis is crowded, and the single color makes the chart difficult to read at a glance.

2. Move Store above Category in the Axis Fields (Categories) area. This creates one series, with blue columns, and the legend entry of Total. The store numbers are the outer labels on the horizontal axis, and category names are the inner labels. This layout lets you compare the sales for all stores and all categories, but the horizontal axis is crowded, and the labels are hard to read.

3. Move Category to the Legend Fields (Series) area. This creates a different colored series for each category. The store numbers are labels on the horizontal axis, and you can compare how well the categories sold, within each store.

4. Move Store to the Legend Fields (Series) area, above Category. This creates a different colored series for each store's sales of each category. The legend contains a lengthy list of store and category names, and the chart is crowded and difficult to read.

How It Works

The Insert Chart Type dialog box shows a list of chart types at the left. At the right are the subtypes available for each chart type. You can point to a subtype and see its name in a tooltip.

Selecting a Chart Type

Unless you changed the setting, the default chart type in Excel is a clustered column chart. Several chart types are available in Excel:

- *Column* and *bar charts* are almost the same, except bars are displayed horizontally across the chart and columns are vertical. Both of these chart types work well for comparing specific values, as you're doing in your chart.

- *Line charts* and *area charts* connect the points that represent values and are good for illustrating changes over time. The charts are the same, except the area charts are filled with color.

- *Pie charts* and *doughnut charts* show the percentage each value comprises in the overall total. The pie chart type works well when there is a single series and value, such as total quantity per region. A doughnut chart can show multiple series.

- *Surface charts* and *radar charts* are specialized chart types you can use to show differences in the data or aggregated data.

■**Note** Although they are available in the list of chart types, you cannot use the X Y (Scatter), Bubble, or Stock chart types when creating a pivot chart.

Selecting a Chart Subtype

After you select a chart type in the Insert Chart Type dialog box, its default chart subtype is automatically selected. You can select a different subtype, to meet the requirements of your current chart. The following are a few of the options:

- Clustered column and bar subtypes are useful if you want to compare the individual values in a series. In the current example, a clustered column lets you compare the category sales at each store, side-by-side.

- Stacked column and bar subtypes combine individual values in a single column or bar, and they let you compare totals. For example, if you select Stacked Column as the subtype for the current chart, with Store in the Axis Fields (Categories) area, and Category in the Legend Fields (Series) area, the chart will have a single column for each store. Each category is represented by a different color.

- The 100 percent Stacked column and bar subtypes combine individual values in a single column or bar that represents 100 percent of each item's value. This lets you compare percentages within each item. For example, if you select 100 percent Stacked Column as the subtype for the current chart, with Store in the Axis Fields (Categories) area, and Category in the Legend Fields (Series) area, the chart will have a single column for each store. All the columns are the same height, and within each column, each category's color shows its percentage of the store's sales.

- Line charts and area charts also have stacked and 100 percent stacked subtypes similar to those for the column and bar charts.

- The remaining chart types have subtypes you can test on your pivot charts. Most of these, such as Line with Markers or Exploded Pie, are simply a different format, rather than a different layout of the data.

■**Tip** Avoid using the 3-D chart subtypes, because they distort the representation of the data in your charts.

10.2. Quickly Creating a Pivot Chart

Problem

You frequently create pivot charts using the clustered column chart type, and you would like a quick way to create one on a chart sheet. You're tired of navigating through the Ribbon's tabs, and performing so many steps, just to create a simple chart. This problem is based on the Regions.xlsx sample file.

Solution

You can press one key on the keyboard, to create a pivot chart on a new chart sheet:

1. Select a cell in the pivot table.

2. On the keyboard, press the F11 key.

A pivot chart is created, on a new chart sheet, in the default chart type and subtype. You can format the pivot chart, or change its layout, if required.

How It Works

If you have not changed the setting, the default chart type is a clustered column chart. If you usually select a different chart type, you can set that type as the default. You can also create your own chart templates, and set one of those as the default.

Setting the Default Chart Type

Follow these steps to change the default chart type:

1. Select an empty cell on any worksheet.

2. On the Ribbon's Insert tab, click the dialog launcher at the bottom right of the Charts group.

3. In the Insert Chart dialog box, select the chart type and chart subtype you want to set as the default type. For example, click Line as the chart type, and then click the Line subtype (see Figure 10-2).

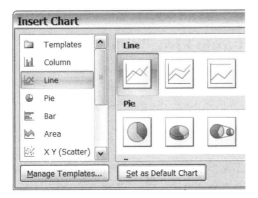

Figure 10-2. *Select a chart type and subtype.*

▪Note The X Y (Scatter), Bubble, and Stock chart types are unavailable when creating a pivot chart. If you select one of these as the default chart type, you will be unable to create a pivot chart with the F11 shortcut.

---

4. Click Set as Default Chart, and then click Cancel, to close the dialog box without creating a chart.

Creating a Chart Template

You can create a chart template that stores all the settings you would like to apply to other charts. For example, if you frequently create a clustered column chart, change the columns to green, and then add a title and other formatting, you could save a GreenCluster template. Follow these steps to create a chart template:

1. Create a chart with the chart type, formatting, and layout you want to save as a template. The chart can be located on a chart sheet, or on a worksheet.

2. Select the chart, and on the Ribbon's Design tab, in the Type group, click Save As Template.

3. In the Save Chart Template dialog box, type a file name for the template, such as **GreenCluster**. The file extension, crtx, is automatically added to the file name when it is saved. Leave the Save In folder unchanged, and your template is saved in the default folder for chart templates.

4. Click Save, to save the template.

To make the template the default chart type, follow these steps:

1. Select an empty cell in the workbook, and on the Ribbon's Insert tab, click the dialog launcher at the bottom right of the Charts group.

2. In the list of chart types, click Templates, and then click your template.

3. Click Set As Default Chart, and then click Cancel, to close the dialog box.

4. If you created a chart as a model for the template, you can delete it—click the chart, and then press the Delete key.

10.3. Creating a Normal Chart from Pivot Table Data

Problem

The sales manager asked you for a pivot chart that shows the number of days customers wait for service in the East region. You summarized the data from your company's service work orders, with Wait days in the Row Labels area, District in the Report Filters area, and Count of WO (work orders) in the Values area.

The best chart type for this would be an *X Y (Scatter) chart*, because the chart will have numbers on both axes—the number of wait days and the count of work orders. However, when you try to create the chart, you get an error message that says, "You cannot use an X Y (Scatter), Bubble, or Stock chart type with a chart that has been created from PivotTable data. Please select a different chart type." This problem is based on the WaitDays.xlsx sample workbook.

Workaround

Although you can't create some types of charts from pivot table data, you can link the data to another worksheet, and then use the linked data as the source for a chart.

1. In the pivot table, select the cells you want to include in the chart. In this example, select cells A4:B21, which contain the wait days and the count of work orders.

2. Right-click one of the selected cells, and then click Copy.

3. Right-click the cell where you would like to paste the linked cells, and then click Paste Special. In this example, the data is pasted onto the PivotLink worksheet.

4. In the Paste Special dialog box, click Paste Link. Add headings above the linked data, such as **Days** and **WOs**.

5. To create a chart, select a cell in the linked data.

6. On the Ribbon's Insert tab, click the Scatter command, and then click the first chart subtype. This creates a scatter chart on the same worksheet as the linked data.

7. Format the chart as desired.

10.4. Filtering the Pivot Chart

Problem

You created a pivot chart for the sales manager to use at the upcoming budget meeting. The pivot chart is on its own chart sheet, and when you want to select a different category in the Report Filter, you have to go to the pivot table and make the changes.

You want it to be easy for the sales manager to select a different category or change the chart layout during the meeting, without having to leave the chart sheet. This problem is based on the Filter.xlsx sample file.

Solution

If you display the PivotChart Filter pane and the PivotTable Field List pane, you can make the layout and filter changes while working on the chart. Follow these steps to display these panes:

1. Select the pivot chart, and on the Ribbon, click the Analyze tab.

2. In the Show/Hide group, click Field List, to display the PivotTable Field List pane, and then click PivotChart Filter, to show the PivotChart Filter pane (see Figure 10-3).

Figure 10-3. *Field List and PivotChart Filter commands*

Tip Hide the PivotTable Field List pane and the PivotChart Filter pane after you finish modifying the pivot chart. This makes more room to view the chart's data.

How It Works

The *PivotTable Field List* lets you change the pivot chart layout, and the *PivotChart Filter pane* lets you filter the fields in the pivot chart.

Using the PivotTable Field List

The PivotTable Field List can be visible or hidden when a pivot chart is active. Use it to move fields in and out of the chart layout, or to a different area of the pivot chart layout.

When the pivot chart is active, two of the area names change, to match the areas in the chart:

- The Column Labels area changes to the Legend Fields (Series) area.

- The Row Labels area becomes the Axis Fields (Categories) area.

Move fields from one area of the PivotTable Field List to another, or add or remove fields from the pivot table layout. This changes the chart's appearance, as well as the pivot table on which the pivot chart is based.

Using the PivotChart Filter Pane

The PivotChart Filter pane (see Figure 10-4) enables you to filter the fields in the pivot chart's Report Filter, Axis Fields (Categories), or Legend Fields (Series) areas. You can also use it to sort the axis fields and legend fields.

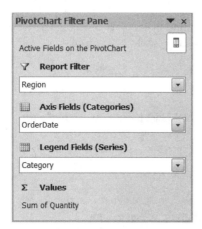

Figure 10-4. *The PivotChart Filter pane*

- At the top right of the PivotChart Filter pane is a button that toggles the PivotTable Field List from visible to hidden (see Figure 10-4).

- To filter a field, click the arrow in the field's drop-down list, and then check the items you want to show. These filters work just as they do for the fields in the pivot table. For the axis and legend fields, you can also apply Value, Date, and Label filters from the filter drop-down lists.

- To sort the axis or legend fields, click the arrow in the field's drop-down list, and then click one of the sort options.

10.5. Changing the Series Order

Problem

You created a line chart to show the sales per category over several months. The categories are listed in the legend, and you would like them sorted alphabetically. This problem is based on the SalesDate.xlsx sample file.

Solution

When you create a pivot chart, the series order is automatically applied, based on the sort setting for the field in the pivot table on which the pivot chart is based. To change the sort order, follow these steps:

1. Select the pivot chart, and then display the PivotChart Filter pane.

2. Click the arrow in the drop-down list for the field you want to sort. In this example, click the arrow for the Legend Fields (series), where the Category field is listed.

3. Click Sort A-Z, to sort the categories in ascending order (see Figure 10-5).

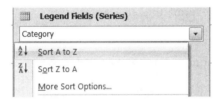

Figure 10-5. *Sort Options in the PivotChart Filter pane*

10.6. Changing Pivot Chart Layout Affects Pivot Table

Problem

When you change the pivot chart layout, the related pivot table is also changed. You want the pivot chart and pivot table to work independently. This problem is based on the SalesDate.xlsx sample file.

Workaround

If you rearrange the fields in a pivot chart, the same changes are made to the related pivot table. You can create a second pivot table, by copying the first one, and arrange it as you'd like. Then, when you change the pivot chart, only the original pivot table is affected. You can hide the first pivot table that's connected to the pivot chart and use the second pivot table for displaying or printing.

If you require several charts based on the same pivot table, but with different layouts, create multiple pivot tables as copies of the original pivot table. Create one pivot chart from each of the secondary pivot tables, and rearranging one won't affect the others.

10.7. Changing Number Format in Pivot Table Affects Pivot Chart

Problem

For the sales manager's presentation, you'd like the sales amounts on the pivot chart's axis formatted as thousands, so the numbers take less room. If you change the number format in the pivot table, the pivot chart's number format also changes, but you'd like the pivot table to show the full number. This problem is based on the `Numbers.xlsx` sample file.

Solution

You can change a setting in the pivot chart, so the numbers are formatted separately.

1. In the pivot chart, right-click a number in the axis, and then click Format Axis.

2. In the Format Axis dialog box, click Number.

3. Click the Custom category. This automatically removes the check mark from Linked to Source, which disconnects the axis labels from the formatting in the pivot table.

4. In the Format Code box, type a code for the formatting, such as

   `#,"K";-#,"K"`

5. Click Add, to create the custom number format code, and then click Close.

10.8. Formatting the Data Table

Problem

You spent an hour applying conditional formatting to the data cells in the pivot table, and formatting the numbers as currency. Then you added a data table to the pivot chart, from the Ribbon's Layout tab. The number formatting was displayed correctly, but the conditional formatting didn't appear. You'd like to show all the formatting in the data table. This problem is based on the `CondFormat.xlsx` sample file.

Workaround

The number formatting from the source data will be used in the chart's data table, but other formatting won't be displayed. Instead of displaying a data table, you could place the pivot chart on a worksheet, close to the pivot table, where the formatted data will be visible.

10.9. Including Grand Totals in a Pivot Chart

Problem

The grand total row is visible in the pivot table, and you want to include the totals in the pivot chart. You can't find any setting that lets you include them. This problem is based on the `Totals.xlsx` sample file.

Workaround

The pivot chart is limited to showing the data from the pivot table's Values area. Other data, such as subtotals, or grand totals or additional series, such as a target line, can't be added.

You could create a normal chart from the data, as described in Section 10.3, and include the grand totals in the linked data.

10.10. Converting a Pivot Chart to a Static Chart

Problem

The sales manager asked you to send each store a copy of the pivot table you created. Before you send them, you want to change the pivot chart to a static chart that isn't connected to the pivot table. That way, you can send the pivot chart without the underlying detailed data. This problem is based on the Sales10.xlsx sample file.

Solution

To change a pivot chart to a static chart, you can copy the pivot chart to a different workbook:

1. Right-click the pivot chart's Chart area, and then in the context menu, click Copy.

2. Activate the workbook into which you want to paste the pivot chart.

3. Right-click the cell where you would like to place the upper-left corner of the chart, and in the context menu, click Paste.

10.11. Showing Field Names on the Pivot Chart

Problem

You created a pivot chart to show the sales of your low-fat and low-calorie products, and two of the fields contain Yes/No values. When you add these fields to the pivot chart, the field names aren't visible, and it's impossible to tell which fields are represented in the pivot chart. You can see the field names in the PivotChart Report Filter, but that won't be visible when you print the chart. You want to display the field names on the pivot chart, so readers can understand the data. This problem is based on the YesNo.xlsx sample file.

Workaround

There's no setting you can change that will display the field names in the pivot chart. To describe the chart contents, you can add a chart title, and you can add axis titles to clarify the items on the vertical and horizontal axes. For fields where ambiguity exists, you can add a text box to the pivot chart, to explain the data that's displayed.

Adding a Chart Title

Follow these steps to add a chart title:

1. Select the pivot chart, and then on the Ribbon, click the Layout tab.

2. In the Labels group, click Chart Title, and then click Centered Overlay Title or Above Chart.

3. Select the placeholder text in the chart title that was added, and type the text you want in your title.

Adding Axis Titles

Follow these steps to add an axis title:

1. Select the pivot chart, and then on the Ribbon, click the Layout tab.

2. In the Labels group, click Axis Titles, and then click Primary Horizontal Axis Title or Primary Vertical Axis Title.

3. Click one of the options for the selected axis title.

4. Select the placeholder text in the axis title that was added, and then type the text you want in the axis title.

Adding a Text Box

Follow these steps to add a text box:

1. Select the pivot chart, and on the Ribbon, click the Layout tab.

2. In the Insert group, click Text Box, and then use the pointer to draw a text box on the pivot chart.

3. In the text box, type the text you want to add to the pivot chart.

Formatting the Titles and Text Boxes

After you add titles or text boxes to the pivot chart, you can format them, using the commands on the Ribbon's Home tab and the Format tab. Select a title or text box in the chart, and then use these commands to change the colors, fonts, and effects.

Creating Dynamic Titles and Text Boxes

To make a title or text box more flexible, you can link it to a worksheet cell. The cell can contain text or a formula. For example, if your pivot table has a Report Filter for Region, you could link the chart title to the cell that shows the selected region's name.

Follow these steps to link a chart title to a cell:

1. In the pivot chart, click the chart title to select it.

2. Click in the formula bar, and then type an equal sign.

3. Activate the sheet that contains the pivot table, and then click the cell that contains the region name.

4. Press the Enter key to complete the link.

5. Select a different region in the PivotChart Filter pane and the chart title will change, to show the new selection.

Note If you are linking a text box to a cell, click the border of the text box to select it. The cursor should not be flashing inside the text box.

10.12. Refreshing the Pivot Chart

Problem

You want to refresh the pivot chart, instead of going to the pivot table and doing the refresh there. However, when you right-click near the center of the pivot chart, the context menu doesn't contain a Refresh command. This problem is based on the Sales10.xlsx sample file.

Solution

The context menus show different commands, based on where the pointer is when you right-click. If you right-click the plot area, you see a short context menu, which has commands including Format Plot Area and Select Data. If you right-click the chart area, which is outside the plot area, you see a longer context menu. It includes such commands as Format Chart Area, Assign Macro, and Refresh Data.

To determine where the chart area is, point to part of the pivot chart, and hold the pointer still. A tooltip shows the name of the chart element (see Figure 10-6).

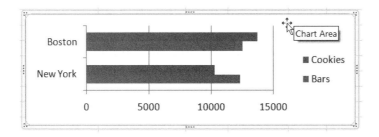

Figure 10-6. *A tooltip shows the name of a chart element.*

10.13. Creating Multiple Series for Years

Problem

The service manager asked for a chart that compares the service data for the past two years. You created a line chart from two years of data, but the chart has a single line, with two years of dates on the horizontal axis. You want each year to have a separate line in the chart, so you can compare the number of work orders for each month (see Figure 10-7). This problem is based on the `Service.xlsx` sample file.

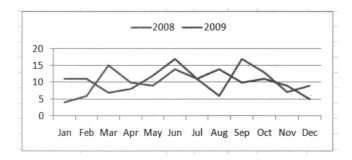

Figure 10-7. *Compare years with a line chart.*

Solution

Follow these steps to group the dates and create a line for each year:

1. In the pivot table, right-click a cell in the date field, and then in the context menu, click Group.

2. In the Grouping dialog box, select Years and Months, and then click OK.

3. In the PivotTable Field List, move the Years field to the Column Labels area.

4. Activate the pivot chart, where the years will each be represented by separate lines.

10.14. Locating the Source Pivot Table

Problem

The sales manager sent you a workbook that contains multiple pivot charts and pivot tables, and he asked you to make some changes. You aren't sure which charts are based on which tables, and you would like to figure it out before you start making changes. This problem is based on the `Source.xlsx` sample file.

Solution

You can use the Ribbon commands to find the pivot table that is the source for a pivot chart.

1. Select a pivot chart, and on the Ribbon, click the Design tab.

2. In the Data group, click Select Data.

3. In the Chart Data Range box, you see a formula that includes the workbook name, sheet name, and range in which the source pivot table is located (see Figure 10-8). Click Cancel to close the dialog box.

Figure 10-8. *Find the pivot chart's source data range.*

Note You can't change the source table for the pivot chart, but the Select Data Source dialog box can help you identify the source table for each pivot chart. If you need to base the pivot chart on a different pivot table, you will have to re-create the pivot chart.

10.15. Creating a Combination Pivot Chart

Problem

You created a clustered column pivot chart to show the sales per category in each city. You'd like to change the column for New York to a line, so it stands out from the other cities and acts as a target line. You can't find any combination chart types, so you aren't sure how to create the line and column chart you need. This problem is based on the Combo.xlsx sample file.

Solution

After you create a pivot chart, you can select a series in the chart and change it to a different chart type.

1. In the pivot chart, right-click a column in the New York series that you want to change.

2. In the context menu, click Change Series Chart Type.

3. In the Change Chart Type dialog box, click the Line chart type and the chart subtype you prefer, and then click OK.

10.16. Moving a Pivot Chart from a Chart Sheet

Problem

When you right-click the pivot chart, the Move Chart command isn't available in the context menu. You'd like to use this quick way to move the chart, instead of finding the command on the Ribbon. This problem is based on the Sales10.xlsx sample file.

Solution

The context menus show different commands, based on where the pointer is when you right-click. If you right-click the Plot area, you see a short context menu, that has commands including Format Plot Area and Select Data. If you right-click the Chart area, which is outside the Plot area, you see a longer context menu. It includes such commands as Format Chart Area, Change Chart Type, and Move Chart.

10.17. Removing a Pivot Chart

Problem

You finished working on the pivot chart, and you would like to remove it from the workbook and create a different pivot chart from the data. This problem is based on the Sales10.xlsx sample file.

Solution

You can delete a pivot table, to completely remove it from the workbook, or you can clear all the fields and formatting from the pivot chart layout, and start over.

■**Caution**   Clearing the pivot chart also clears the pivot table on which it is based.

Deleting a Pivot Chart on a Worksheet

If you no longer need a pivot chart that's on a worksheet, you can delete it.

1. Select the pivot chart.

2. On the keyboard, press the Delete key.

Deleting a Pivot Chart on a Chart Sheet

If you no longer need a pivot chart that's on a chart sheet, you can delete it.

1. Right-click the sheet tab for the chart sheet, and then click Delete.

2. In the confirmation message, click Delete.

Clearing a Pivot Chart

If you want to start from scratch with a pivot chart layout, you can clear it.

1. Select the pivot chart.

2. On the Ribbon, under the PivotChart Tools tab, click the Analyze tab.

3. In the Data section, click the Clear command, and then click Clear All.

This leaves the pivot chart frame on the worksheet, but it removes all the fields from the pivot chart and pivot table. To rebuild the chart, use the PivotTable Field List.

■■■

CHAPTER 11

Programming a Pivot Table

Although you can create complex pivot tables without programming, some pivot table settings can only be changed by using programming. As a developer, you can use programming to limit the ways users can manipulate your pivot tables, or to simplify a complex set of tasks. For example, you can provide a button on the worksheet that users can click to format, refresh, and preview a pivot table before printing.

This chapter addresses programming issues related to pivot tables and provides code examples for macros that can't be recorded. The chapter begins with a brief introduction to using Excel's macro recorder and the Visual Basic Editor (VBE), where you can view and edit the code stored in the workbook's modules. Many excellent books are available with instructions and examples for learning how to program in Excel. Also, extensive documentation is in the VBE help files and Excel's help files.

For an overview of the Excel 2007 object model, see "Excel Object Model Reference" on the Microsoft web site at `http://msdn2.microsoft.com/en-us/library/bb332345.aspx`.

Except where noted, the problems in this chapter are based on the `Sales11.xlsm` workbook. The code, in text format, is also available in the file named `Code.txt`. You can copy the code from the text file into your own workbooks, or experiment with the code in the sample workbooks.

11.1. Using Sample Code

Problem

You've obtained sample code from this chapter, and you would like to use it in your workbook. You aren't sure where to store the code, or how to run it.

Solution

To use the code examples in this chapter, you can add them to your workbooks. Some code may require modification, as described in Section 11.3, to match names and ranges in your workbooks. You'd then run the code using one of the methods described here.

■**Note** When a workbook contains code, it must be saved as an Excel Macro-Enabled Workbook. This type of file has an `xlsm` file extension, as you can see in the sample files for this chapter.

Storing the Code

Most of the code samples are stored in a regular code module:

1. Download the sample files, and then copy the code you want to use.

2. Open the workbook in which you want to store the code.

3. On the keyboard, hold the Alt key, and then press the F11 key to open the Visual Basic Editor.

4. Click the Insert menu, and then click Module.

5. Right-click where the cursor is flashing, and then click Paste.

■**Note** If an "Option Explicit" line of code is at the top of the worksheet, position the cursor below that line.

Some code is event code, and it runs automatically when something specific occurs in the workbook. For example, if you type in a cell and press the Enter key, the worksheet is changed. This could trigger the Worksheet_Change event. Worksheet event code is stored on a worksheet code module. To add the code to a worksheet, do the following:

1. Download the sample files, and then copy the code you want to use.

2. Select the worksheet in which you want to use the code.

3. Right-click the sheet tab and click View Code to open the Visual Basic Editor.

4. Right-click where the cursor is flashing, and then click Paste.

Running the Code

To run the macros you create, you can store the workbook that contains the macros in a trusted location, or change your macro settings to enable macros. Follow these steps to enable all macros:

1. Click the Microsoft Office button, and then click Excel Options.

2. Click the Trust Center category, and then click Trust Center Settings.

3. Click the Macro Settings category, and in the Macro Settings section, either click Disable All Macros with Notification, or click Enable All Macros.

■**Note** If you click Disable All Macros with Notification, you are asked to enable or disable macros whenever you open a workbook that contains macros.

---

4. Click OK, twice, to close the dialog boxes.

Macros can be run by using several methods. For example, you can use a shortcut key, a Ribbon command, or a button on the Quick Access Toolbar (QAT).

Using a Shortcut Key

When recording a macro, you can assign a shortcut key, as described in Section 11.2. To run the macro, press the shortcut key combination.

Using a Ribbon Command

To run a macro, you can click the Macros command on the Ribbon's View tab or the Developer tab. If the Developer tab is not visible on the Ribbon, follow these steps to display it:

1. Click the Microsoft Office button, and then click Excel Options.

2. Click the Popular category, and in the Top Options For Working With Excel section, add a check mark to Show Developer Tab in the Ribbon (see Figure 11-1).

Figure 11-1. *Displaying the Developer tab in the Ribbon*

3. Click OK, to close the Excel Options dialog box.

Follow these steps to run a macro from a Ribbon command:

1. On the Ribbon's Developer tab, in the Code group, click Macros.

Tip The Macros command is also available on the Ribbon's View tab.

---

2. In the center of the Macro dialog box is a drop-down list with the caption, Macros In. From that list, select the location in which you stored your macro.

3. In the list of macros, click your macro, and then click Run.

Using a Quick Access Toolbar (QAT) Button

To run a macro, you can add a button to the QAT:

1. At the right end of the QAT, click Customize Quick Access Toolbar, and then click More Commands.

2. In the Excel Options dialog box, click the arrow on the Choose Commands From drop-down list, and then click Macros (see Figure 11-2).

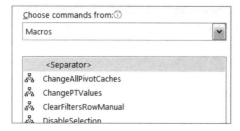

Figure 11-2. *Selecting a macro to add to the QAT*

3. In the list of macros, click the macro you want to add to the QAT.

4. Click the Add button, to move the macro to the QAT.

5. To change the macro's icon, select the macro in the Customize Quick Access Toolbar list. Click Modify and select a different icon, and then click OK.

6. Click OK to close the Excel Options dialog box.

7. To run the macro, click the macro's button on the QAT.

11.2. Recording a Macro While Printing a Pivot Table

Problem

At the beginning of each work day, you format and print your pivot table, and several steps are in the process. First, you apply a light PivotTable Style that you use when printing, and then you refresh the data, and, finally, you preview the report. You're not really a morning person, so you'd like to create a macro that performs all these steps automatically, to make the process easier and faster. This problem is based on the OrderDates pivot table in the Sales11.xlsm workbook.

Solution

Excel programming is done in the Visual Basic for Applications (VBA) language. When manually changing or creating a pivot table, you can use Excel's macro recorder to create code as you work. Later, you can run the macro as recorded, or adjust the code to make it more flexible, enabling it to run correctly if the worksheet data or layout changes.

The macro recorder doesn't create ideal code. It records what you do with the mouse and keyboard as you manually perform a task but, occasionally, it's unable to record one or more steps, so the resulting code is incomplete. The macro recorder also includes many recorded steps that may be unnecessary in the final code, such as multiple clicks on the scroll bar button to move down the worksheet. However, for simple tasks, or for learning about Excel's object model and programming syntax, the macro recorder is a useful tool.

Before You Begin Recording

When creating a macro, you can select a range as the first step in the macro and operate on that range, or you can record steps that operate on the currently selected range. In this example, you want the macro to prepare a specific pivot table, so select a cell outside the pivot table, and then select a different worksheet. In the Sales11.xlsm sample file, you can select the Sales Data sheet before you begin recording. You select the OrderDates worksheet and a cell in the pivot table after you begin recording, so those steps will be part of the recorded code.

Recording a Macro

1. On the Ribbon's Developer tab, in the Code group, click Record Macro.

Tip You can also click the Record Macro button at the left side of the Status bar.

---

2. Type a one-word name for the macro, for example, **Prepare_Pivot**.

3. If you want to run the macro by using a keyboard shortcut, type an upper- or lowercase letter in the Shortcut Key box. In this example, uppercase P is used (see Figure 11-3). This setting is optional; there are other ways to run the macro after you create it. To run the macro later, using the shortcut, press the Ctrl key, and the Shift key, and then tap the P key. If you use lowercase p as the shortcut, then you press Ctrl and tap the P key, without pressing the Shift key.

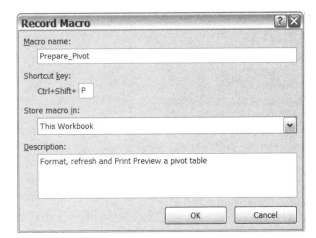

Figure 11-3. *Ctrl+Shift+P is entered as the macro's shortcut key.*

Caution Don't use a shortcut key that's the same as the Excel shortcuts you like to use. For example, Ctrl+c copies the selection in Excel. If you use Ctrl+c as your macro shortcut, it will overwrite Excel's copy shortcut while the workbook with the macro shortcut is open. However, the shortcut keys are case-sensitive; you could hold the Shift key, and use an uppercase C as your shortcut, and it won't overwrite the Copy shortcut.

---

4. From the Store Macro In drop-down list, select a location in which to save the macro. In this example, the macro is specific to the active workbook, so you would select This Workbook. If it's a macro you want to use in many workbooks, you could store it in your Personal Macro Workbook. The third option is to store it in a new workbook.

5. To help you, or other users, understand what the macro does, you can enter a brief message about the macro's purpose in the Description box.

6. Click the OK button to start recording the macro.

7. Perform the steps you want to record. In the Sales11.xlsm example, select the Order-Dates worksheet, where the pivot table named PT1 is located. Then, select a cell at the top left of the pivot table. On the Ribbon's Design tab, open the PivotTable Styles gallery, and then click Pivot Style Light 1. Then, right-click a cell in the pivot table, and click Refresh. Finally, click the Microsoft Office button, point to Print, click Print Preview, and click the Close Print Preview button.

■**Note**   While recording the macro, Live Preview is disabled, so you won't see a preview when you select a different PivotTable Style.

---

8. After you complete the steps you want to record, click the Stop Recording button at the left side of the status bar (see Figure 11-4).

Figure 11-4. *The Stop Recording button on the status bar*

Viewing the Recorded Code

1. On Ribbon's View tab, at the far right, click the top section of the Macros command, to open the Macro dialog box.

2. From the Macros In drop-down list, select This Workbook, or the location in which you stored your macro.

3. In the list of macros, select your macro, and then click Edit.

4. This opens the VBE, where you can see the recorded code.

5. At the left, you should see the Project Explorer, which lists the open Excel files. Your active workbook is in the list, with its modules and Excel objects listed. The recorded code was stored in a module, which is highlighted in the list (see Figure 11-5).

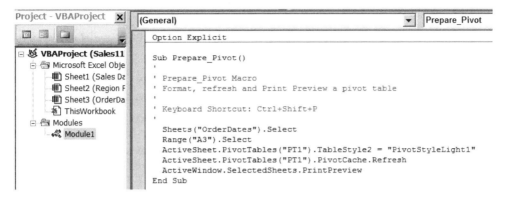

Figure 11-5. *The VBE shows the recorded code.*

■**Note** If the Project Explorer is not visible, on the VBE menu, click View, and then click Project Explorer.

---

6. In the code window at the right, you can see the recorded code. The code is in a procedure, which starts with a line that contains the word "Sub," followed by the name you gave the macro and a set of parentheses.

7. Following the Sub line are comment lines that start with a single quote mark. The comments don't affect the code, but they can make it easier to understand. Some comments are added by the macro recorder, and you can add your own comments to the code. Lines that don't start with a single quote mark are the lines of code that control what steps are performed when you run the macro.

■**Note** Although the recorder was on when you closed the Print Preview window, that step was not recorded. Some actions cannot be captured by the macro recorder.

---

8. In the code window, you can edit the existing code or type new code. In this example, you leave the code as it is. To make changes later, you can follow the instructions in Section 11.3.

9. To close the VBE and return to Excel, click the File menu, and then click Close and Return to Microsoft Excel.

Running a Macro

When you're ready to print the pivot table, you can run your macro to perform the preparation steps:

1. On the Ribbon's Developer tab, in the Code group, click Macros.

2. From the drop-down list for Macros In, select the location in which you stored your macro.

3. In the list of macros, select your macro, and then click Run.

Changing a Macro Keyboard Shortcut

After creating a macro that runs from a keyboard shortcut, you may want to change the letter used in the shortcut. Or, if you recorded a macro, and did not assign a keyboard shortcut to it, you can use this technique to add a keyboard shortcut later. To add or change a shortcut, follow these steps:

1. On the Ribbon's Developer tab, in the Code group, click Macros.

2. From the Macros In drop-down list, select the location in which you stored your macro.

3. In the list of macros, select your macro, and then click Options.

4. In the Shortcut key box, type a different uppercase or lowercase character.

5. Click OK to close the Macro Options dialog box.

6. Click Cancel to close the Macro dialog box.

11.3. Modifying Recorded Code

Problem

To make your morning tasks easier, you followed the steps in Section 11.2—you turned on the macro recorder as you formatted the pivot table, refreshed the data, and previewed the worksheet. The following code was created in the Sales11.xlsm workbook:

```
Sub Prepare_Pivot()
'
' Prepare_Pivot Macro
' Format, refresh and Print Preview a pivot table
' Keyboard Shortcut: Ctrl+Shift+P
'
    Sheets("OrderDates").Select
    Range("A3").Select
    ActiveSheet.PivotTables("PT1").TableStyle2="PivotStyleLight1"
    ActiveSheet.PivotTables("PT1").PivotCache.Refresh
    ActiveWindow.SelectedSheets.PrintPreview
End Sub
```

Things were going well, and you ran the macro without problems every morning last week. However, yesterday you changed the pivot table's name from **PT1** to **OrderPivot**, and when you ran the macro this morning, an error message appeared that said, "Run-time error '1004': Unable to get the PivotTables property of the Worksheet class."

Solution

The recorded code includes the name of the pivot table at the time of the recording:

```
ActiveSheet.PivotTables("PT1").PivotCache.Refresh
```

You can replace the recorded name with the new name, and then the macro will run correctly.

1. To edit the code, open the VBE, as described in Section 11.2.

2. Because the pivot table's new name is OrderPivot, change all occurrences of the recorded name, PT1, to OrderPivot. For example:

```
ActiveSheet.PivotTables("OrderPivot").PivotCache.Refresh
```

3. Click the Save button, and then click the File menu, and click Close and Return to Microsoft Excel.

11.4. Changing the Summary Function for All Value Fields

Problem

When you add fields to the Values area, sometimes they appear as Count of Field instead of Sum of Field. You would like the Sum function to be the default for all Values fields. This problem is based on the `Summary.xlsm` workbook.

Workaround

You can't change the default settings for the pivot table's Values fields. If a field in the source data contains blank cells, or cells with text, it defaults to Count; otherwise, it defaults to Sum. After the Values fields are added, you can run a macro to change the summary function. The following macro changes all the Values fields in the first pivot table on the active sheet to use the Sum function. Store the code on a regular code module.

```
Sub SumAllValueFields()
  Dim pt As PivotTable
  Dim pf As PivotField
  Dim ws As Worksheet

  Set ws = ActiveSheet
  Set pt = ws.PivotTables(1)
  Application.ScreenUpdating = False
```

```
    pt.ManualUpdate = True
    For Each pf In pt.DataFields
      pf.Function = xlSum
    Next pf
    pt.ManualUpdate = False

  Application.ScreenUpdating = True

  Set pf = Nothing
  Set pt = Nothing
  Set ws = Nothing
End Sub
```

To run the code, use one of the methods described in Section 11.1.

How It Works

The SumAllValueFields procedure changes the Function property for each field in the Values area (pt.DataFields), setting it to xlSum. Because the ws variable is set to the ActiveSheet instead of a specific worksheet, you can run the code on any worksheet that contains a pivot table. The code refers to the pivot table by index number (1), instead of using a specific name ("PT1"), and that also makes it more flexible.

11.5. Naming and Formatting the Show Details Sheet

Problem

The sales manager frequently opens your workbook to check the results in the OrderDates pivot table. To investigate the records included in a number in the Values area, he often double-clicks a cell, and the underlying records are exported to a new sheet. This can occur several times during each session, and you have to clear out all the extra sheets the next time you open the workbook.

You'd like to automatically name the sheets created by the Show Details feature, so they're easy to identify. This problem is based on the SheetsName.xlsm workbook.

Solution

You can name the new sheet using an event procedure that runs automatically when a sheet is added to the workbook.

1. In the VBE, click the Insert menu, and then click Module.

2. At the top of the module, where the cursor is flashing, type the following line of code to create a public variable. This variable can be used by other procedures in the workbook.

   ```
   Public SheetType As String
   ```

3. You want code to run when a cell is double-clicked on the OrderDates sheet, so you'll add event code to that sheet's module. In Excel, right-click the OrderDates worksheet tab, and then click View Code. Add the following code to the worksheet module, below the Option Explicit line:

```
Private Sub Worksheet_BeforeDoubleClick(ByVal Target As Range, _
    Cancel As Boolean)
  Dim pt As PivotTable

  If Me.PivotTables.Count = 0 Then Exit Sub
  For Each pt In Me.PivotTables
    If Not Intersect(Target, pt.DataBodyRange) Is Nothing Then
      SheetType = "Show"
      Exit For
    End If
  Next pt
  Set pt = Nothing
End Sub
```

4. In the VBE, in the Project Explorer, double-click the ThisWorkbook object for the SheetsName.xlsm workbook. Add the following code to its module, as shown in Figure 11-6.

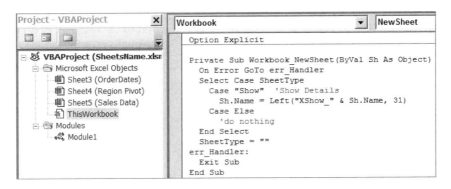

Figure 11-6. *Add code to the ThisWorkbook module.*

```
Private Sub Workbook_NewSheet(ByVal Sh As Object)
  On Error GoTo err_Handler
  Select Case SheetType
    Case "Show"  'Show Details
      Sh.Name = Left("XShow_" & Sh.Name, 31)
    Case Else
      'do nothing
  End Select
  SheetType = ""
```

```
err_Handler:
    Exit Sub
End Sub
```

To run the event code, double-click a cell in the OrderDates pivot table's Values area. A worksheet is created with the extracted data, and a sheet name that starts with XShow_.

How It Works

When any cell on the pivot table's sheet is double-clicked, the BeforeDoubleClick event is triggered. If no pivot tables are on the worksheet, or if the double-clicked cell is not in the Values area (pt.DataBodyRange) of a pivot table, the procedure is exited. Otherwise, the public variable, SheetType, is set to a value of Show. If the double-click creates a new sheet, the workbook's NewSheet event code runs.

If SheetType is set to the value of Show, the sheet is given a name that starts with XShow_. This makes the sheets easy to identify, and they can be deleted automatically when the workbook closes. See Section 11.6 for sample code to delete the worksheets.

11.6. Automatically Deleting Worksheets When Closing a Workbook

Problem

Once a week, you send a printed copy of the Region Pivot report to the manager of each region. On the Ribbon's Options tab, in the PivotTable group, you can click the Options drop-down arrow, and then click Show Report Filter Pages, to create a worksheet with a copy of the pivot table for each region in the Report Filter Field.

This command is useful for printing customized copies of the pivot table, but it adds extra sheets to the workbook. You'd like these sheets to be automatically deleted when the workbook is closed to prevent the buildup of sheets. This problem is based on the SheetsDelete.xlsm sample workbook.

Solution

You can use an event procedure that runs when a sheet is added to the workbook to rename the new sheets, so they're easy to identify and delete when the workbook closes.

1. In the ThisWorkbook module, add the following two procedures:

```
Private Sub Workbook_NewSheet(ByVal Sh As Object)
    If TypeName(Sh)="Worksheet" Then
        If Sh.PivotTables.Count > 0 Then
            If Sh.PivotTables(1).PageFields.Count > 0 Then
                Sh.Name = Left("XShow_" & Sh.Name, 31)
            End If
        End If
    End If
```

```
End Sub
'

Private Sub Workbook_BeforeClose(Cancel As Boolean)
  Dim ws As Worksheet
  Dim Resp As Long
  Dim ShowCount As Long

  ShowCount = 0
  For Each ws In ThisWorkbook.Worksheets
    If UCase(Left(ws.Name, 5)) = "XSHOW" Then
      ShowCount = ShowCount + 1
    End If
  Next ws

  If ShowCount > 0 Then
    Resp = MsgBox("Delete Show Report Filter Pages sheets?", _
              vbYesNo, "Delete Sheets?")
    If Resp = vbYes Then
      Application.DisplayAlerts = False
      For Each ws In ThisWorkbook.Worksheets
        If UCase(Left(ws.Name, 5)) = "XSHOW" Then
          ws.Delete
        End If
      Next ws
    End If
  End If
  Set ws = Nothing
End Sub
```

2. To run the event code that names the sheets, select a cell in the pivot table and on the Ribbon's Options tab, in the PivotTable group, click the Options drop-down arrow, and then click Show Report Filter Pages. Select a report filter in the list, and then click OK.

How It Works

If a new sheet is created, the workbook's NewSheet event is triggered. If the new sheet contains a pivot table, and that pivot table has a report filter, it's assumed to be generated by the Show Report Filter Pages command. The sheet is renamed by the NewSheet code, with XShow_ at the start of the name.

When the workbook closes, the workbook's BeforeClose event is triggered. The event code asks the user if Show Report Filter Pages sheets should be deleted. If the user clicks Yes, the sheets are deleted, and the workbook can be saved without the sheets.

Notes

The ThisWorkbook module can contain only one copy of each event, such as the Workbook_NewSheet event. To use both the sample code from Section 11.5 and the sample code in this section, you can combine the Workbook_NewSheet code into one procedure:

```
Private Sub Workbook_NewSheet(ByVal Sh As Object)
  On Error GoTo err_Handler
  Select Case SheetType
    Case "Show"  'Show Details
      Sh.Name = Left("XShow_" & Sh.Name, 31)
    Case Else
      'do nothing
  End Select
  SheetType = ""

  If TypeName(Sh) = "Worksheet" Then
      If Sh.PivotTables.Count > 0 Then
        If Sh.PivotTables(1).PageFields.Count > 0 Then
          Sh.Name = Left("XShow_" & Sh.Name, 31)
        End If
      End If
  End If

err_Handler:
  Exit Sub
End Sub
```

11.7. Changing the Report Filter Selection in Related Tables

Problem

In your workbook, three pivot tables are based on the same Excel Table, and the Product field is in the Report Filter area for each pivot table. When you're asked for the status of a specific product, you select that product from the report filter in each pivot table, and you print all three pivot tables.

It would be easier if you could change the Product Report Filters in all the pivot tables at the same time, instead of going to each sheet and changing them individually. This problem is based on the ChangeTwo.xlsm sample workbook.

Solution

You can use an event procedure to change the other pivot tables' report filters when the Product report filter is changed in the OrderDates pivot table.

1. Right-click the sheet tab for the OrderDates pivot table, and then click View Code.

2. Enter the following line of code in the General Declarations section at the top of the module (see Figure 11-7). This is a module-level variable:

   ```
   Dim mstrFilter As Variant
   ```

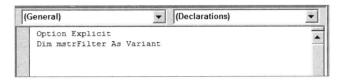

Figure 11-7. *Module-level variable in the General Declarations section*

Tip The Option Explicit setting ensures that all the variables you use are declared in the code. Using this setting is good practice, as it can help you prevent errors when you write or edit code. You can type Option Explicit at the top of each module, or you can change a setting, so it automatically appears in new modules. In the VBE, click the Tools menu, and then click Options. On the Editor tab, add a check mark to Require Variable Declaration.

---

3. Below the General Declarations section, add the following code, which includes the sheet names where the other pivot tables are located, and the name of the report filter:

```
Private Sub Worksheet_PivotTableUpdate(ByVal Target As PivotTable)
  Dim wsOther1 As Worksheet
  Dim wsOther2 As Worksheet
  Dim pt As PivotTable
  Dim strFilter As String

  On Error GoTo err_Handler

  Set wsOther1 = Worksheets("Region Pivot") 'second PT sheet name
  Set wsOther2 = Worksheets("CitySales")    'third PT sheet name
  strFilter = "Product"                     'Report Filter name

  Application.EnableEvents = False

  If UCase(Target.PivotFields(strFilter).CurrentPage) _
    <> UCase(mstrFilter) Then
   mstrFilter= Target.PivotFields(strFilter).CurrentPage
   For Each pt In wsOther1.PivotTables
     pt.PageFields(strFilter).CurrentPage = mstrFilter
   Next pt
   For Each pt In wsOther2.PivotTables
     pt.PageFields(strFilter).CurrentPage = mstrFilter
   Next pt
  End If
```

```
err_Handler:
  Application.EnableEvents = True
End Sub
```

To run the event code, change the selection in the OrderDates pivot table's report filter.

How It Works

A variable within a procedure is stored only as long as the procedure that declared it is running. A module-level variable is used in this example, because it can store the current report filter selection while the workbook is open. When the pivot table is updated, the variable named mstrFilter is compared to the current selection in the Product Report Filter. If they're different, the new report filter value is stored in the variable, and the report filter in each related pivot table is changed to match the report filter in the main pivot table.

11.8. Removing Filters in a Pivot Field

Problem

When you want to remove a filter from a pivot table field, you can manually check the Show All box to show all items in that pivot table field. When you record this step, the code shows a list of all the items in the pivot field, instead of using a Show All command. When you run the code later, it can be very slow, if the list of items is long, such as in an OrderDate field. Also, if you add new items to the field and run the macro, the new items aren't made visible, because the macro contains a list of the original items only. This problem is based on the Filters.xlsm sample workbook.

Solution

Instead of using the recorded code, with its long list of items, you can use the ClearManualFilter method. For example, the following code shows all items, in all visible fields, in all tables on the active sheet. Store the code on a regular module.

```
Sub ClearFilters ()
  Dim pt As PivotTable
  Dim pf As PivotField
  Dim ws As Worksheet

  On Error GoTo err_Handler

  Set ws = ActiveSheet

  Application.ScreenUpdating = False
  Application.DisplayAlerts = False
```

```
  For Each pt In ws.PivotTables
    For Each pf In pt.VisibleFields
      On Error Resume Next
      pf.ClearManualFilter
    Next pf
  Next pt

exit_Handler:
  Application.ScreenUpdating = True
  Exit Sub
err_Handler:
  MsgBox Err.Number & ": " & Err.Description
  GoTo exit_Handler
  Set pf = Nothing
  Set pt = Nothing
  Set ws = Nothing
End Sub
```

To run the code, use a method described in Section 11.1. The code refers to ActiveSheet, so you can run the code on any sheet that contains a pivot table.

How It Works

The ClearFilters code uses For Each…Next loops to clear the manual filters in all visible fields, in all pivot tables on the active worksheet.

■**Tip** To show only column fields, change pt.VisibleFields to pt.ColumnFields. To show only the row fields, change pt.VisibleFields to pt.RowFields, and to show report filter fields, change pt.RowFields to pt.PageFields.

The *ClearManualFilter method* only clears the manual filters applied to the pivot field. You apply a manual filter by using the check boxes in the filter list, or by right-clicking an item, clicking Filter, and then clicking Hide Selected Items.

In addition to the manual filters, date, value, or label filters may have been applied to the row or column fields.

To clear value or Top 10 filters, you can use the following method:

```
pf.ClearValueFilters
```

To clear label or date filters, you can use the following method:

```
pf.ClearLabelFilters
```

To clear all filters in the pivot table, you can use the following method:

```
For Each pt In ws.PivotTables
  pt.ClearAllFilters
Next pt
```

■Tip While recording a macro, you can record the ClearAllFilters method. Right-click a filtered field, click Filter, and then click Clear Filter from *FieldName*.

11.9. Changing Content in the Values Area

Problem

You discovered that one of the totals in your OrderDates report is incorrect, but you haven't received the corrected source data yet. You need to print the totals for the sales manager, who's leaving for the airport in 15 minutes. As a temporary fix, you'd like to change the New York total and the Grand Total in the Values area of the pivot table, so you can print the report.

However, when you try to type over a value, you see the error message "Cannot change this part of a PivotTable report." This problem is based on the Change.xlsm sample workbook.

Solution

The best solution is to add a row in the source data, to adjust the New York total, with a comment to explain the entry. Then, refresh the pivot table, to see the updated total. After the corrected source data is received, another row can be added, to reverse the temporary adjustment. This solution would leave an audit trail, explaining the changes.

However, if you change a PivotTable setting programmatically, you can make temporary changes to the PivotTable values. Store the code in a regular code module.

```
Sub ChangePTValues()
  Dim pt As PivotTable

  Set pt = ActiveSheet.PivotTables(1)
  pt.EnableDataValueEditing = True
  Set pt = Nothing
End Sub
```

■Note When the pivot table is refreshed, the manually entered values are overwritten.

To run the code, use a method described in Section 11.1. The code refers to ActiveSheet, so you can run the code on any sheet that contains a pivot table.

How It Works

The EnableDataValueEditing property can only be set programmatically, and it allows temporary changes to the pivot table data area cells.

■**Caution** If you rely on pivot tables to summarize your data, you should be aware that the data can be changed, accidentally or maliciously, and use other methods to verify the data, as a safeguard.

To prevent accidental changes to the pivot table, you should create another macro that turns this setting to False, and run that macro as soon as you finish making changes to the values.

```
Sub BlockPTValues()
  Dim pt As PivotTable

  Set pt = ActiveSheet.PivotTables(1)
  pt.EnableDataValueEditing = False
  Set pt = Nothing
End Sub
```

11.10. Identifying a Pivot Table's Pivot Cache

Problem

You're working on next year's budget, and your workbook contains sales data and a forecast for the upcoming year. Several pivot tables are based on similar Excel Tables, and you want to identify which pivot cache each pivot table uses. This problem is based on the Cache.xlsm sample workbook.

Solution

To determine which pivot cache a pivot table uses, you can run the following code to test the pivot table's CacheIndex property and view the result in a message box. Store the code on a regular code module.

```
Sub ViewCacheIndex()
  On Error GoTo err_Handler
  MsgBox "PivotCache: " & ActiveCell.PivotTable.CacheIndex
  Exit Sub
err_Handler:
  MsgBox "Active cell is not in a pivot table"
End Sub
```

Select a cell in a pivot table, and then run the code, using one of the methods described in Section 11.1. A message box displays the CacheIndex property for the active cell's pivot table. If the active cell is not in a pivot table, an error message is displayed.

How It Works

When pivot caches are created, they are added to the workbook's PivotCaches collection and given an index number. This number is displayed in the macro's message box. If a pivot table is based on the same source data as an existing pivot table, it uses the same pivot cache.

11.11. Changing a Pivot Table's Pivot Cache

Problem

You used the code from Section 11.10 to identify the pivot cache used by each pivot table in your workbook. You want to change the pivot cache of the Category pivot table, so it uses the same cache as the StoreTotals pivot table. This problem is based on the Cache.xlsm sample workbook.

Solution

To change the pivot cache, you can set the pivot table's CacheIndex property. The following code sets the pivot table for the active cell to use pivot cache number 2. Store the code on a regular code module.

```
Sub SetCache2Index()
  On Error GoTo err_Handler
  ActiveCell.PivotTable.CacheIndex = 2
  Exit Sub
err_Handler:
  MsgBox "Cache index could not be changed"
End Sub
```

To run the code, use a method described in Section 11.1. The code refers to ActiveCell, so you can run the code on any sheet that contains a pivot table.

How It Works

The SetCache2Index code sets the CacheIndex property for the active cell's pivot table to 2. If a pivot table cell is not selected, or if there is no CacheIndex 2, an error message is displayed. Instead of setting the CacheIndex property to a specific number, you can obtain an index number in the code, and use that number as the setting. For example:

```
Sub SetCacheIndex()
  Dim i As Integer
  i = Worksheets("StoreTotals").PivotTables(1).CacheIndex
  On Error GoTo err_Handler
  ActiveCell.PivotTable.CacheIndex = i
  Exit Sub
err_Handler:
  MsgBox "Cache index could not be changed"
End Sub
```

11.12. Refreshing a Pivot Table on a Protected Sheet

Problem

You protected the StoreTotals worksheet, so no one is able to change the layout of the pivot table. Now, you want to refresh the StoreTotals pivot table, but the Refresh Data button on the PivotTable toolbar is disabled. This problem is based on the `Refresh.xlsm` sample workbook.

Solution

You can record a macro, modify it slightly, and then run that macro when you need to refresh the pivot table. Before you begin, protect the StoreTotals worksheet, with the password **pwd**.

1. Record a macro as you unprotect the StoreTotals sheet, refresh the pivot table, and then protect the worksheet.

2. View the recorded code in the VBE. For example, your code may look similar to the following:

```
Sub RefreshPivot()
  ActiveSheet.Unprotect
  Range("B1").Select
  ActiveSheet.PivotTables("StorePT").PivotCache.Refresh
  ActiveSheet.Protect DrawingObjects:=True, _
    Contents:=True, Scenarios:=True
End Sub
```

3. In the recorded code, you can add a password to the Unprotect and Protect lines. For example, if your password is pwd, the revised code would be as follows:

```
Sub RefreshPivot()
  ActiveSheet.Unprotect Password:="pwd"
  Range("B1").Select
  ActiveSheet.PivotTables("StorePT").PivotCache.Refresh
  ActiveSheet.Protect Password:="pwd", _
    DrawingObjects:=True, Contents:=True, Scenarios:=True
End Sub
```

4. Run the macro using one of the methods shown in Section 11.1.

How It Works

The RefreshPivot macro stores your password, and then uses it when unprotecting and protecting the worksheet. While the worksheet is unprotected, it refreshes the pivot table.

Notes

If you add your password to the macro, it is visible to anyone who can open your workbook project in the VBE. For information on protecting your code, see the article "Locking Your Solution's VBA Project," at http://msdn2.microsoft.com/en-us/library/ Aa165442(office.10).aspx.

Although the article refers to Excel 2000, it is still applicable to a VBA project in Excel 2007.

11.13. Refreshing Automatically When Source Data Changes

Problem

You frequently update the source data that's in an Excel Table in your workbook, but you forget to update the pivot table that's based on it. Hours later, you realize you printed several reports, all of which contain outdated information. To avoid wasting time and paper, you want the pivot table to automatically refresh when changes are made in the Excel Table on which the pivot table is based. This problem is based on the Update.xlsm sample workbook.

Solution

You can use an event procedure to automatically update the pivot table if the source data changes. In this example, the source data is on the Forecast sheet, and the pivot table is on the Product sheet:

1. Add the following code to the Forecast worksheet module:

```
Private Sub Worksheet_Change(ByVal Target As Range)
  Worksheets("Product").PivotTables(1).PivotCache.Refresh
End Sub
```

2. If you protected the Product worksheet, include code to unprotect the worksheet, and then protect it again, as shown in Section 11.12.

3. To run the event code, make a change to the data in the Excel Table.

How It Works

When a change is made on the Forecast worksheet, that sheet's Change event is triggered. In the Event code, the pivot cache for the Product sheet's pivot table is refreshed.

11.14. Setting a Minimum Width for Data Bars

Problem

You created a pivot table to show the quantity of snacks sold each month, and you added conditional formatting, using the data bars option. Although zero were sold in March and only one sold in April, the data bars for those months are too wide, in proportion to the other bars. You changed the setting for the Lowest Value, as described in Section 4.17, but the bars are still too wide. You'd like to fix the data bars, so the bars that represent zero and one are barely visible. This problem is based on the DataBars.xlsm sample file.

Solution

Although you can adjust the Lowest Value setting in the Edit Formatting Rule dialog box, you can't change the size of the smallest bar, which will be approximately 10 percent the width of the bar for the highest value.

However, the minimum width can be adjusted programmatically. For example, you can change the minimum width to 1 percent, and the bars for the zero and one will be much narrower (see Figure 11-8).

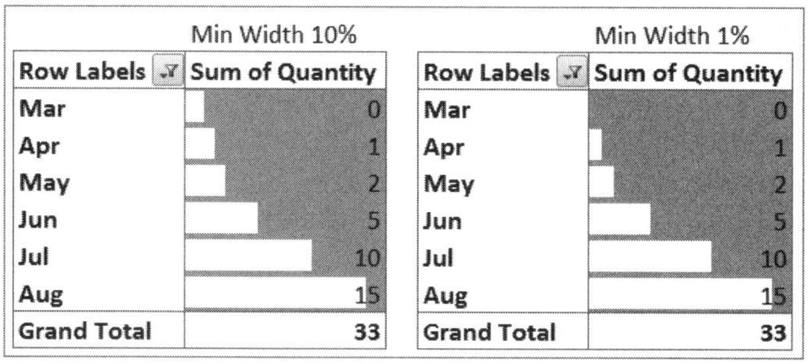

Min Width 10%		Min Width 1%	
Row Labels ⍒	Sum of Quantity	Row Labels ⍒	Sum of Quantity
Mar	0	Mar	0
Apr	1	Apr	1
May	2	May	2
Jun	5	Jun	5
Jul	10	Jul	10
Aug	15	Aug	15
Grand Total	33	Grand Total	33

Figure 11-8. *The minimum width for data bars is reduced to 1 percent.*

In the following code, the minimum width of the data bars that start in cell B6 will be changed to 1 percent. Also, the Lowest Value will be set as a Number, with zero as the value. You can manually change this setting in the Edit Formatting Rules dialog box, but it is included here for convenience.

```
Sub DataBarWidth()

With Range("B6").FormatConditions(1)
    .MinPoint.Modify _
        NewType:=xlConditionValueNumber, NewValue:=0
    .PercentMin = 1
End With

End Sub
```

11.15. Preventing Selection of (All) in a Report Filter

Problem

You're sending a copy of your workbook to the regional managers. In the OrderDates pivot table, you want the managers to view the sales totals by selecting an order date. GetPivotData formulas are on the worksheet that will result in an error if (All) is selected, so you want to prevent them from choosing (All) in the report filter's drop-down list. This problem is based on the BlockAll.xlsm sample workbook.

Solution

You can't remove the (All) option from the report filter's drop-down list, but you can use programming to prevent users from selecting that option. The following code, stored on the OrderDates sheet's module, can undo the report filter change, if (All) is selected or if multiple items are selected in the filter, and displays a message warning:

```
Private Sub Worksheet_PivotTableUpdate(ByVal Target As PivotTable)
  Dim pf As PivotField
  On Error GoTo exit_Handler

  Application.EnableEvents = False
  Application.ScreenUpdating = False

  For Each pf In Target.PageFields
    If pf.CurrentPage = "(All)" Then
        Application.Undo
        MsgBox "Please select a single date."
    End If
  Next pf

exit_Handler:
  Set pf = Nothing
  Application.EnableEvents = True
  Application.ScreenUpdating = True
End Sub
```

To run the code, select (All) from the OrderDate report filter's drop-down list.

How It Works

When an item is selected from a report filter's drop-down list, the PivotTableUpdate event is triggered. If the (All) item was selected, the code undoes the change to the report filter, and displays the previously selected item.

11.16. Disabling Pivot Field Drop-Downs

Problem

In the workbook you're sending to regional managers, you selected the manager's region name from the report filter on the Region Pivot worksheet, and all the stores in their region are in the Row Labels area. To ensure they're viewing the correct data, you want to prevent the managers from selecting a different item in the report filter or in the Row Labels filters. This problem is based on the Protect.xlsm sample workbook.

Solution

You can use programming to disable many pivot table features. For example, the following macro disables selection in each field in the first pivot table of the active sheet. The drop-down arrows disappear, and users can't change the displayed items. Store the code in a regular code module.

Note Instead of PivotFields, you can use VisibleFields, RowFields, ColumnFields, or PageFields.

```
Sub DisableSelection()
  Dim pt As PivotTable
  Dim pf As PivotField

  Set pt = ActiveSheet.PivotTables(1)

  For Each pf In pt.PivotFields
    pf.EnableItemSelection = False
  Next pf
  Set pf = Nothing
  Set pt = Nothing
End Sub
```

To run the code, use a method described in Section 11.1. The code refers to ActiveSheet, so you can run the code on any sheet that contains a pivot table.

How It Works

The code sets the EnableItemSelection property to False for each field in the pivot table, even if they aren't visible in the layout. To reenable selection, create and run a similar macro that sets the EnableItemSelection property to True.

11.17. Preventing Layout Changes in a Pivot Table

Problem

In the workbook you're sending to the regional managers, you created a SalesByDate pivot table that's referenced in GetPivotData formulas on the OrderDates worksheet. You want to prevent the managers from rearranging the SalesByDate pivot table layout. This problem is based on the Protect.xlsm sample workbook.

Solution

The pivot table has DragTo settings you can change programmatically. For example, the following macro prevents dragging fields to any pivot table area or off the pivot table. Store the code in a regular code module.

```
Sub RestrictPTDrag()
  Dim pt As PivotTable
  Dim pf As PivotField
  On Error Resume Next

  Set pt = ActiveSheet.PivotTables(1)

  For Each pf In pt.PivotFields
    With pf
        .DragToPage = False
        .DragToRow = False
        .DragToColumn = False
        .DragToData = False
        .DragToHide = False
    End With
  Next pf
  Set pt = Nothing
End Sub
```

To run the code, use a method described in Section 11.1. The code refers to ActiveSheet, so you can run the code on any sheet that contains a pivot table.

How It Works

The code stops users from moving the pivot table fields to a different location in the Pivot-Table Field List. It also prevents adding or removing fields in the pivot table layout. To allow layout changes again, create and run a similar macro that sets the DragTo properties to True.

In addition to the security features discussed in this and previous sections, you can programmatically control access to the following features:

- PivotTable Field List

- Field Settings

- Refresh

- Ribbon's PivotTable Tools contextual tabs

- Show Details

The following macro turns off each of these features. Store the macro on a regular code module.

```
Sub RestrictPTChanges()
  Dim pt As PivotTable
  Application.EnableEvents = False
  Set pt = ActiveSheet.PivotTables(1)
```

```
  With pt
    .EnableWizard = False 'hides Ribbon tabs
    .EnableDrilldown = False
    .EnableFieldList = False
    .EnableFieldDialog = False 'Field Settings
    .PivotCache.EnableRefresh = False
  End With
  Application.EnableEvents = True
  Set pt = Nothing
End Sub
```

To run the code, use a method described in Section 11.1. The code refers to ActiveSheet, so you can run the code on any sheet that contains a pivot table.

The RestrictPTChanges macro turns off many features in the first pivot table in the active sheet. To allow use of the features, create and run another macro that changes the settings to True.

11.18. Resetting the Print Area to Include the Entire Pivot Table

Problem

The OrderDates pivot table is on a worksheet that contains other data, which you don't want to print. The pivot table frequently changes size, and you have to reset the print area every time you want to print it. This problem is based on the Print.xlsm sample workbook.

Solution

Use programming to reset the print area automatically before printing. Add the following code to a regular code module:

```
Sub SetPivotPrintArea()
Dim ws As Worksheet
Dim pt As PivotTable

  Set ws = ActiveSheet
  Set pt = ws.PivotTables(1)

  With ws.PageSetup
    .PrintTitleRows = ""
    .PrintTitleColumns = ""
    .PrintArea = pt.TableRange2.Address
  End With

  pt.PrintTitles = True
  ws.PrintOut Preview:=True
  Set pt = Nothing
  Set ws = Nothing
End Sub
```

To run the code, use a method described in Section 11.1. The code refers to ActiveSheet, so you can run the code on any sheet that contains a pivot table.

How It Works

The SetPivotPrintArea macro clears the print titles for the active sheet, sets the print area based on the current layout of the pivot table, turns on the pivot table's print titles options, and prints the worksheet. In this example, the ws.PrintOut line has Preview set to True, so the worksheet will preview instead of printing. When you finish testing the code, you can change the setting to False, and the sheet will print when the code runs.

11.19. Printing the Pivot Table for Each Report Filter Field

Problem

You're preparing for a sales meeting, and you want to print a copy of the pivot table for each item in the Category report filter. This problem is based on the PrintCat.xlsm sample workbook.

Solution

The following code prints the pivot table once for each item in the Category report filter. Store the code in a regular code module.

```
Sub PrintPivotFilters()
  Dim pt As PivotTable
  Dim pf As PivotField
  Dim pi As PivotItem
  Dim ws As Worksheet
  On Error Resume Next

  Set ws = ActiveSheet
  Set pt = ws.PivotTables(1)
  Set pf = pt.PageFields("Category")

  For Each pi In pf.PivotItems
    pf.CurrentPage = pi.Name
    ws.PrintOut Preview:=True
  Next pi

  Set pf = Nothing
  Set pt = Nothing
  Set ws = Nothing
End Sub
```

To run the code, use a method described in Section 11.1. The code refers to ActiveSheet, so you can run the code on any sheet that contains a pivot table.

How It Works

The PrintPivotFilters macro selects each item in the pivot table's first report filter, and then prints the worksheet. In this example, the ws.PrintOut line has Preview set to True, so the worksheet will preview instead of printing. When you finish testing the code, you can change the setting to False, and the sheet will print when the code runs.

Notes

The procedure can be modified slightly to print a copy of a pivot chart on a chart sheet for each item in the Category report filter. Store the code on a regular code module.

```
Sub PrintPivotChartFilters()
  Dim pt As PivotTable
  Dim pf As PivotField
  Dim pi As PivotItem
  Dim ch As Chart
  On Error Resume Next

  Set ch = ActiveChart
  Set pt = ch.PivotLayout.PivotTable
  Set pf = pt.PageFields("Category")

  For Each pi In pf.PivotItems
    pf.CurrentPage = pi.Name
    ch.PrintOut Preview:=True
  Next pi

  Set ch = Nothing
  Set pf = Nothing
  Set pt = Nothing
End Sub
```

11.20. Scrolling Through Report Filter Items on a Pivot Chart

Problem

On the OrderDates Chart sheet, you have a list of categories in the Pivot Chart report filter. Instead of selecting the next category from the drop-down list to view its chart, you'd like scrolling buttons on the chart, so you can quickly view each category's data. This problem is based on the PrintCat.xlsm sample workbook.

Solution

You can add arrow shapes to the chart, and assign a macro to each shape, and then click the arrows to select the next or previous report filter item.

1. Add the following two procedures to a regular code module:

```
Sub PivotPageNext()
  Dim CountPI As Long
  Dim i As Long
  Dim pt As PivotTable
  Dim pf As PivotField
  Dim pi As PivotItem

  Set pt = ActiveChart.PivotLayout.PivotTable
  Set pf = pt.PageFields("Category")
  CountPI = 1
  i = 1

  For Each pi In pf.PivotItems
    If pf.CurrentPage.Name = "(All)" Then
      CountPI = 0
      Exit For
    End If
    If pi.Name = pf.CurrentPage.Name Then
        Exit For
    End If
    CountPI = CountPI + 1
  Next pi

  For i = CountPI + 1 To pf.PivotItems.Count + 1
    On Error Resume Next
    If i = pf.PivotItems.Count + 1 Then
      pf.CurrentPage = "(All)"
      Exit For
    End If
    pf.CurrentPage = pf.PivotItems(i).Name
      If Err.Number = 0 Then
        Exit For
      End If
  Next i
  Set pf = Nothing
  Set pt = Nothing
End Sub

Sub PivotPagePrev()
  Dim CountPI As Long
  Dim i As Long
  Dim pt As PivotTable
  Dim pf As PivotField
  Dim pi As PivotItem
```

```
Set pt = ActiveChart.PivotLayout.PivotTable
Set pf = pt.PageFields("Category")
CountPI = 1

For Each pi In pf.PivotItems
  If pf.CurrentPage.Name = "(All)" Then
    CountPI = pf.PivotItems.Count + 1
    Exit For
  End If
  If pi.Name = pf.CurrentPage.Name Then Exit For
  CountPI = CountPI + 1
Next pi

For i = CountPI - 1 To 0 Step -1
  On Error Resume Next
  pf.CurrentPage = pf.PivotItems(i).Name
    If Err.Number = 0 Then Exit For
  If i = 0 Then
    pf.CurrentPage = "(All)"
    Exit For
  End If
Next i
Set pf = Nothing
Set pt = Nothing
End Sub
```

2. Select the OrderDates Chart sheet, and on the Ribbon's Insert tab, in the Illustrations group, click Shapes.

3. Click the Left Arrow shape, and then click the chart, to add that shape.

4. On the chart, right-click the Left Arrow shape, and then click Assign Macro.

5. In the list of macros, select PivotPagePrev, and then click OK.

6. Add a Right Arrow shape, and assign it the PivotPageNext macro.

7. To scroll through the report filter items, click the arrows (see Figure 11-9).

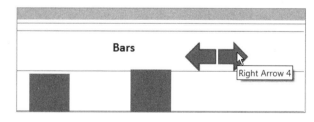

Figure 11-9. *Scrolling arrows at the top of a pivot chart*

How It Works

The two macros check the current report filter item and calculate its position in the list of items. If the Left Arrow shape is clicked, the PivotPagePrev macro runs, and the visible item with the next lower number is shown. If the Right Arrow shape is clicked, the PivotPageNext macro runs, and the visible item with the next higher number is shown.

Index

You Need the Companion eBook

Your purchase of this book entitles you to buy the companion PDF-version eBook for only $10. Take the weightless companion with you anywhere.

We believe this Apress title will prove so indispensable that you'll want to carry it with you everywhere, which is why we are offering the companion eBook (in PDF format) for $10 to customers who purchase this book now. Convenient and fully searchable, the PDF version of any content-rich, page-heavy Apress book makes a valuable addition to your programming library. You can easily find and copy code—or perform examples by quickly toggling between instructions and the application. Even simultaneously tackling a donut, diet soda, and complex code becomes simplified with hands-free eBooks!

Once you purchase your book, getting the $10 companion eBook is simple:

❶ Visit **www.apress.com/promo/tendollars/**.

❷ Complete a basic registration form to receive a randomly generated question about this title.

❸ Answer the question correctly in 60 seconds, and you will receive a promotional code to redeem for the $10.00 eBook.

THE EXPERT'S VOICE™

2855 TELEGRAPH AVENUE | SUITE 600 | BERKELEY, CA 94705

Offer valid through 6/10/08.